JO-ANN®

Your Guide to Quilting™

Cutting · Piecing · Appliquéing · Quilting

Your Guide to Quilting

Better Homes and Gardens®
CREATIVE COLLECTION

Director, Editorial Administration   Michael L. Maine
Editor-in-Chief   Beverly Rivers

Editorial Manager   Ann Blevins
Art Director   Brenda Drake Lesch

Copy Chief   Mary Heaton
Contributing Graphic Designer   Patty Crawford
Administrative Assistant   Lori Eggers
Contributing Writers   Jill Abeloe Mead, Sandra Neff, and Terri Pauser Wolf
Copy Editors   Diane Doro and Jennifer Speer Ramundt
Proofreaders   Angela Ingle, Katherine C. Nugent, and Marcia Teeter
Photostylists   Janet Pittman, Jill Abeloe Mead, and Christa Bahr
Illustrators   Chris Neubauer   *Antique Quilt Collection*   Xenia Cord
Photographers   Perry Struse and Scott Little

Publisher   Stephen B. Levinson
Senior Marketing Manager   Suzy Johnson

Chairman, President and CEO   Alan Rosskamm
Executive Vice President of Merchandising and Marketing   Dave Bolen
Vice President, Marketing   William J. Dandy

Director of Sales and Promotion   Bill Hasslen

Meredith CORPORATION

Vice President, Publishing Director   William R. Reed

Chairman and CEO   William T. Kerr

Publishing Group President   Stephen M. Lacy
Magazine Group President   Jack Griffin

Production   Marjorie J. Schenkelberg
Book Retail Marketing Administration and Sales   George Susral
Circulation Newsstand   Gary Koerner

WELCOME

Whether you're new to quilting or have generations of experience, you'll turn to this all-inclusive reference book time and time again. It includes virtually everything you need to know about creating a quilt that will become a family heirloom.

From the tools you use to the colors you choose, the information on these pages will streamline your start-up steps. And that's important: A good start gives you the confidence to forge ahead—and fuels the excitement that compels the first cut.

As important, you'll find precise instructions for every stitch of hand and machine sewing. New techniques will help you achieve better results in less time and with more ease than ever before. This guide to color use, fabric selection, piecing, quilting, embellishing, and finishing is designed to ensure your success on patchwork projects of all sizes.

Your Guide to Quilting is also designed to share the joy that has made this a heritage art. It features ten notable quilts from the past to demonstrate how patchwork reflects the lives and times of their makers.

These quilts represent a mere fraction of the heartfelt art that has warmed us over the centuries. The designs are among hundreds that endured wars and weddings to earn their place as favorites among quilters of all ages. Elements from these quilts are re-created by each quilter, in fabrics that reflect their times and preferences.

As the world becomes smaller, our fabric selection becomes larger. But one hundred years ago, or even fifty, that was not the case. Textiles were treasured for their unique origin as well as their spectacular color or intriguing pattern. Swatches of fabric, like

designs, were shared among friends and family. Printed patterns were either unavailable or financially inaccessible.

Today, we have the advantage of the world at our fingertips. At Jo-Ann Stores across the nation, you can sample the personality of Africa, Asia, and Australia as well as Europe, North and South America, or the poles—by the bolt or fat quarter. This abundance of textiles is an unprecedented opportunity to personalize the art of quilting: Reflect individual tastes by mingling vintage and abstract prints, homespun fabrics with satin or wool.

Whatever your choice, you'll find that this book works as a personal tutor. Written for beginners and experts alike, *Your Guide to Quilting* covers the full gamut of steps involved in making a quilt. This series of carefully presented how-to techniques can be applied to your own patchwork projects, no matter how simple or complex.

And there are special tips from the people you've learned to trust most: Jo-Ann's veteran employees. They share their personal experience, and magnify it with hints and suggestions from hundreds of people they've helped over the years.

The tools and materials demonstrated in this book are usually available at your Jo-Ann Store. If you can't find a specific item at your local store, stretch your creativity and substitute fabric of a similar print, color, or texture.

So go ahead and get started. You'll be amazed how delightful it is to create a quilt when you have the advantage of a tutorial as thorough as this one. The easy-to-understand directions will help you enjoy the process—so you can relax and enjoy the creation of an heirloom quilt.

Table of CONTENTS

Chapter 1

TOOLS
AND MATERIALS

Whether you're quilting by hand or by machine,

make your quilting tasks easier, more accurate,

and more fun by using the right supplies.

GERMAN BAPTIST WEDDING QUILT

As a token of friendship in the early 1900s, a bride's friends often got together to make a special quilt for her. Sometimes they used fabrics from dresses they had made, knowing that the bride would think of them as she remembered them wearing those dresses. In 1906, 36 women who were friends and relatives of Anna Cripe Miller made a wedding quilt for her, signing their names in dark red thread in the centers of the blocks. Because the women were members of the conservative German Baptist church, the fabrics they chose were traditional indigo blues with tiny figures. They all used the same white fabric with tiny black dots for contrast. Easy Four-Patch units, set with larger squares to form Nine-Patch blocks, make this simple yet subtle design.

Tools *and Materials*

One of the joys of quilting is that the supplies needed can be as simple as scissors, needle, and thread, or more complex with specialty tools designed for specific purposes. Whether you're a gadget lover who wants every tool or a minimalist looking to acquire the basics, knowing what the tools are, what to use them for, and why they're useful is essential to quilting success.

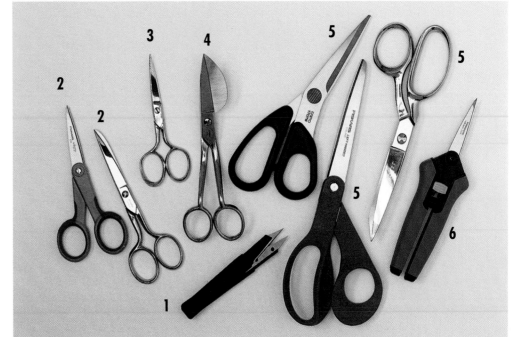

Photo 1A

SCISSORS

Quilting requires a good pair of scissors (see Photo 1A, *right*). Most quilters use several pairs, each designed for a different purpose. Choose your cutting tools with care, making certain they are of the highest quality you can afford. It's better to have two or three sharp pairs of scissors than a drawer full of seldom-used, dull pairs.

Choose your scissors and shears from the following:

Thread Clippers – 1
Use for cutting threads. Single style used by both left- and right-handed persons.

Craft Scissors and Knife-Edge Straight Trimmers – 2
Use for cutting threads and trimming fabric edges. Left- and right-handed styles available.

Embroidery Scissors – 3
Use for thread cutting. Left- and right-handed styles available.

Appliqué Scissors – 4
Use for close trimming; special duckbill protects underneath layers of fabric. Left- and right-handed styles available.

Knife-Edge Bent Trimmers or Shears – 5
Use for general cutting and sewing. Bent handle and flat edge provide accuracy when cutting on a flat surface. Left- and right-handed styles available.

Spring-Action Scissors – 6
Small and large sizes available. Ideal for use by persons with weakened hands or for lengthy cutting sessions. Single style used by both left- and right-handed quilters.

ROTARY-CUTTING TOOLS

Although scissors are still often used for cutting fabric, the rotary cutter and mat board have revolutionized the industry and streamlined the process. To rotary-cut fabrics you need a ruler, mat, and rotary cutter (see Chapter 4—Cutting Techniques for information on how to rotary-cut).

Rotary Cutters

Rotary cutters (see Photo 1B, *below*) come with different types and sizes of blades and a variety of handle sizes. Try out the cutters before buying to find the grip and size that work for you.

A rotary cutter will cut through several layers of fabric at one time. Because the blade is sharp, be sure to purchase a cutter with a safety guard and keep the guard over the blade when the cutter is not in use.

Rotary cutters are commonly available in three sizes—28 mm, 45 mm, and 60 mm. A good first blade is 45 mm. The 28-mm size is good for small-scale projects, miniatures, and corners. The 60-mm cutter can easily and accurately cut up to six layers of cotton fabrics.

Specialty blades, such as the 18-mm size, are used for cutting curves, miniatures, and appliqués; trimming seams; and cutting templates. Pinking and wave blades are used for novelty effects.

Acrylic Rulers

Accurate measurement is important for accurate piecing. To make straight cuts with a rotary cutter, choose a ruler of thick, clear plastic. Look for clear markings and accurate increments by measuring the ruler. Check to see if the 1" marks are the same crosswise and lengthwise.

Rulers come marked in a variety of colors. Try different rulers on cutting surfaces to see which is most easily visible (see Photo 1C, *opposite*).

There are rulers for every type of project and cutting need. Some rulers are almost like templates in that they create squares or right triangles in varying sizes. Some triangle rulers enable you to trim the points before joining the pieces together. If possible, try out rulers before making a purchase, or ask for a demonstration at a quilt shop and understand how to use them to get the maximum benefit from your purchase.

Rectangular Rulers

These rulers, such as a 6×24" ruler marked in ¼" increments with 30°, 45°, and 60° angles, are a good beginner's purchase (see Photo 1D, *opposite*). As you become more proficient you may wish to purchase additional acrylic rulers and templates in a variety of sizes and shapes.

A good second ruler is the 6×12" size (see Photo 1E, *opposite*). It is easier to handle than the 24" ruler and can be used for smaller cuts and to make crosscut strips. It can also be used with the 6×24" ruler to cut 12" blocks or to make straightening cuts.

Photo 1B

Photo 1C

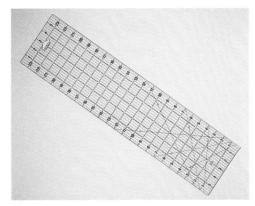

Photo 1D

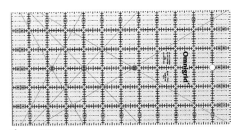

Photo 1E

Square Rulers
Good for secondary cuts and cutting and squaring blocks, square rulers are available in a variety of sizes (see Photo 1F, *right*).

For squaring up large blocks and quilt corners a 12½" or 15½" square ruler works well. This ruler can also be used for making setting triangles (see Photo 1G, *far right*).

Other Common Shapes
There are many rulers available that make cutting triangles, diamonds, and hexagons easy (see Photo 1H, *below right*).

45° Triangle Rulers
Cutting half- and quarter-square triangles, mitering corners, and cutting some diamonds and parallelograms is much easier with a 45° triangle ruler (see Photo 1I, *far right*).

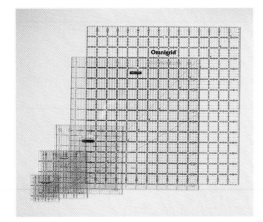

Photo 1F

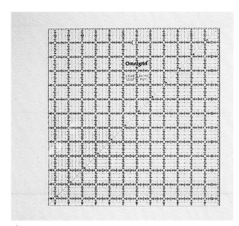

Photo 1G

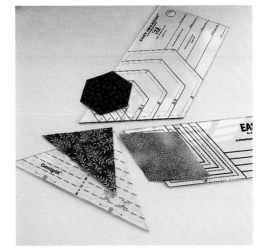

Photo 1H

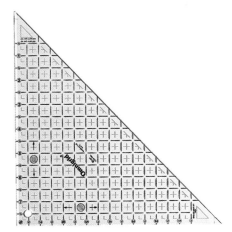

Photo 1I

60° Triangle Rulers

Use a 60° triangle ruler (see Photo 1J, *right*) when cutting equilateral triangles, diamonds, and hexagons.

Specialty Rulers and Templates

These tools are designed for cutting fans, arcs, Dresden Plates, Kaleidoscopes, some star patterns, and more (see Photo 1K, *below left*).

Curved Rulers and Templates

Cut precise Double Wedding Ring and Drunkard's Path pattern pieces (see Photo 1L, *below right*) with curved rulers and templates.

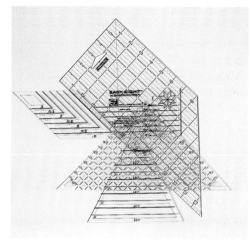

Photo 1J

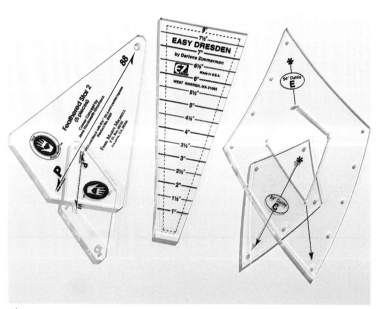

Photo 1K

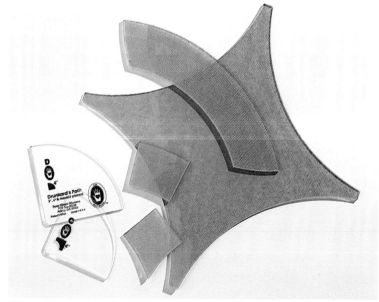

Photo 1L

Rotary-Cutting Mats

A rotary cutter should always be used with a mat designed specifically for it. The mat protects the work surface and keeps the fabric from shifting while you cut. Often mats are labeled as "self-healing," meaning the blade does not leave slash marks or grooves in the surface even after repeated usage. Many sizes, shapes, and styles are available (see Photo 1M, *below*), but a 16×23" mat marked with a 1" grid, hash marks at ⅛" increments, and 45° and 60° angles is a good first choice. For convenience, purchase a second smaller mat to take to workshops and classes.

Cutting mats usually have one side with a printed grid (see Photo 1N, *below*) and one plain side. To avoid confusion when lining up fabric with preprinted lines on a ruler, some quilters prefer to use the plain side of the mat. Others prefer to use the mat's grid.

Mats are also available with a mat board on one side and an ironing surface on the other side. This combination ironing board/cutting mat is great to have at workshops. Some mats have a lazy-Susan-type turnstile affixed underneath so they can be swiveled easily. The smallest mat boards (less than 12") work well for trimming blocks while you are seated at the sewing machine.

Store cutting mats flat or hanging on a wall. To avoid permanent bends do not store a mat on an edge or rolled up. Heat will cause a mat to warp and become unstable, so keep all mats out of direct sunlight, don't iron on them unless they have an ironing surface, and never leave them in a hot car.

Periodically treat a mat to a good cleaning with warm (not hot) soapy water or window cleaner. Dry gently with a towel.

Marking Supplies

Many products are available for marking sewing lines and quilting designs on a quilt top (see Photo 1O, *below left*). Useful supplies include fabric markers, templates, and pattern guides.

Variances in fabric contrast (light to dark) and fabric quality make marking different for each project, and a variety of markers may be needed for a single project. Try markers on fabric scraps and wash the test scraps in the same way the quilt will be washed to be sure marks will wash out. Templates and pattern guides will vary according to the needs of each project.

Fabric Markers
Artist's Pencil
This silver pencil often works on both light and dark fabrics.

Chalk Pencil
The chalk tends to brush away, so it is best to mark as you go with this pencil.

Mechanical Pencil
Use hard lead (0.5) and mark lightly so that stitching or quilting will cover the marks.

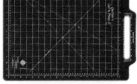

Photo 1M

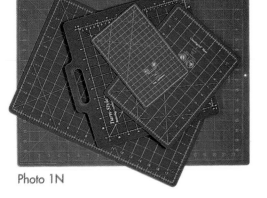

Photo 1N

Photo 1O

Pounce
This is chalk in a bag (see Photo 1P, *right*). Pounce or pat the bag on a stencil, leaving a chalk design on the fabric. The chalk disappears easily, so mark as you go with a pounce.

Soap Sliver
Sharpen the edges of leftover soap for a marker that washes out easily.

Soapstone Marker
If kept sharp, these markers will show up on light and dark fabrics.

Wash-Out Graphite Marker
Keep the sharpener handy for these markers that work well on light and dark fabrics.

Wash-Out Pen or Pencil
These markers maintain a point and are easy to see. Refer to the manufacturer's instructions to remove the markings and test them on scraps of your fabric to make sure the marks will wash out.
Note: Humidity may make the marks disappear, and applying heat to them may make them permanent.

Templates and Pattern Guides
A template is a pattern made from extra-sturdy material so it can be traced around many times without wearing away the edges.

Quilting Templates and Stencils
Precut templates and stencils (see Photo 1Q, *top, far right*) in a variety of shapes and sizes are available from quilt shops. These may be made from template plastic or a heavier-weight acrylic plastic. They can be traced around multiple times without wearing away any edges.

Some quilting stencils are made from paper. They are designed to be stitched through and torn away after the design is complete.

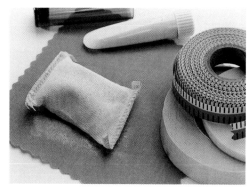
Photo 1P

Template Plastic
Template plastic (see Photo 1R, *right*) is an easy-to-cut, translucent material. Its translucency makes it possible to trace a pattern directly onto its surface with pencil or permanent marker to make a stencil or template.

Test a variety of materials, as some are heat-resistant (helpful when ironing over template edges) and some are not. Other varieties have grided for accuracy in tracing or are shaded for better visibility.

Freezer Paper
Create iron-on templates with freezer paper. Simply trace a shape onto the dull side of the freezer paper, cut it out, and press the shiny side directly onto fabric with a warm iron.

Graph Paper Templates
Use the printed lines on graph paper to draw a pattern piece. Glue the graph-paper pattern to template plastic, tag board, or cardboard. Allow the adhesive to dry before cutting through all layers at once to make an accurate template.

Clear Vinyl
Also known as upholstery vinyl, this material is used by hand quilters to make overlays for accurately positioning appliqué pieces on foundation fabric (see Chapter 6—Appliqué Techniques for more information on the overlay method).

Photo 1Q

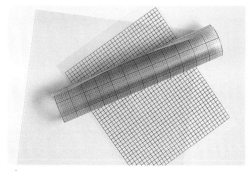
Photo 1R

Tape
Several types of tapes—quilter's tape, painter's tape, paper tape, and masking tape —are used to mark quilting and stitching lines. Quilter's tape is exactly $\frac{1}{4}$" wide; place it at the edge of the fabric and stitch alongside it for a perfect $\frac{1}{4}$" seam allowance.

Specialty tapes in widths from $\frac{1}{16}$" to 1" and wider are preprinted with lines to aid quilters in evenly spacing hand quilting or decorative stitches, such as a blanket stitch.

Some quilters use masking tape as a guide for straight-line machine or hand quilting.
Note: Do not leave masking tape on fabric for an extended period of time as the adhesive from the tape may leave a residue. Painter's tape is less sticky than masking tape and also can be used as a guide for straight-line quilting.

Cotton-Wrapped Polyester

Wrapping cotton around a polyester core creates a stronger thread with the finish characteristics of cotton thread. This thread is best used with fabric blends because it provides a little stretch. It's important to use a needle with a large eye to prevent stripping the cotton wrap from the polyester core.

Bobbin-Fill or Lingerie

Made from polyester or nylon and available in black or white, bobbin-fill works for machine embroidery, machine appliqué, or other decorative thread projects where multiple colors might be used in the needle. Prepare several bobbins filled with this thread and you can sew continuously without stopping to refill a bobbin. This thread is lighter weight than 100% cotton thread, which will cause the top thread to pull slightly through to the back side of the piece. Bobbin-fill is a more economical alternative to filling bobbins with specialty threads.

Metallic

The sheen and variety of colors available make metallic threads appealing for decorative stitching. However, metallic threads have a tendency to fray and break more often than cotton thread.

Using the right equipment will make the sewing process smoother. Work with a metallic or large-eye needle and a lightweight polyester, rayon, or nylon thread in the bobbin. Depending on the sewing machine manufacturer's specifications, liquid silicone drops may be added to the spool to make the thread run through the machine more easily.

Monofilament

Available in clear or smoke color, this synthetic, lightweight thread comes in nylon and polyester. It generally is used for machine quilting when the quilting thread

THREAD

Thread and needles are at the heart of quilting as the two elements that literally hold everything together. Choosing the right type and size needle and thread can make a big difference in the success of a quilting project. Follow three general guidelines:
• match the thread type to the fabric fiber content
• select the needle type based on the fabric being used
• select the needle size to match the thread

Thread Types

Thread has multiple roles, from holding together patchwork to anchoring the fabric to the batting. Thread also adds color, design, and texture to the quilt surface.

For piecing and most quilting, it's best to match the thread fiber to the fabric. Since most quilters use cotton fabric, 100% cotton thread is the best thread choice. Cotton thread is equal in strength to cotton fabric and should wear evenly. Synthetic threads, such as polyester, rayon, and nylon, are quite strong and can wear cotton fibers at the seams. For decorative quilting or embellishing, threads other than cotton may be appropriate (see Chapter 10—Specialty Techniques). Be sure your thread choice is suitable for the task; thread made for hand quilting, such as glazed cotton thread, should not be used in a sewing machine.

100% Cotton

Cotton thread is a staple in quilting. This thread works well with cotton fabric and is strong enough to create pieces that are durable. Hundreds of color choices are available in a variety of weights, although not all weights are created equal. Most cotton threads are two- or three-ply (see *page 17* for information on ply).

should not show or where thread color may be an issue (i.e. quilting on multicolor prints). In the bobbin, use a lightweight cotton thread or bobbin-fill in a color that matches the backing.

Perle Cotton

Soft and yarn-like, perle cotton is used for needlework projects or quilt embellishment. Typical weights used in quilting include Nos. 3, 5, 8, and 12. The higher the number, the finer the thread.

Polyester

This thread is designed for sewing with knits because the filament has the same stretch as knit fabric. Polyester thread should not be used with cotton fabrics for piecing or quilting because it can be abrasive to soft cotton fibers and cause the fabric to tear at the seams.

Rayon

The soft, lustrous characteristics of rayon thread and the hundreds of colors available make it ideal for embellishment. It's often used for decorative quilting or embroidery. This thread is not strong enough and doesn't wear well enough to be used in piecing a quilt. It should be alternated with a cotton thread when quilting a project that will get lots of wear.

Silk

Silk thread is stronger than cotton because it is a continuous filament, unlike the short, spun fibers of cotton. Silk also has more stretch than cotton thread. Some quilters prefer to use silk thread for hand appliqué because it glides through the fabric more easily than cotton and is usually finer, thus making it easier to hide the stitches. It also is less prone to fraying, allowing a longer length of thread to be used.

Variegated

This term applies to thread in which the color changes back and forth from light to dark throughout the strand or revolves through a range of colors to create a rainbow effect. It is available in both cotton and rayon.

Water-Soluble

This thread dissolves in water. Use it to baste a quilt and anchor trapunto or reverse appliqué. Once the project is completed, immerse it in water to dissolve the thread. Be sure to store the thread in a dry, humidity-controlled location.

Thread Finishes

After thread is made, finishes are often added to enhance its ability to perform under certain sewing conditions.

Mercerized Cotton

Mercerization enhances the dyeability, increases the luster, and adds strength to cotton thread. Mercerized cotton thread is often used for machine piecing and quilting.

Glazed Cotton

Glazed cotton threads are treated with starches and special chemicals under controlled heat, then polished to a high luster. The glazing process results in a hard finish that protects the thread from abrasion. Glazed cotton thread is used for hand quilting; it should not be used in a sewing machine.

> **Tip:** Thread marked 50/3 (50 weight and 3 ply) works for both hand and machine quilting on cotton fabric. It's considered a medium-weight thread.

Bonded Threads

These are continuous-filament nylon or polyester threads that have been treated with a special resin to encapsulate the filaments. The tough, smooth coating holds the plies together and adds to the thread's ability to resist abrasion.

Thread Quality

Buy the highest quality thread you can afford for your projects. Skimping in the thread department can create frustration with breakage, bleeding, and other problems. Consider the total cost of quilting materials and your time, and know that saving a dollar on a spool of thread may not be worth it in the long run.

Cotton thread is made from cotton fibers, which are only as long as what the plant produces. The fibers are spun into a yarn and yarns are twisted into a thread. Poor quality threads are made from the shortest fibers and appear fuzzy along the length of the thread. They tend to fray and break easily. Higher quality threads are made from longer fibers of cotton and have a smoother finish.

Ply

Thread is made from yarns that are twisted together into a single ply yarn. Plies are then twisted together to produce two-ply or three-ply threads, which are the kinds most commonly used for piecing.

Filament

This term is generally applied to man-made threads, such as polyester, nylon, or rayon, created from a chemical spinning process where a single strand or "filament" is produced. Silk is the only naturally occurring filament. Polyester and nylon threads are quite strong and are not normally used for piecing cotton since the fabric will tear before the thread breaks.

Thread Breakage

If you're having trouble with thread breaking, check these possible causes:

- **Damaged or incorrect needle** Change the needle, as it may have dulled from overuse or could have a burr or nick. If the needle is new, check that it is the correct size and the eye is large enough for the thread type and weight being used.
- **Defective or old thread** Lower-quality threads may have thick and thin spots that lead to breakage. Thread becomes dry and brittle as it ages, causing it to break more easily.
- **Improperly threaded machine** Check to see that the spool is properly positioned on the sewing machine. The thread may be getting caught on the spool cap end as it comes off the top of the spool. The solution may be as simple as turning over the spool on the spool pin.

  If the presser foot wasn't raised when the machine was threaded, the thread may not be caught between the tension discs inside the machine. Remove the spool and rethread the machine with the presser foot raised.
- **Operator error** Pushing, pulling, or allowing drag on the fabric by hanging a heavy quilt over a work surface can increase stress on the thread and cause breakage.
- **Tension too tight** Refer to the machine's manual and *page 30* to determine if this is the cause of thread breakage.
- **Wrong thread** You may have the wrong thread type for the fabric. Change the thread and sew on a scrap of fabric to see how a different thread performs.

Photo 1S

NEEDLES

Whether you sew by hand or machine, using the correct needle size and type will make the task easier and the results more polished (see Photo 1S, *above*).

Machine- and hand-sewing needles have some similarities, but be aware that once you've mastered the numbers for machine-needle sizes, you'll need to learn a whole new set for hand-sewing needles.

It is important to change needles frequently, as both kinds become dull with use. If a machine needle strikes a pin or the machine bed, it can develop a nick or burr that can tear your fabric.

Sewing-Machine Needles

A notions wall can be intimidating if you're not sure what you need. There are dozens of sizes and shapes of sewing-machine needles, each designed for a different task (see Photo 1T, *right*). Understanding the terminology associated with machine needles can take the mystery out of making a selection and make piecing and quilting go smoother.

Machine Needle Sizes

When looking at a package of machine needles, you will often see two numbers separated by a slash mark. The number on the left of the slash is the European size (range of 60 to 120); the right-hand number is the American size (range of 8 to 21). Sizes 70/10, 80/12, and 90/14 are most commonly used for quilting. A lower number indicates a finer machine needle.

Machine Needle Points

The needle point differentiates the type and purpose of a needle and is a key characteristic to consider when selecting a needle for a project. The needle point should match the fabric type. For sewing on quilting cotton, for example, use a needle labeled as a "sharps."
Note: *Needles last longer when the fabric and batting used are 100% cotton. Polyester or polyester/cotton blend batting tends to dull needles quicker.*

Machine Needle Eyes

A needle's eye must be large enough for the thread to pass through with minimal friction. If the eye is too large for the thread, it may produce a seam that is loose and weak. Large needles make large holes, so use the smallest needle appropriate

for the thread. Some needles have eyes specially shaped for certain thread types, such as metallic threads, to minimize breakage.

Machine Needle Types
- Sharps are the preferred needle type for piecing and quilting woven fabrics such as cotton. Sharps needles come in a variety of sizes and brands.
- Universal needles can be used on both woven and knit fabrics but are not ideal for piecing because the needle points are slightly rounded. Choose this needle type if you want versatility when working with different fabrics.
- Metallic needles are designed for use with metallic threads. A larger needle eye accommodates the thread, which tends to be fragile yet rough enough to create burrs in the eye of the needle. Burrs can cause the thread to fray and break.
- Topstitch needles can handle heavier decorative threads but also leave larger holes in the fabric.
- Specialty needles include double or triple needles, leather needles, and heirloom-sewing needles.

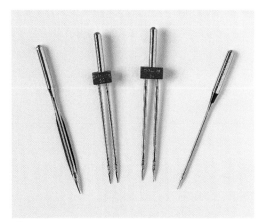

Photo 1T

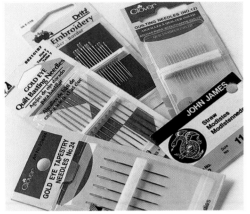
Photo 1U

Hand-Sewing Needles

Make hand sewing easier by selecting the right needle. A wide variety of hand-sewing needles are available through quilt shops and fabric stores (see Photo 1U, *left*). Understanding the type, size, and uses of each needle will help you select the one most suitable for your project.

Hand Needle Sizes

The size of a hand needle is determined by its diameter. There are two ranges in diameter size: 1 to 15 and 13 to 28. The diameter of a specific size remains consistent across the various needle types. In each case, the larger the number, the finer the needle; all size 12 needles are finer than size 8, for example.

Hand Needle Points

Hand-quilting needles have sharp points that pierce fabric readily. Working with a dull needle can be frustrating and produce less desirable results. Just as with machine sewing, switching to a new needle after several hours of sewing is optimal.

Hand-Sewing Needles

SMALL ROUND EYES	TYPE	LENGTH / DIAMETER	SIZES	USES
#8 Sharps	SHARPS	Medium / 41–76 mm	4–12	Hand piecing; general sewing; fine thread embroidery; sewing binding
#8 Betweens	BETWEENS/ QUILTING	Short / 41–76 mm	4–12	Hand piecing and quilting; appliqué; sewing binding
#9 Straw #8 Glovers	STRAW/ MILLINERS	Long / 53–76 mm	4–10	Basting; gathering; appliqué
	GLOVERS	Medium with a triangular point / 86–102 mm	1–3	Leather
		53–76 mm	4–10	Leather
LONG NARROW EYES				
#8 Embroidery	EMBROIDERY	Medium / 53–102 mm	1–10	Wool thread embroidery
#9 Darners	DARNERS	Long / 46–102 mm	1–11	Basting; weaving; tying comforters
		127–234 mm	14–18	
#9 Long Darners	LONG DARNERS	Double long / 61–183 mm	1–15	Weaving; tying comforters
#10 Beading	BEADING	Double long / 25–46 mm	10–15	Bead and sequin work
LONG OVAL EYES				
#26 Chenille	CHENILLE	Medium / 61–234 mm	12–26	Heavy thread embroidery; tying comforters
#26 Tapestry	TAPESTRY/ CROSS-STITCH	Medium with blunt point / 46–234 mm	13–28	Needlepoint; cross-stitch

Hand Needle Eyes

Needles with small, round eyes carry fine thread (approximately equal in diameter to the needle itself) that slides easily through the fabric. Longer needle eyes accommodate thicker threads and yarns. The oval eye found in tapestry and chenille needles helps create an opening in the fabric for thick, sometimes coarse fibers to pass through. Use the smallest needle appropriate to the thread to minimize holes in the fabric.

Hand Needle Types

Quilters have many different uses for hand-sewing needles—hand piecing, hand quilting, appliqué, embroidery, tying, and securing binding. The point of the needle, the shape of the eye, and the needle's length in proportion to the eye determine its type. Short needles are easier to maneuver in small spaces. There are longer needles for tasks that require long stitches or lots of stitches on the needle, like basting, weaving, and gathering.

- **Betweens** have a small, round eye and come in sizes 4 to 12. Betweens are short and made of fine wire, resulting in a strong, flexible needle that's ideal for hand quilting, appliqué, and sewing binding. This is the most commonly used needle for hand quilting.
- **Sharps** have a small, round eye and come in sizes 4 to 12. They are used for hand piecing, appliqué, general sewing, embroidery work that uses fine threads, and sewing binding.
- **Straw, or milliners, needles** come in sizes 4 to 10. They have a small, round eye and are very long. These needles are often used for basting, gathering, and appliqué.
- **Beading needles** are extra long with long, narrow eyes. Available in sizes 10 to 15, these needles are used for embellishment, beading, and sequin work.

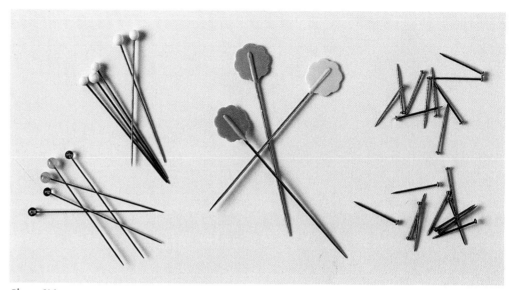

Photo 1V

- **Chenille needles** have long, oval eyes and come in sizes 12 to 26. A chenille needle is often used for heavyweight thread, embroidery, and tying quilts.
- **Darners** have long, narrow eyes. This needle type comes in sizes 1 to 11 and is used for basting, weaving, and tying quilts. Darners are available in finer sizes ranging from 14 to 18. Long darners (double-long needles) are available in sizes 1 to 15.
- **Embroidery needles** come in sizes 1 to 10 and have long, narrow eyes. They are most often used for embroidery work with thicker decorative thread or wool thread.

PINS

Experiment with different pins to determine which ones work best for your needs (see Photo 1V, *above*).

- **Extra-fine, or silk, pins** have thin shafts and sharp points. These pins make a small hole and are easy to insert.
- **Glass-head pins** allow you to press fabric pieces with pins in place without melting the pin heads.
- **Flat flower pins** have heads shaped like flowers. The long shaft makes them easy to grab and helps the pins stay put in the fabric.
- **Appliqué pins** range from ¾" to 1¼" in length. They are designed to securely hold work in place yet prevent the sewing thread from getting snagged with each stitch.
- **Safety pins** (not shown) are clasps with a guard covering the point when closed. Use safety pins that are at least 1" long to pin-baste a quilt. Choose stainless-steel pins that are rust-proof and will not tarnish. There are several devices, including a spoon, that can be used to help close the pins, preventing hand fatigue. In addition, there are curved basting safety pins that slide in place without moving the quilt sandwich.

General Sewing Supplies

Whether you like to hand- or machine-quilt, there are a variety of general sewing supplies that are handy to have.

Needle Threaders

A needle threader, whether handheld or a machine attachment, makes getting the thread through the needle eye easier (see Photo 1W, *right*). Try several models to see which works best for your vision and coordination skills. Keep one close at hand to prevent eye strain.

Seam Rippers

Although quilters don't enjoy "reverse sewing," sometimes it is necessary to remove a line of stitching. A sharp, good quality seam ripper can make the task of removing stitches easy and cause the least damage possible to the fabric (see Photo 1X, *top, far right*). Choose one that is sharp and fits comfortably in your hand.

Graph Paper

For pattern making or quilt designing use ⅛" (8 squares per inch) graph paper (see Photo 1Y, *right*). If you're drawing a design on ¼" paper, enlarge the design on a copier by 400% to have a full-size copy. **Note:** *Be sure to measure photocopies for distortion before using them as templates.*

Measuring Tapes

A measuring tape is essential for large measurements, such as border lengths or squaring up quilts (see Photo 1Z, *right*). Purchase one that is long enough to cover the largest possible quilt measurement so you don't have to move the tape midway. Be aware that over time, a well-used cloth measuring tape may stretch and thus become inaccurate.

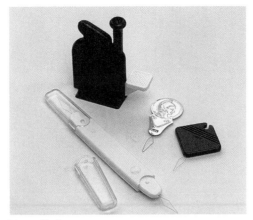

Photo 1W

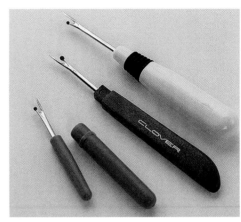

Photo 1X

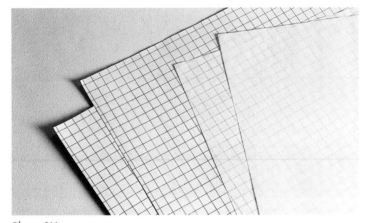

Photo 1Y

Photo 1Z

✂Creative Tip

Remove any pins or hand-sewing needles from a project within 48 hours of placement. Pins and needles left too long can leave a mark.
—SUE, EDUCATION/MARKETING CONTENT SPECIALIST

Pincushions

Pincushions are available in numerous styles, from the familiar standard tomato shape, to wrist, magnetic tabletop, and even decorative pincushions. Select a style that's easy to use. Computerized machines may have problems with magnetic pincushions placed on or near the computer display screen. Check the sewing machine manual for specific warnings.

The strawberry-shape needle cushion filled with emery that is often attached to a tomato-shape pincushion is an important aid in keeping needles sharp and tarnish-free. Run all hand-sewing needles through the emery cushion before using them to remove any slight burrs, nicks, or residue.

Stabilizers

Stabilizers are used beneath machine appliqué or machine embroidery work to add support to the foundation fabric, helping to eliminate puckers and pulling.

Stabilizers may be temporary or permanent. Temporary stabilizers are removed after stitching is complete. Permanent stabilizers remain in the quilt or are only partially cut away after stitching. Many brands are commercially available. Two of the most common types are tear-away and water-soluble. Freezer paper may also be used as a stabilizer.

Check the manufacturer's instructions on the package to select a stabilizer that is appropriate for your fabric and type of project. It is wise to experiment with a variety of stabilizers to determine which works best for a specific project.

Bias Bars

These heat-resistant metal or plastic bars may be purchased in a size to match the desired finished width of the bias tube you wish to make. They are a handy tool for making appliqué stems (see Chapter 6—Appliqué Techniques for more information on making bias stems).

Reducing Lens or Door Peephole

A reducing lens or door peephole (see Photo 2A, *below right*) allows quilters to view fabrics and projects as if they are several feet away. Distance is valuable in determining design qualities (see Chapter 2—Fabric and Color for more information).

PRESSING EQUIPMENT

Proper pressing is essential to successful quilting. Even with the right equipment, understanding how to press can make a significant difference in the quality of your finished quilt. See Chapter 5—Piecing for information on how to press.

Irons

Choose an iron that can be adjusted to a cotton setting and can be used with or without steam (see Photo 2B, *opposite*). There are a variety of irons available, including some small portable models that work well for classes or for special purposes, such as pressing bias strips or appliqués. If the iron will be used with fusible web, be sure to place a protective, nonstick sheet between the fabric and the iron to prevent the fusing adhesive from sticking to the sole of the iron. Consider purchasing a soleplate cover or second iron for use only with fusible web.

Photo 2A

Creative Tip

Hang your tools on the wall with Self Stick Velcro.

Apply the hook side to the wall and a small piece of the loop side

to the wrong side of your rotary rules.

—COLLEEN, SALES ASSOCIATE

Ironing Boards

Quilters have many choices in pressing surfaces, from the traditional ironing board with a tapered end to portable pressing surfaces/cutting boards in one. There are products available to create a pressing surface on a table, and there are large rectangular boards that fit over the traditional ironing board. The pressing surface can be covered with a purchased cover, or one made with batting and flannel or extra cotton fabric.

Do not choose a silver-color, nonstick-coated cover for a pressing surface, as it reflects the heat, rather than allowing steam to pass completely through the fabric pieces.

Starch and Sizing

Some quilters like to work with fabric that has been starched, because they believe the fabric pieces are easier to handle and hold their shape better while pinning and stitching. Use a spray starch to add stiffening to prewashed fabrics or appliqué projects. Use spray sizing when more body but not as much stiffening is desired, such as when working with flannels. Wash the quilt after assembling.

ADHESIVES

Basting Spray

Many brands of basting spray are available (see Photo 2C, *below*). The main point of difference is the ability to reposition the fabric. The sprays are often a good option for temporarily holding appliqués in place or for basting a small quilt or wall hanging together. Follow label directions and work in a ventilated area.

Fabric Glue

Fabric glue comes   Photo 2C
in several different forms. Whether it comes in a bottle with a needle-tip applicator or on a glue stick, make certain it is designed for use with fabric and is water-soluble and acid-free. When dry, fabric glue is more pliable than standard glue, and often its temporary bond allows you to reposition pieces without leaving permanent residue on a quilt.

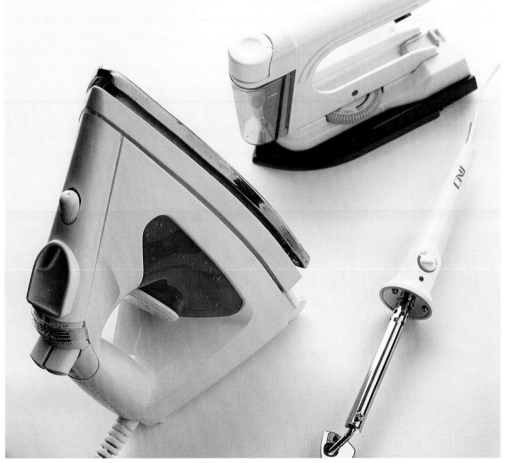

Photo 2B

Photo 2D

Photo 2E

Photo 2F

Fusible Web

Available in prepackaged sheets or rolls, by the yard off the bolt, and as a narrow-width tape, fusible web is an iron-on adhesive that in nearly every case creates a permanent bond between layers of fabric.

Fusible web has adhesive on both sides with a paper backing on one side. It is most often used for machine appliqué.

The standard version for quilting is a lightweight, paper-backed fusible web specifically designed to be stitched through. When purchasing this product, check the label to make sure it is a sew-through type. If the fused fabric will not be sewn through, (e.g. unfinished appliqué edges), it may be wise to use a heavyweight, no-sew fusible web.

The manufacturer's instructions for adhering fusible web vary by brand. Follow the instructions that come with the fusible web regarding the correct iron temperature

setting and whether to use a dry or steam iron. These factors, along with the length of time the fabric is pressed, are critical to attaining a secure bond between the fusible web and the fabric.

BATTING

The material that goes between the quilt top and quilt backing—batting—can vary from quilt to quilt (see Photo 2D, *above left*). Learn the characteristics and properties of batting for the ideal match (see Chapter 8—Quilting Ideas for complete information).

MACHINE QUILTING ACCESSORIES

Besides needles and threads appropriate to a specific project, a variety of tools make machine quilting more successful. Personal preference dictates the use of many of these optional accessories.

Quilt Clips

Use quilt clips, or bicycle clips, to secure the rolled-up edges of a large quilt that will be machine-quilted. These will better control the bulk of the quilt as you move it around while stitching.

Walking or Even-Feed Foot

This foot evenly feeds multiple layers of fabric and batting for machine quilting, effectively providing feed dogs for the upper fabrics to work in conjunction with the feed dogs on the machine bed (see Photo 2E, *above middle*). Some sewing machines come with a built-in dual-feed system, eliminating the need for a special foot. Some machines have brand-specific walking feet, while others will accept a generic walking foot. (See Additional Accessory Feet on *page 30* for information on other specialty machine presser feet.)

HAND QUILTING ACCESSORIES

Beyond the all-important needle and thread choices that hand quilters make, there are few other tools required. Personal preference dictates the use of many of the optional accessories.

Thimbles

Protect your fingers while quilting with a variety of thimbles (see Photo 2F, *opposite*). Choose from metal or leather, or consider special pads that stick to your finger. Try them all to determine the style that works best for you. For difficult-to-fit fingers or simply increased comfort, custom-made thimbles are widely available.

Quilting Frames and Hoops

Wooden hoops or frames are often used to hold quilt layers together, keeping them smooth and evenly taut for hand quilting (see Photo 2G, *below*). The layers of a quilt should be basted together before inserting them into a hoop or frame.

Some quilters prefer hoops because they are smaller and lighter in weight than frames, take up less storage space, are portable, and can be retightened as needed.

Quilting hoops, which generally are sturdier than embroidery hoops, may be round, oval, square, or rectangular. Semicircular hoops, which are good for stitching borders or other areas close to a quilt's edges, are also available.

Hoops come in all sizes, but one with a diameter of 10 to 20" should be able to accommodate most quilting needs. Some hoops have a detachable floor stand that frees your hands for stitching and permits the hoop to be tilted and/or raised.

Most quilting frames consist of wooden top rails in a rectangular shape supported by sturdy legs. They come in a wide range of sizes (30 to 120") so they can handle quilts up to king size. When using a frame, a quilt's edges are pinned or stitched flat to the rails so the layers are smooth, straight, and secure. One or both pairs of frame rails can be rotated to roll up the quilt and facilitate working on a small area at a time. A quilt frame must remain set up and in place until the quilting is complete.

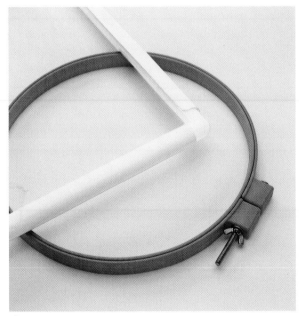

Photo 2G

Creative Tip

Plug your sewing machine, iron, and Ott light fixture into a power strip. When you're done sewing or ironing, just flip off the one switch for ease and peace of mind. If the light's off, the iron's off.

—VIRGINIA, SALES ASSOCIATE

WORK SPACE DESIGN FOR EFFICIENCY AND COMFORT

Although quilting may seem like a sedentary activity, it takes energy, and the repetitive actions can stress joints and muscles. To keep sewing comfortably, follow a few simple tips for posture and position.

Posture

Be aware of your body posture. A straight back with your head and neck aligned and feet flat on the floor provides the most support. Sitting or working at awkward angles and performing repetitive motions create situations that can cause injuries.

90 Degrees

Keep this angle in mind whenever you sit down to perform a task.

Your back and legs should be at a 90° angle. Your upper and lower legs should form a 90° angle at the knees. When your feet are flat on the floor, your ankles will also be at a 90° angle. Next look at your arms. Elbows should be at a 90° angle, with your forearms parallel to the work surface. Keep your elbows close to your sides and your shoulders straight.

Table or Large Work Surface

A large work surface allows you to lay out long yardages of fabric when cutting or to handle a medium- to large-size quilt for basting. In addition, a large surface provides ample space to spread out a project for machine quilting, preventing the project from dragging or pulling, which can result in uneven stitches.

Adjust the Work Surface

Once your 90° positions are determined, raise or lower the work surface and/or chair to the proper height so you can hold these positions and work comfortably.

When the chair is raised so your arms are at the work surface, it may not be possible to keep your feet flat on the floor. Put a sturdy box or platform step under your feet so that your knees and ankles remain at 90° angles.

Several products are available that can adjust the tilt of a sewing machine or foot pedal to make it more comfortable to use and easier to see the machine bed. Many quilters find these products ease the stress and strain on their bodies when they sew for extended periods. If possible, sit down and try the products at the shop to see whether they would aid in making your work space more comfortable.

Give this good posture time. Your body may have adapted to working at awkward angles, and it may feel strange when your posture is adjusted. Stay with the correct posture, and you will benefit in the long run.

Align the cutting surface to hip height to eliminate the need to bend over and unnecessarily put strain on back and shoulder muscles. When rotary cutting, use sharp rotary blades and rulers with nonskid material to decrease the amount of pressure needed to cut fabric, thus reducing the strain on your body.

When hand-quilting with a frame, it is best to first position the chair with your body at 90° angles. Next measure the distance between your elbows (bent at 90°) and the floor. Set the front roller bar of the quilting frame at this height, then adjust the back of the quilting frame.

Design Wall

Having a vertical surface on which to lay out fabric choices can help you visualize how they might look in a quilt (see Photo 2H, *opposite*). For a permanent or portable design wall, cover foam core or board insulation with a napped material, such as felt or flannel, that will hold small fabric pieces in place. Some designers use the flannel backing of a vinyl tablecloth, which can be rolled up between projects or hung on a hanger.

Creative Tip

Cramped on space, but need a full-size ironing board close by? Install a

wall-mountable ironing board above your cutting counter or sewing desk.

—LESLIE, STORE ASSOCIATE

Lighting

Quilting requires overall lighting and nonglare directional lighting to avoid eyestrain and produce high-quality results. Review your quilting areas for lighting and invest in the appropriate fixtures to eliminate the headaches and vision problems that can result from eyestrain.

Several specialty lamps and bulbs specifically designed for quilters are available at quilt shops. Some are designed to more accurately reflect the colors of fabrics, filtering out excess yellow and blue tones that common household bulbs can cast. These can be especially helpful when you are selecting fabric combinations for your quilts and if your quilting area does not have abundant natural daylight.

Workshop and Retreat Setup

Plan for posture and comfort needs when going to workshops and retreats. Bring a portable table and chair, or anticipate the type of chair (often folding) and table (often portable and 30" high). Borrow a folding chair ahead of time and note your posture and the 90° positions. Use pillows or boxes to adjust your height, and take them to class. Being properly positioned will allow more productivity and reduce the chances of developing joint and muscle pain.

Keep Moving for Personal Comfort

Though it's easy to get lost in quilting, it is important to to pause for a few minutes every hour to step away from the sewing machine or quilting frame and stretch. Reposition yourself periodically to reduce muscle fatigue and eyestrain, and enjoy several hours of quilting. Speak with your health care provider about specific exercises that can help strengthen your neck, back, shoulders, arms, wrists, and hands.

Creative Tip

Use an Ott light or just an Ott lightbulb in a regular lamp in your sewing area. Colors appear as true as in daylight and the light is kinder to the eyes. I can sew much later at night without fatigue.

—SUE, EDUCATION/MARKETING CONTENT SPECIALIST

Photo 2H

Sewing Machines

Essential to machine piecing and quilting is the sewing machine. A serviceable, basic machine in good working order is sufficient for most purposes. Newer machines offer some features and optional accessories that make piecing and quilting easier and more enjoyable. Select a brand that can have its annual maintenance and repairs handled conveniently.

Understanding the machine's features can help avoid problems or fix them when they arise. The machine's manual is the best resource for specific information and problem solving. Some basic information applicable to most sewing machines follows.

How Machines Stitch

Two threads coming together to hold pieces of fabric in place may appear to be magic. In reality, it takes sophisticated engineering for the two threads to create straight and decorative stitches. Understanding how thread travels through the sewing machine can be useful in preventing and solving problems.

The seams created by machine are a series of lockstitches or knots. To create lockstitches on most machines, the thread runs from the spool through tension discs and into the take-up lever. As the needle goes down into the bobbin case, the take-up lever also moves down. In the bobbin case, the bobbin hook creates a loop that interlaces with the thread coming through the needle eye. As the take-up lever and needle come back up through the fabric, the loop formed with the bobbin and needle threads is pulled up to create a stitch.

Sewing Machine Features

Only one basic function is needed to piece and quilt by machine—sewing straight, uniform stitches to create a seam that doesn't pucker or pull the fabric. Optional features may include some or all of the following.

Adjustable Stitch Length

This feature enables the change in stitch length from long stitches for basting to tiny stitches used to secure thread at the beginning or end of a seam or quilted area. In many newer machines, this feature is expressed in millimeters (10 to 12 stitches per inch equals a 2.0- to 2.5-mm setting). If knowing the stitches per inch is important to the project, create a sample swatch and measure the number of stitches in an inch.

Adjustable Stitch Width

With this feature, zigzag and other decorative machine stitches can be widened. This is an important feature for crazy quilting with decorative stitches (see Chapter 10—Specialty Techniques).

Zigzag and Satin Stitch

For a zigzag stitch, often used in machine appliqué, the needle swings from left to right. Adjusting the stitch length will produce stitches that are closer together. When the stitches form one against the other, filling any gaps, this creates satin stitching (see Chapter 6—Appliqué Techniques). Often the width of the stitch also can be varied.

Needle-Down Option

Once engaged, this feature allows the needle to stop sewing in the down position every time, allowing you to pivot or adjust the fabric without losing your stitching position. If disengaged, the needle will always stop in the up position.

Photo 2I

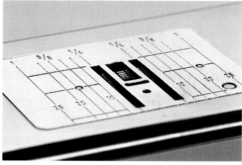

Photo 2J

Adjustable Feed Dogs

The ability to drop or cover the feed dogs is important for free-motion quilting (see Chapter 10—Specialty Techniques). When the feed dogs are in the up position, they grab onto the fabric as it moves under the presser foot (see Photo 2I, *top*).

With the feed dogs in the down position and a darning presser foot on, the fabric can be moved freely on the machine bed, controlling where and at what rate the fabric feeds beneath the presser foot (see Photo 2J, *above*).

Easily Accessible Bobbin Case

When a bobbin runs out of thread, especially in the middle of a project, being able to easily change or refill it is important. Look for a machine that offers easy access to the bobbin so you don't have to take apart the machine bed or remove the machine from the cabinet.

Extended Machine Bed Surface

An extended surface is important if a machine is not in a cabinet with the arm in line with the cabinet surface, especially for piecing or quilting large projects. Some portable machines come with a snap-on or slide-on tray that extends the bed of the machine. Or purchase a surround that is customized to fit around the arm of the sewing machine to extend the work area. The larger, level work surface prevents the fabric from pulling and stretching under its own weight as you work with it.

Knee-Lift Presser Foot

This feature enables you to lift and lower the presser foot by pressing your knee on a bar that extends down from the machine front (see Photo 2K, *below*). It can be especially helpful when you need both hands free to hold the fabric.

Sewing Machine Accessories

Many machines come with a kit of standard accessories. Some have optional accessories available for purchase.

There are also a number of generic sewing accessories designed to work with a variety of machine models. Knowing the sewing machine model brand and number when purchasing generic accessories is helpful, as the packaging often states the machines and brands with which the accessories will work.

Straight-Stitch Throat Plate

A straight-stitch throat plate has a small, round hole for the needle to pass through, rather than the larger opening of a standard throat plate (see Photo 2L, *below*). This smaller opening allows less area for the sewing machine to take in or "swallow" the fabric as it is being stitched and results in more uniform stitches.

Photo 2K

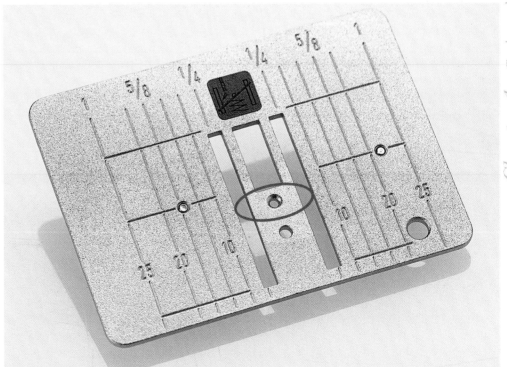

Photo 2L

¼" Foot

Some machines allow the needle to be repositioned so that it's ¼" from the edge of the standard presser foot. In addition, many machine models offer a special ¼" presser foot (see Photo 2M, *below*). With this foot and the needle in the standard position, the edge of the foot serves as the seam guide. For piecing, it is a useful accessory as you can watch only the edge of the fabric along the presser foot edge; it isn't necessary to watch or mark a line along the throat plate or machine bed.

Additional Accessory Feet

An array of specialty feet, including open-toe appliqué (see Photo 2N, *below*) and darning (used for free-motion quilting; see Photo 2O, *below*), cording, and binding feet, are available for a variety of machines. (See Machine Quilting Accessories on *page 24* for information on a walking, or even-feed, foot.) Check with the sewing machine's manufacturer for a complete list, or check the packaging of generic accessory feet to determine which models might be compatible with your machine.

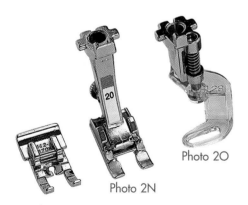

Photo 2O

Photo 2N

Photo 2M

TENSION

When tension is balanced, stitches appear on both sides of the fabric without loops, surface knots, or broken thread.

For most piecing, the machine's tension will not need to be adjusted. Tension problems tend to be more prevalent when sewing with fabrics of different weights, heavy or decorative threads, or specialty needles. As with all sewing machine adjustments, check the machine's manual first when attempting to solve a tension problem.

Adjusting Upper Thread Tension

When a "bird's nest" of thread appears either on top of or underneath the fabric, the likely culprit is upper thread tension. To determine what to correct, follow these guidelines:
- If loops appear on the underside of the fabric, the upper thread tension may be too loose.
- If knots appear on top of the fabric, the upper tension may be too tight.

Before adjusting the machine's tension dial, check to be sure the machine is properly threaded. If the presser foot was lowered as the machine was threaded, it is likely the upper thread is not between the tension discs inside the machine. Or one of the tension guides or the take-up lever may have been missed. Simply raise the presser foot and rethread the machine.

If the problem still occurs, it may be necessary to adjust the upper tension dial. If the tension is too tight, adjust the dial to a lower number to loosen it. If the upper thread tension is too loose, adjust the dial to a higher number to tighten it. Refer to the machine's manual for specific instructions about making tension dial adjustments.

Adjusting Bobbin Thread Tension

Although many machines allow for adjustment of the upper thread tension, the bobbin thread tension is generally set by the machine's manufacturer. It doesn't usually need to be adjusted except for work with decorative or specialty threads (see Extra Bobbin Case, *opposite*).

If the bobbin thread is knotting up on the underside of the fabric, try removing the bobbin and reloading it, making sure to properly insert the thread through the bobbin tension slots as directed in the sewing machine's manual.

In some cases, it may be necessary to thread the bobbin through the hole in the bobbin case "finger" to increase the tension. The machine manual will have instructions for this procedure if it is an option.

BOBBINS

For general piecing and quilting, use the same type of thread in the bobbin as in the top of the machine. Metallic and decorative threads are the exceptions (see *pages 15–16*). Trying to save money by using a less expensive or different type of thread in the bobbin can lead to tension difficulties.

Use bobbins that are specifically designed for the sewing machine.

There are two basic types of bobbin mechanisms. The first is a front-loading bobbin, in which a filled bobbin fits into a bobbin case that then snaps into the opening on the front of the machine (see photos 2P and 2Q, *opposite*).

The second type of bobbin mechanism is the top-loading, or drop-in, bobbin (see Photo 2R, *opposite*). This type usually does not have a separate bobbin case. Instead, the

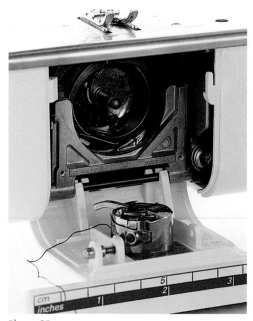

Photo 2P

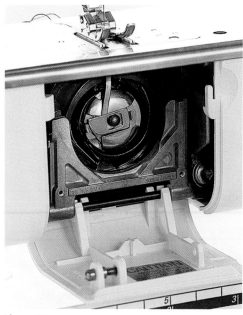

Photo 2Q

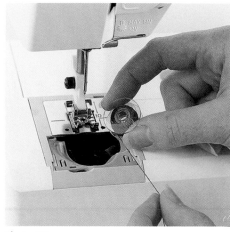

Photo 2R

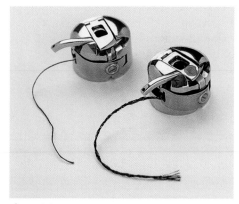

Photo 2S

filled bobbin simply drops into the bobbin casing in the bed of the machine, usually in front of the presser foot.

Winding Bobbins

For large projects, keep multiple bobbins filled by winding several at one sitting.

Follow the sewing machine manufacturer's directions for bobbin winding. Be sure to start the thread in the correct direction and wind at a speed that allows for even filling. Winding a bobbin at too fast a speed can stretch the thread, resulting in a puckered seam.

Disposable, prewound bobbins are another option, depending on what the machine will accept and project requirements.

Extra Bobbin Case

The bobbin case that comes with a machine has been factory set for sewing with basic threads. To sew with specialty threads, consider purchasing an additional bobbin case (if the machine accepts one) for use with decorative or thicker threads (see Photo 2S, *above right*).

It is necessary to adjust the tension for these threads by turning the screw on the bobbin case's tension spring. Turn it to the left to loosen the tension and to the right to tighten the tension.

For heavy, thick threads the tension generally needs to be loosened, and this should be accomplished in less than two complete rotations of the screw. Work over a bowl, box, or plastic bag in case the screw comes out.

Always sew a test sample after adjusting the screw.

Place a dot of nail polish or permanent marker on the second case to designate it as the case that has had its tension adjusted.

If there is only one bobbin case, make notes in the sewing machine manual to indicate changes in screw or tension settings when using different threads. For example, write "left 1½ turns for No. 5 perle cotton."

Creative Tip

Adhere the hook side of self-sticking Velcro on the bottom of serger and sewing machine foot pedals to keep them from creeping on carpeted floors.

—NANCY, SALES ASSOCIATE

Chapter 2

FABRIC
AND COLOR

Shopping for fabrics that have the contrast, color,

and character you desire is worth the time spent

as they will give your quilt its own personality.

LOG CABIN

The Log Cabin block has been a popular pattern with quilters for more than a century. The simple strips of cloth, set around a traditional red center, were meant to resemble the logs of a house with a hearth warming the middle. Because there were many ways to arrange the blocks, quilters named the design variations after things they saw around them: Courthouse Steps, Windmill Blades, Straight Furrow, Streak of Lightning. Even when people no longer lived in log houses, the design remained popular. This "Light and Dark" setting of Log Cabin blocks, dated 1953, was pieced in pastel prints and solid whites with multiprint "hearth" centers.

Fabric and Color

Selecting just the right fabrics in just the right colors is part of the fun of quilting. For some quilters, however, this step in the quiltmaking process can be the most daunting. Appreciating how your fabric and color choices affect the overall appearance of a finished quilt can help make the selection process easier.

FABRIC

Understanding how fabric is made and what kind of finishes are applied can make it easier to select fabric for each project.

Fabric Manufacturing Basics

Most quilting fabrics begin as greige (gray-zh) goods, which means unbleached and undyed. Fabrics in this state must be cleaned and prepared before any color can be added or design printed. Greige goods can range in weave from loose to tight and their surfaces may have imperfections. The number of threads per square inch varies according to each manufacturer's specifications. Each of these characteristics affects the finished product's quality, durability, hand (or feel), and price.

Because manufacturers try to meet different market demands for products and prices, it's common for a manufacturer to print the same design on different quality greige goods. The fabrics may appear the same and have the same manufacturer and designer names printed on the selvages, but may vary in terms of durability or quality.

Homespuns are one of the few fabric types that don't begin as greige goods. Instead, they are woven with colored threads.

Producing a Finished Product

Color and design are dyed, screen printed, or roller printed onto greige goods. Occasionally dyed fabrics may be overprinted, meaning they are first dyed, then printed.

Finishes are added to greige goods through mechanical or chemical means and range from temporary to permanent. Permanent finishes, as the label implies, endure for the life of the fabric. Durable finishes lose some of their properties with each cleaning, but, with proper care, should last nearly as long as the fabric. Semidurable finishes will last through several launderings, while temporary finishes are lost after the first washing.

Many quilting cottons have a finish applied to reduce wrinkling, which can make it easier to work with a fabric. It's important to know if the fabric has such a finish, as it may prevent the fabric from holding a sharp crease, making it more difficult to press seams flat.

Fabrics with a polished appearance on one side have been glazed. This finish tends to wear off over time, but some quilters find it helpful during quiltmaking as it adds a stiffness to the fabric.

More loosely woven fabrics are sometimes finished with a process called napping, which creates flannel. The fabric runs over a series of napping rolls that raise the surface nap of the fabric. Fabrics can be napped on one or both sides. Because of the looser yarns and weave required to create the nap, flannel fabrics tend to shrink more than other woven fabrics do.

Cotton fabrics with an especially soft feel may have had a mechanical sueding finish applied.

Fiber Content

The preferred fabric fiber content for quilting is 100% cotton. However, even within this category, there are choices to make. Other fiber content options also are available.

100% Cotton

Cotton is woven in many ways to create a variety of products. Some of these products work well in quilts, and others are better suited for home decorating and garment making. Poplin, chino, chenille, and velveteen can be 100% cotton, for example, but may not work well for intricately pieced quilts.

Always consider the intended use when choosing quilting fabrics, as different fabrics behave in different ways when sewn, pressed, hung, or laundered. If different types of 100% cotton fabrics will be combined in a quilt, know that the pieced units will only be as strong as the weakest fabric, and there may be complications such as puckering, sagging, and pulling.

Several types of 100% cotton fabrics are often used in quiltmaking. They include broadcloth or plain-weave cotton, homespun, flannel, and chintz (see Photo 1A, *right*).
- **Broadcloth or Plain-Weave Cotton** This fabric, often called quilters' cotton, has several benefits, including a weight, or body, that allows it to be sewn with little slippage. It creases well, so seams open flat. It is durable and doesn't readily fray. It also will tear along the grain line. When used in bedding, cotton's natural fibers wick moisture away from the body, increasing comfort.
- **Homespun** Already-dyed threads are woven into a solid, plaid, striped, or checked design for these fabrics. They are often used when a primitive look is desired.
- **Flannel** This fabric is woven of a bulkier cotton thread with a looser fiber, then brushed to give it a nap.
- **Chintz** A high thread count and glazed finish make this fabric more difficult to needle than other 100% cottons. It frequently puckers when stitched, and needles and pins may cause permanent holes.

Other Fiber Choices

Fabrics with a fiber content other than 100% cotton, including wool and silk (see Photo 1B, *below right*), can be used in quilting, though it's best to stick with the same content within a single quilt.
- **Wool** Working with wool offers quilters nearly as many options as working with cotton. Felted wool is especially easy to use in appliqué, as the edges don't need to be turned under since they will not ravel.

To felt wool, machine-wash it in a hot-water wash/cool-water rinse cycle with a small amount of detergent, machine-dry on hot, and steam press. If using wool from a piece of clothing, cut it apart and remove the seams before washing so it can shrink freely.
- **Silk** This natural fiber has luster and can be smooth or have slubs (small threads) on the surface. Silk generally requires more care in cleaning than cotton does.

Photo 1A

Photo 1B

Check the Fabric Bolt End

The percentage of fibers is usually listed on the end of the fabric's cardboard bolt, along with information about special finishes, such as if the fabric is chintz or is permanent press (see Photo 1C, *below*). Care instructions, style number, the fabric and manufacturer's name, and any processing, such as preshrinking, will also be noted.

Note: *Some fabric stores rewrap fabric flat folds around unused cardboard bolts. Be sure to confirm that the information on the bolt end matches the manufacturer and fabric name on the fabric selvage.*

Photo 1C

Thread Count

The number of threads per square inch determines the quality and weight of a fabric. If the thread count is the same for both length and width, the fabric is said to have an even weave.

Quilting cotton has a higher thread count (68×68 threads per square inch) than lighter-weight cotton. Fabrics with low thread counts (less than 60×60 threads per square inch) are too lightweight to use successfully in a quilt, as they will ravel excessively when they are handled. Low thread counts also mean more shrinkage, less durability, and bearding (batting coming through the quilt top or backing). Pieces can fray and fall apart if seams need to be removed.

Higher thread counts and extremely tight weaves can be difficult to needle. It may be tempting to use a sheet for a quilt back, for example, but the finish and thread count make it difficult to work with and create puckering.

Grain Line

Cutting pieces according to a fabric's grain line makes for more accurate piecing and a stronger finished quilt top. Following the grain line reduces stretching and distortion, enhancing the overall appearance of the finished quilt (see Illustration 1, *below*).

In weaving fabric, manufacturers place the lengthwise threads (warp) tightly in the loom to eliminate stretch. The crosswise (weft) threads are then woven into the lengthwise threads, but are not stretched as tightly, leaving a little "give" in the finished fabric.

Fabric pieces cut diagonally across the grain line, or on the bias, are susceptible to stretching because there are no stabilizing threads along the edges. If the design motif can only be cut on the bias, backing it with a lightweight fusible web can help to stabilize it.

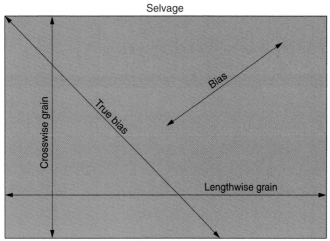

Illustration 1

Photo 1D

Right Side/Wrong Side

Most manufacturers print on one side of the greige goods. This means the fabric has two sides (right and wrong, or front and back; see Photo 1D, *left*). The back of the fabric, or the wrong side, may have some color from the dye bleeding through. If a lighter shade of a fabric is needed in a quilt, use the "back" or wrong side of the fabric as the right side.

Batiks have very little difference between the right and wrong sides. Homespuns, which are woven from already-dyed threads, look the same on both sides.

Specialty Fabric Cuts

Two common specialty cuts of fabrics—fat quarters and fat eighths—are found in a majority of quilt shops. Many quilters find these sizes offer more versatility for cutting templates or strips than the actual ¼-yard and ⅛-yard cuts.

Fat Quarter

Although a traditional ¼-yard cut and a fat-quarter cut are the same amount of fabric, the difference is the shape. A traditional ¼-yard cut measures 9×44". A fat quarter is ¼ yard of fabric cut crosswise from a ½-yard piece of fabric—an 18×44" rectangle of fabric cut in half to yield an 18×22" "fat" ¼-yard piece (see Illustration 2, *far left*).

Fat Eighth

A traditional ⅛-yard cut and a fat-eighth cut are also the same amount of fabric. A traditional ⅛-yard cut is 4½×44". A fat eighth is cut crosswise from a ¼-yard piece of fabric—a 9×44" rectangle of fabric cut in half to make a 9×22" "fat" ⅛-yard piece (see Illustration 3, *left*).

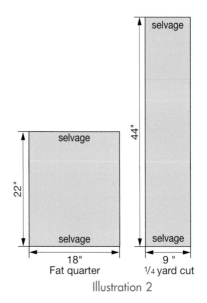

Illustration 2

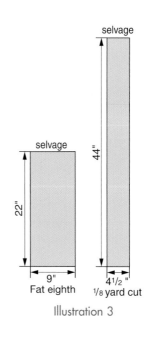

Illustration 3

Before Buying Fabric

Determine how much fabric is necessary for a project before shopping. Graph paper helps take out the guesswork.

Use graph paper to create a cutting diagram. Let each square equal 1" and map out the needed pieces. It's wise to purchase ⅛ to ¼ yard more fabric than the layout requires to allow for inches that may be lost in squaring up fabric edges, shrinkage during prewashing, and/or cutting errors.

Make template windows out of sturdy paper or cardboard to take to the fabric store for previewing fabric options (see Photo 1E, *below*). Do not include seam allowances in the window cut, but do leave a healthy margin of paper around each window to help differentiate what's showing through from the rest of the bolt. Viewing a fabric through a template window can make it easier to see what individual pieces look like than looking at the whole bolt.

Photo 1E

The array of fabric colors and designs available today can be both exciting and intimidating. When selecting fabrics for a project, consider the following suggestions:

- Separate the bolts you're interested in from the other fabrics. Examine them away from other fabrics to avoid confusion or interference from other colors.
- Stack the bolts horizontally to view how the fabrics may appear when cut into smaller shapes and how they work together. Or use template windows.
- Stand back about 10 feet and look at the bolts stacked horizontally. A view from this distance gives a good idea of how a fabric combination will work in a quilt.
- Find optimum light. Fluorescent lighting can sometimes cast a yellow glow, altering the appearance of a fabric's true colors. Take the bolts to the area of the store that has the most natural light. Stand with the light at your back and let it wash across the bolts.

Fabric Preparation

All fabrics are subject to loss of color from washing, exposure to light, and abrasion. Whether or not to prewash fabrics is a topic of much debate among quilters.

Many of those who don't prewash find it easier to work with fabrics that have the sizing and finish from the manufacturing process still on them. Others don't prewash because the shrinkage of the fabric after a quilt is complete can create the rumpled, old look of an antique that they desire.

Some quilters favor prewashing fabrics to reduce uneven shrinkage or colors bleeding once a quilt is complete.

The decision about prewashing may change from one project to the next. Consider these color-retention factors when deciding.

Color-Retention Factors

Whether prewashing fabric or laundering a finished quilt, consider several factors that affect a fabric's ability to retain its color.

- **Hot water** can be damaging to any fabric's color and finish. Cold water is safest for washing cotton. Check first to see if any color is released at this temperature by filling a clear glass with cold water and dropping in a swatch of the fabric. If the water changes color as a result of dyes being released, prewashing the fabric will be necessary to rid the fabric of excess dye before using it in a quilt. After prewashing, retest a swatch in a clear glass to see if the dye-bleeding problem has been resolved.
- **Detergents** can break down the binding agents that hold pigment on cloth. Detergents with chlorine bleach can damage fiber-reactive dyes. Gentle soaps and cleansers made specifically for cleaning quilts are widely available at quilt shops and some fabric stores. As with any product, it is important to follow the manufacturer's instructions and use the correct amount. Soils remain if too little is used, and fabric is affected if too much is used and it's not rinsed out properly.
- **Abrasion**, or the friction of fabrics rubbing against each other, may cause crocking, which is a transfer of color from one fabric to another. The friction may be caused by handling or from contact in the washer and dryer. Colors may leach out of a piece of fabric, causing a color loss in that piece, but the real concern is whether or not the dye will then permanently reattach itself to other fabrics.

If you are working with high-contrast fabrics, such as red and white, one method of testing for crocking is to pretreat the fabrics as desired, then vigorously rub them against one another. If any of the darker color rubs off on the lighter fabric, pretreat it again until the fabric passes the rub test.

Another test to determine if color will migrate from one fabric to another is to put the suspect fabric (usually a dark, intensely colored fabric) in a jar of water with 1 teaspoon of laundry detergent. Check for color loss after 10 minutes. If color is present in the water, add a piece of the light fabric to the water and shake the jar several times. Leave both fabrics in the water for 10 minutes, then remove the lighter sample and compare it to the original light fabric. If there is no transfer of color, the dark fabric should be safe to use even with color loss in the water.

FABRIC AND QUILT CARE

Caring for fabrics properly, both before and after they're sewn into a quilt, can increase their longevity. Whether quilts are stored for a long period of time (see Photo 1F, *opposite*) or are periodically rotated on display, follow these guidelines to protect them from fiber damage and keep them at their best.

Sources of Fiber Damage
Light

Fluorescent lights and ultraviolet radiation from sunlight cause fabric dyes to fade and fibers to become brittle. Rotate quilts frequently to prevent damage from exposure to light. Watch quilts displayed on beds, as the side exposed to sunlight from a nearby window may fade. Cover windows with shades when sunlight is direct. Make sure that quilts are not stored in an area exposed to direct sunlight to prevent the exposed portions from fading.

Creative Tip

City water contains chlorine, which can cause dye loss. One cup of vinegar will neutralize chlorine when washing your quilt.

—LYNN, SALES ASSOCIATE

Folds and Creases

When folded fabrics or quilts are stored for long periods of time, the fibers along the folds begin to weaken, and permanent creases can develop. Some quilters refold their fabrics periodically to keep this from occurring. It's best to roll, rather than fold, quilts for storage, adding acid-free tissue paper between the layers of the quilt to help prevent creasing.

Acid

Paper, cardboard, plastics, and unfinished wood in shelves, drawers, and trunks release acid, which is damaging to plant-derived fabrics, such as cotton and linen. Prevent fabrics and quilts from coming in contact with these surfaces by rolling them in acid-free tissue paper and storing them in acid-free boxes or white, cotton pillowcases.

Mold/Mildew

Mold and mildew flourish in warm, moist environments, so quilts shut in closed containers or wrapped in plastic and stored in areas of temperature extremes and excess moisture (attics, basements, garages) are susceptible to the growth of these fungi.

To avoid the irreversible damage caused by mold and mildew, and to protect quilts from dust and other elements, store them in a cool, dry location (less than 50% humidity). Wrap them in white, cotton pillowcases to allow air to pass through and let the quilts breathe.

Time

Antique fibers need to be handled with care. Vintage fabrics can be prone to damage by laundering. Unstable dyes and pigments, weave, and age make these fabrics especially sensitive to today's cleaning methods.

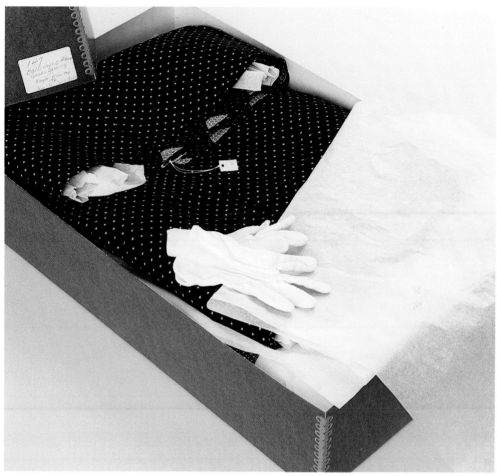

Photo 1F

For example, some older fabrics were made with unstable dyes, and any contact with moisture may cause them to bleed. This is especially noticeable with brown and black dyes in antique quilts. Other fabrics become brittle with time and may turn to powder.

Contact an expert, such as a quilt preservationist or appraiser at a museum or university, for recommendations on handling, cleaning, and preserving older quilts.

Caring for Quilts on Display

Rotate the quilts on display often to give them a rest. This will diminish their exposure to dust, light, and other potential sources of fiber damage (see Sources of Fiber Damage on *page 40* for more information).

A quilt that doesn't have an obvious top or bottom can be turned periodically to prevent distortion or damage to the fibers along one end. It is a good idea to add a hanging sleeve to more than one edge, which will make rotating the quilt easier. (See Chapter 9—Finishing Techniques for information on adding hanging sleeves.)

Cleaning Methods

Avoid washing a quilt unless it's absolutely necessary. Washing, even when done on a gentle cycle, causes fabrics to fade and is abrasive to fibers. Clean and freshen a quilt using one of these methods.

Airing Outdoors

Annually take quilts outdoors on an overcast, dry, and windy day to be refreshed. Place towels or a mattress pad on the dry ground and lay the quilts on them. Cover the quilts with a sheet to prevent debris from falling on them. Avoid placing quilts on a clothesline to prevent stress on the seams.

Using a Dryer

Quilts can be freshened in a dryer on a gentle-cycle/air-dry setting without heat.

Vacuuming

Vacuuming both the front and back of a quilt can help preserve it by removing dust and dirt. Place a nylon hose or net over the end of a vacuum hose and gently draw the hose over the quilt's surface without rubbing it (see Photo 1G, *below*). You can also lay a piece of clean screening on the quilt, then vacuum it. Always clean a quilt with at least a quick vacuuming to remove airborne dust and dirt before storing it.

Washing

As a last resort, cotton quilts can be washed in cold water with a gentle soap (see Photo 1H, *opposite*) by hand or in the machine on a gentle cycle. Do not wring or twist a quilt;

Photo 1G

instead gently squeeze out the water. Wet quilts are heavy and need to be supported when they are being moved to a flat area to dry.

Washing by Hand

1. Use a clean tub that is free from other soaps or cleaning materials.

2. Place a large towel or cotton blanket in the tub to support the quilt.

3. Thoroughly dissolve soap in water prior to adding the quilt to the tub. Be sure you have enough water in the tub to cover the quilt.

4. Place the quilt in the tub. Gently agitate (do not wring or twist) the quilt to release the dirt and soil.

5. Rinse the quilt by draining and refilling the tub. Repeat as needed to remove soap, as residue can build up on a quilt's surface.

6. Press excess water out of the quilt, starting at the end farthest from the drain and working your way across the quilt. Use towels to blot up excess water.

7. Remove the quilt from the tub, using the large towel or cotton blanket beneath it.

8. Spread the quilt flat on a clean sheet that has been placed out of direct sunlight. Let it air-dry, using a fan to speed the process.

Washing by Machine

1. Fill the washing machine with water and dissolve the soap.

2. Place the quilt in the machine. Let it soak for up to 15 minutes, checking it frequently to make sure the fabric dyes are stable and not running onto neighboring fabrics. If

Photo 1H

desired, agitate the quilt on a gentle cycle for up to five minutes.

Note: A front-loading washing machine will not allow the quilt to soak in the washer drum. Agitating on a gentle cycle is necessary in this type of washing machine.

3. Repeat steps 1 and 2 with fresh soap and water if a quilt is heavily soiled.

4. Use a gentle spin cycle to rinse the quilt and remove the excess water. Continue to rinse and spin until the rinse water is free of soap.

5. Remove the quilt from the machine and spread it flat on a clean sheet that has been placed out of direct sunlight. Let it air-dry, using a fan to speed the process.

Dry Cleaning

It is wise to check references before selecting a dry cleaner to handle quilts, as dry cleaning can cause cotton dyes to bleed or change color.

Take special precautions when dry-cleaning a wool or silk quilt. Dry cleaning should be a last resort, used only if vacuuming or spot cleaning doesn't remove the soil.

CONSIDERING FABRIC DESIGN

Use the three Cs when selecting fabrics for a quilt—contrast, color, and character.

Although color is fun and exciting, it is contrast, or differences in values, that often makes a design successful. Without contrast in value between pieces in a block or the blocks in a quilt top, the colors will blend together and the design itself may get lost.

It's important to choose colors that are appealing and suit the design. A block design may work with odd colors that have good contrast, but it may not be as visually pleasing.

The character of the fabric also influences a quilt. Motifs can range from polka dots or stripes to florals, calicoes, novelty prints, plaids, and large-scale patterns.

Seeing Design at Work

Different quilts and styles of quilting attract different quilters for different reasons. Before selecting fabrics, many quilters find it helpful to thumb through quilting books, magazines, and patterns. Note the common qualities among the quilts that attract your eye.

Do you like quilts with stark contrast between colors, such as a quilt composed solely of red and white? Are you attracted to scrappy quilts with dozens of different fabrics included? Do you like quilts with muted tones where the colors seem to meld together?

Knowing what you like is the first step in selecting fabrics.

CONTRAST (VALUE)

One of the first design concepts to consider when composing a quilt is contrast. Many quilt patterns list the fabrics needed for a project in terms of their contrast or values—light, medium, or dark. Learning to see fabrics in these categories of contrast can enhance fabric selection success.

Why Contrast?

Contrast clarifies the design and makes depth apparent. Without contrast between the medium gold and the medium green in the Photo 1I block *far left,* the pieces in the block blend together, and the design appears flat.

The shapes take on new dimensions when the fabrics—a dark purple, medium green, and light yellow—have more contrast (see Photo 1J, *left*).

Contrast, however, is a relative concept. The block in Photo 1K, *far left,* uses a medium-value purple for the center star and a darker purple for the background. Because there isn't too much difference between the medium and dark values, the contrast in the resulting block is subtle.

When the same medium-value purple is paired with a light purple background fabric, the resulting block in Photo 1L, *left,* has a higher contrast than the first one because of the difference in values between the purples.

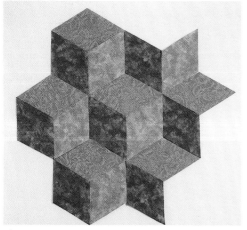

Photo 1I

Photo 1J

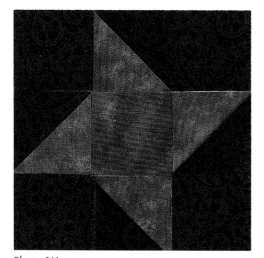

Photo 1K

Photo 1L

Understanding the relative contrast of color choices is helpful when selecting fabric for a quilt, because the difference determines whether the desired contrast between elements is achieved.

Visualizing Contrast

Trying to ignore color and just study contrast is not an easy task. When looking at fabrics in a store or from a fabric stash, try these techniques to see the contrast or value (see Photo 1M, *right*).

Select fabrics for a project, then perform one or more of these tests to see if there is enough contrast in the group. If more contrast is needed, substitute lighter or darker fabrics until the variety of values is satisfactory.

- Try squinting This limits the amount of light received and reduces the perception of color, making contrast more evident (see Photo 1N, *below*).
- Use a reducing tool Purchase a reducing glass or a door peephole. These tools reduce an image, making color less obvious and contrast more apparent when the fabrics are viewed. Taking instant photographs or looking through a camera also works in this regard.

- Look through red cellophane This technique obliterates the color so that the continuum of values from light to dark can be seen (see Photo 1O, *bottom middle*).

- Make black and white photocopies Photocopying completely masks color and can give an indication of contrast between and within pieces of fabric (see Photo 1P, *bottom right*).

Photo 1M

Photo 1N

Photo 1O

Photo 1P

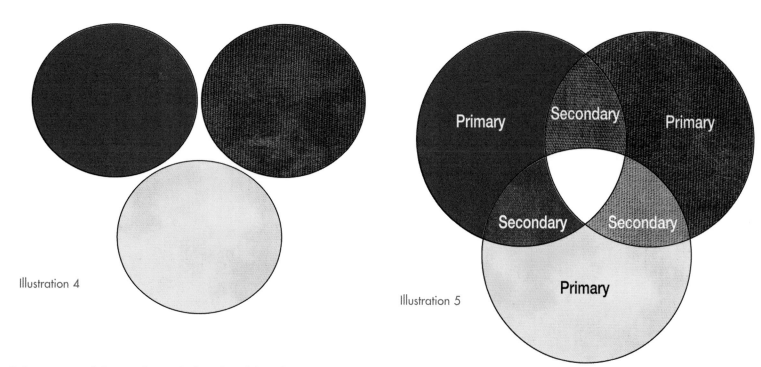

Illustration 4

Illustration 5

(Illustration 5 labels: Primary, Secondary, Primary, Secondary, Secondary, Primary)

Primary and Secondary Color Combinations

PRIMARY COLOR	ANALOGOUS COLORS Neighboring colors that coordinate with the primary color. These colors share the primary color, so they'll always work together.	COMPLEMENTARY COLOR The color opposite a primary color on the color wheel that contains the other two primary colors. A small amount of a color's complement can serve as an accent.
Red	Orange Violet	Green
Blue	Violet Green	Orange
Yellow	Green Orange	Violet

COLOR

Color, or hue, becomes the next design element to consider when selecting quilt fabrics. Where contrast is an objective quality, color is more subjective and often evokes emotion.

Successfully combining colors takes observation, practice, and a little help from the color wheel. Study the color palettes of quilts, artwork, or fashions that appeal to you. Note the main color and how it is combined with other hues.

Using the Color Wheel in Quilting
Artists in many mediums use the color wheel. With paint the result of blending colors is a little more predictable than with fabric because paint is solid; it doesn't have pattern or texture. Even so, the color wheel is a useful guide in choosing fabric colors.

Primary Colors

All colors are derived from the three primary colors: red, blue, and yellow (see Illustration 4, *opposite*). Though many people think of them in terms of color, black, gray, and white are not on the color wheel.

Secondary Colors

When primary colors are mixed in different combinations, the secondary colors of orange, violet, and green are created (see Illustration 5, *opposite*). Brown is not on the color wheel because it has all colors in it.

Complementary Colors

The color that sits opposite a color on the wheel is its complementary color. When combined in equal amounts, complementary colors can vibrate. A popular pair of complementary colors is red and green. True red and true green are a vibrant combination. When they are shaded with a bit of black, they become the calmer colors that are often used for traditional holiday designs.

A little complementary color can go a long way in adding excitement to a design. For example, include a sprinkle of orange in an otherwise all-blue quilt for a little punch.

Tertiary Colors

Further divisions of colors are created in a 12-Piece Color Wheel on *page 49*. This wheel shows the primary colors (red, yellow, blue), secondary colors (orange, purple, green), and the tertiary colors, which are a combination of the primary and secondary colors—red-orange, yellow-orange, yellow-green, blue-green, blue-violet, and red-violet.

Primary and Secondary Color Wheel

The six-piece color wheel *below* shows the relationship of the primary and secondary colors. Use the information in the chart *opposite* to understand how analogous and complementary colors work together.

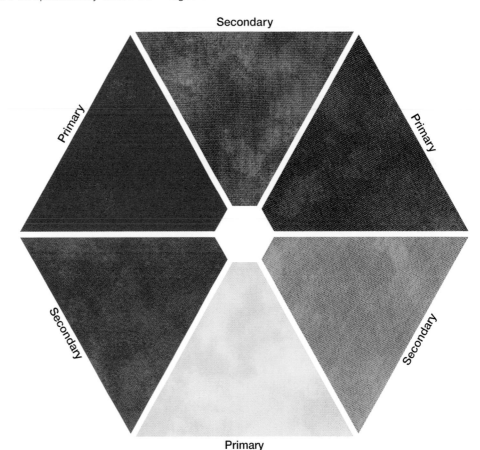

Tints and Shades of Primary, Secondary, and Tertiary Colors

COLOR	TINT White is added for a lighter color.	SHADE Black is added for a darker color.
Red	Pink	Cranberry
Red-Violet	Magenta	Grape
Violet	Lavender	Eggplant
Blue-Violet	Lilac	Ultramarine
Blue	Periwinkle	Navy
Blue-Green	Aqua	Teal
Green	Seafoam	Forest Green
Yellow-Green	Mint	Olive
Yellow	Daffodil	Gold
Yellow-Orange	Peach	Mustard
Orange	Melon	Cinnamon
Red-Orange	Salmon	Burnt Orange

Tints and Shades

Also shown in the 12-Piece Color Wheel *opposite* are some variations in the colors when they are tinted (white is added) or shaded (black is added), which alters the true-color values. When you consider the infinite amounts of black and white that can be added to make different tints or shades, it's easy to see that the number of colors is limitless.

If the fabric world only had primary, secondary, and tertiary colors, all quilts would be bright and vibrant. Fortunately for those who enjoy a more subtle palette, fabric designers create additional color options by adding white or black to colors.

Temperature

Fabrics, like paints, have a warmth, or lack thereof. In a quilt of predominantly cool fabrics (blues), a dash of orange or yellow can add warmth to the quilt.

Temperature, like contrast, is relative. The temperature of a color depends on what colors are around it. Look at the color wheel for guidance. Yellow-green and red-violet can be warm or cool depending on what the adjacent ones (or neighbors) are. For example, yellow-green feels cool when used with pure yellow, which is warmer in comparison. The same yellow-green feels warm when paired with greens or blues, which are cooler in comparison. (See the dashed line on the 12-Piece Color Wheel. It delineates the warm and cool sections of the color wheel.)

12-Piece Color Wheel (Primary, Secondary, and Tertiary Colors)

The middle ring of this color wheel shows the true color, or hue. The outer ring is the shaded color; black has been added for a darker value of the original color. The inner ring shows the tinted color; white has been added for a lighter value of the original color.

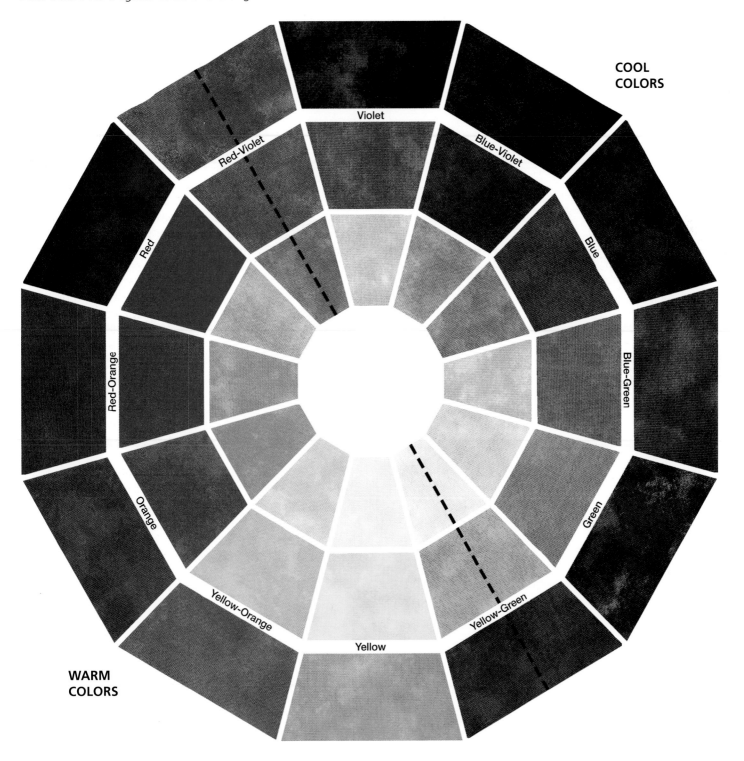

COOL
COLORS

WARM
COLORS

Split Complement Color Combinations

The split complement combination includes a primary, secondary, or tertiary color and the colors on either side of its complement.

COLOR	SPLIT COMPLEMENTS	
Red	Yellow-Green	Blue-Green
Red-Violet	Yellow	Green
Violet	Yellow-Orange	Yellow-Green
Blue-Violet	Orange	Yellow
Blue	Red-Orange	Yellow-Orange
Blue-Green	Red	Orange
Green	Red-Violet	Red-Orange
Yellow-Green	Red	Violet
Yellow	Red-Violet	Blue-Violet
Yellow-Orange	Violet	Blue
Orange	Blue-Violet	Blue-Green
Red-Orange	Green	Blue

Intensity

When looking at a fabric, determine if the color is pure (saturated, brilliant) or muted (grayed, subdued). The answer indicates the fabric's intensity.

Contrast differs from intensity. A dark navy fabric can be brilliant, and a pale yellow can have a low intensity.

In general, use intense colors sparingly, and choose less intense colors for larger areas. Intense colors will appear to come forward, while less intense colors will recede.

Intensity is also a relative characteristic; it changes according to the fabrics that surround it. Observe in Photo 1Q, *below,* how intense the small red square looks when placed on the larger black square; it pops out from the background.

Photo 1Q

When the same red square is placed on the larger white square, it appears to recede.

When combined with the muted gray square, the intensity of the red seems to lessen.

Combining Colors

Remember that the color wheels and charts presented in this book are created from pictures of solid or marbled fabrics. The colors are bright and pure. Fabrics may have similar colors, but can be influenced by pattern and additional colors in the fabric. Use these charts only as a guide.

Study individual fabrics and note their color combinations. Often the fabric manufacturer has printer's dots on the selvage that show the colors used to create the fabric design. Replicating these colors exactly can create a flat quilt, but using tints and shades of the colors, as well as a variety of intensities (pure colors versus muted, grayed colors) and temperatures (warm versus cool colors) can enhance a design.

Consider the following guidelines and types of color combinations when choosing fabrics for a quilt.

Triad Color Combinations

The triad combination uses three primary, secondary, or tertiary colors that are equidistant on the color wheel. There are four possible triad combinations, but your choice of tints, shades, and intensities within each is unlimited. Each triad shown below includes an example of colors that would work well together in a three-color quilt.

TRIAD 1	EXAMPLE	TRIAD 2	EXAMPLE
Red	Cranberry	Violet	Eggplant
Blue	Navy	Orange	Melon
Yellow	Gold	Green	Seafoam

TRIAD 3	EXAMPLE	TRIAD 4	EXAMPLE
Blue-Violet	Lilac	Blue-Green	Teal
Red-Orange	Salmon	Red-Violet	Magenta
Yellow-Green	Yellow-Green	Yellow-Orange	Mustard

Monochromatic Combinations

While a monochromatic quilt uses a single color, every color has tinted and shaded variations. If you're interested in composing a single-color quilt, refer to the Tints and Shades of Primary, Secondary, and Tertiary Colors chart on *page 48* for possible color combinations in planning a monochromatic quilt. Choose one of the primary, secondary, or tertiary colors, then consider including all of the tints through shades of that color. A one-color quilt is most successful when the designs, textures, and contrasts of the fabrics vary.

Split Complements

A split complement color scheme includes a primary, secondary, or tertiary color and the colors on either side of its complement.

For example, to determine the split complement colors of violet, look at the 12-Piece Color Wheel on *page 49*. Yellow-orange and yellow-green are on either side of violet's complementary color, yellow—directly across from violet on the color wheel. If these pure colors seem strong, consider that violet, yellow-orange, and yellow-green could be eggplant, olive, and mustard, three warm and mellow colors. Use the Split Complement Color Combinations chart, *opposite*, to devise a split complement color scheme.

Analogous Color Combinations

Think of analogous colors as neighbors. To make a quilt of this type, select a favorite fabric as the feature fabric and find its closest companion on the color wheel. Pull the remaining fabrics for the quilt from neighboring, or adjacent, colors.

For example, if the feature fabric is a green, then pick a variety of light and dark fabrics in yellow-green, yellow, blue-green, and blue. This is one of the safest palettes to work with, but it can look dull if the fabrics don't have some interest in their patterns and variety in contrast.

Triad Combinations

A triad combination—three colors that are equidistant on the color wheel—results in a harmonious quilt. There are four triad combinations from which to choose, and an unlimited number of tints, shades, and intensities within those colors from which to select. The Triad Color Combinations chart at *left* shows the four triad combinations and a color combination example for each.

Tetrad Combinations

A tetrad combination—four colors that are equidistant on the color wheel—is another way to select quilt fabrics. There are three combinations from which to choose. Again, you can select from an unlimited number of tints, shades, and intensities within those colors. The Tetrad Color Combinations chart *below left* shows the three tetrad combinations and a color combination example for each.

Polychromatic Combinations

Polychromatic, or multicolor, combinations are often scrap quilts—those composed of myriad fabrics in a wide range of colors and textures. Varying contrast, intensity, and temperature helps tie these quilts together. Adding neutral fabrics to the mix provides balance among colors that might otherwise compete for attention.

CHARACTER

The third element that affects quilt design is the character of the fabrics, the features that change how each one works in a block or an overall quilt top. Prints may contain the same hues, for example, but may look different when placed in a block. One may be an elegant floral reproduction fabric, while the other is perhaps a stripe or a conversation print of animals. Consider the character of each fabric when making selection decisions.

Scale

Scale refers to the relative size of the print's elements. Quilts benefit from a range—small, medium and large—in scale (see Photo 1R, *opposite*).

Small-scale prints may look as though they're solid, but will contribute additional color and add visual texture.

Tetrad Color Combinations

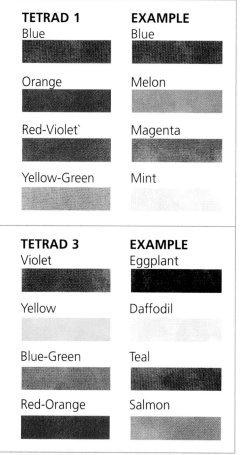

The tetrad combination uses four primary, secondary, or tertiary colors that are equidistant on the color wheel. There are three possible tetrad combinations, but the choice of tints, shades, and intensities within each is unlimited. Each tetrad shown here includes an example of colors that would work well together in a four-color quilt.

TETRAD 1	EXAMPLE
Blue	Blue
Orange	Melon
Red-Violet`	Magenta
Yellow-Green	Mint

TETRAD 2	EXAMPLE
Red	Red
Green	Forest Green
Blue-Violet	Blue-Violet
Yellow-Orange	Mustard

TETRAD 3	EXAMPLE
Violet	Eggplant
Yellow	Daffodil
Blue-Green	Teal
Red-Orange	Salmon

Medium-scale prints tend to be quilters' favorites because they are easy to use and most readily available. Even when cut or viewed from a distance, they tend to retain their design.

Large-scale prints are visually appealing on the bolt but require a little extra care when incorporating them into a design. Test large-scale prints with a window template to see what colors or parts will appear when cut into smaller pieces. (See *page 39* for information on making window templates.) Use care because a large-scale print can appear fragmented if used for small pieces within a block. Large-scale prints are best in borders and setting blocks.

Mood

Is the print busy or calm? Is the fabric elegant and formal or playful and lively? Coordinate fabric moods to convey the desired effect (see Photo 1S, *top, far right*).

Print Style

Variations in Contrast

When selecting fabrics, be sure to look for variety in contrast, or values, within each color family (see Photo 1T, *right*). This adds more life to a quilt. Consider that an individual fabric can have contrast within itself—a red print, for example, that has areas of pink and burgundy. This brings interest to a monochromatic block or quilt.

Solid and Tone-on-Tone Prints

Solid-color fabrics or tone-on-tone prints (prints that look like solids when viewed from a distance) help set areas of the quilt apart from other prints or linear designs. Tone-on-tone prints add subtle visual texture without competing for the eye's attention (see Photo 1U, *far right*).

Photo 1R

Photo 1S

Photo 1T

Photo 1U

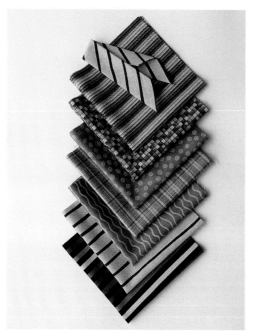

Photo 1V

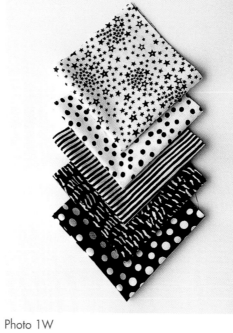

Photo 1W

Photo 1X

Photo 1Y

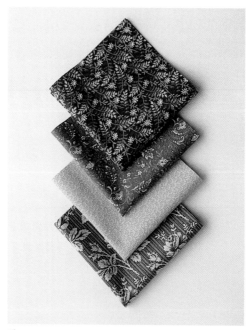

Photo 1Z

Photo 2A

Striped, Checked, or Plaid Fabric

Available in structured designs or wavy lines, stripes, checks, and plaids can add pizzazz to blocks or units (see Photo 1V, *opposite*). Try them as sashing or small inner borders.

Stripes also make fun binding. For example, cutting a striped fabric on the bias can produce the effect of a barber-pole stripe around the edge of a quilt.

Black-and-White Fabric

Don't overlook black-and-white fabrics when shopping for color. Sometimes such a print adds exactly the right punch to a quilt design (see Photo 1W, *opposite*).

Large-Scale Prints

Large-scale prints, such as floral motifs, leaves, and paisleys, are often used as feature or focus fabrics (see Photo 1X, *opposite*). Use a window template to determine how a large-scale print might look when cut into smaller pieces. (See *page 39* for information on making window

templates.) Purchase additional yardage if the fabric is going to be used as a border. Using a large print in both the quilt center and border helps bring unity to a quilt top.

Conversation or Novelty Prints

These prints depict themes, including sewing tools, holiday symbols, corporate logos, and even hobbies (see Photo 1Y, *opposite*). If it is difficult to work a favorite conversation print into a quilt top, use it for the backing instead. Or, if it is the main motif in a block, try fussy-cutting it to center the desired area. (See Chapter 4— Cutting Techniques for information on fussy cutting.)

Reproduction Fabrics

A multitude of fabric collections re-create prints from bygone days—from the Civil War era to the 1930s. The color and design elements of these reproduction prints may be such that it's easiest to combine them with other reproduction fabrics from the same collection or era (see photos 1Z and 2A, *opposite*).

Abstract or Painterly Fabrics

Batiks and hand-dyed fabrics can be great choices when you're looking for subtle changes in color and texture, such as where you want a transition between colors (see Photo 2B, *left*).

AUDITIONING FABRICS

Combining fabrics successfully may take experimentation, patience, and experience. Understanding the basics of contrast, color, and character will take some of the trial and error out of putting fabrics together.

Distance

One of the best ways to tell if a fabric combination will work is to step back from it. Fabrics that don't appear to work when viewed up close may be perfect from a distance, where each fabric's contribution to the whole can be seen. Remember that each piece is just a fraction of the total finished product.

Color Photocopy

Photocopy fabric choices on a color copier to test all options. (See Chapter 3—Planning Your Quilt for more information on testing fabric choices using photocopies.)

Design Wall

Having a surface to vertically lay out fabric choices can make it easier to visualize how they will look in a quilt. For a permanent or portable design wall, cover the surface of foam-core board with a napped material, such as flannel, that will hold small pieces in place for viewing. Some quilters use the flannel back of oilcloth for a design wall, rolling it up between projects or hanging one in front of the other to view different quilts.

Photo 2B

ꙮCreative Tip

I cut my cotton scraps into strips so when

I start a new quilting project, I have some

already cut. I can see how much usable fabric

I have to start a project. I keep each of the

different sizes in a separate clear organizer

marked with the size on it.

—CORLESS, SALES ASSOCIATE

Chapter 3

PLANNING
YOUR QUILT

Understanding how blocks are created can make

it easier to dissect a quilt design and duplicate its

elements or formulate a design of your own.

OCEAN WAVES

Hundreds and hundreds of different prints are used in the triangles in this Ocean Waves design. To organize the pattern, the quiltmaker used solid red triangles where the blocks come together to create pinwheels that cleverly spin in different directions. To make designs with small pieces such as this one, Nine-Patch, Cut Glass Dish, and Grandmother's Flower Garden, quilters often asked for the free samples dry goods stores received several times a year from textile manufacturers. The small fabric pieces, sent to promote the newest lines, were large enough to be cut in half and shared with friends.

Planning *Your Blocks*

Quilts and quilt designs often arise from a single block or the strategic grouping of units. Knowing what goes into a block allows you to more easily re-create it or to use it as the basis for a design that's uniquely yours.

COMBINING GEOMETRIC SHAPES INTO UNITS

Individual geometric shapes and their combinations are the foundation of every quilt block. On the following pages, several common shapes are shown. Study the different shapes in blocks. Knowing the shapes will make cutting and piecing easier to understand.

The term *unit* is used frequently in block design and pattern directions. Units are composed of at least two shapes sewn together. In this chapter, the shapes that combine to make a unit are illustrated. For specific instructions on piecing methods for these units, see Chapter 5—Piecing.

Many blocks are built from common units such as the triangle-square and Flying Geese. Knowing how a block is divided into units can help determine how a quilt is put together and allows efficiency in piecing.

Squares
Whether it is a simple setting block, the foundation for an appliqué block, or part of a unit, the square is one of the most common geometric shapes used in quilt designs (see Illustration 1, *left*).

Four-Patch Unit
Four equal-size squares sewn in two rows of two become a Four-Patch unit. This unit can act as a block (see Illustration 2, *left*).

Nine-Patch Unit
Nine equal-size squares sewn in three rows of three form a Nine-Patch block or a unit within a block. Often these units are composed of two alternating colors (see Illustration 3, *left*).

Rectangles
Rectangles can be combined into square units (see Illustration 4, *right*).

Illustration 4

Two- and Three-Bar Units
Depending on the size of the rectangles and the desired size of the finished square, any number of bars can be used to create a square (see Illustration 5, *below*).

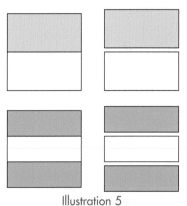

Illustration 5

Alternating the direction of those squares produces a Rail Fence block (see Illustration 6, *below*).

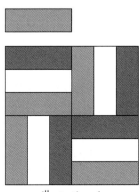

Illustration 6

Illustration 1

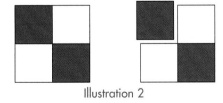

Illustration 2

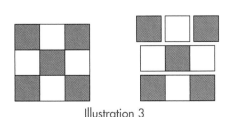

Illustration 3

Three-Piece Square Unit

Two squares and a rectangle can be pieced into a square unit (see Illustration 7, *below*).

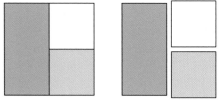

Illustration 7

90° Triangles

The square is also the starting point for many other shapes commonly used in quilting. Infinite design opportunities arise when squares are cut into 90° (right) triangles.

Two 90° triangles, or half-square triangles, are created when a square is cut in half diagonally (see Illustration 8, *below*). When triangles are cut from a square in this manner, the two short sides are cut on the straight grain and the longest side is cut on the bias.

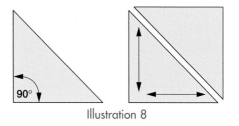

Illustration 8

Four 90° triangles, or quarter-square triangles, are created when a square is cut diagonally twice in an X (see Illustration 9, *below*). When triangles are cut from a square in this manner, the longest side of the triangle is cut on the straight grain and the two short sides are cut on the bias. Knowing which edge is cut along the straight grain becomes important when joining shapes into units and blocks. The straight grain should run along the outer edge of the block whenever possible to minimize stretching and distortion (see Chapter 4—Cutting Techniques for more information on fabric grain).

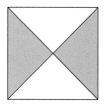

Illustration 9

Triangle-Square Unit

Two 90° half-square triangles combine to make a triangle-square unit (see Illustration 10, *below*). Note that by using half-square triangles to create this unit, the bias edges are sewn together, leaving the straight grain along the outer edges (see Chapter 5—Piecing for more information on making triangle-square units).

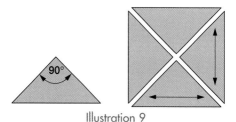

Illustration 10

Hour Glass Unit

An Hour Glass unit is made with pairs of contrasting quarter-square triangles (see Illustration 11, *below*). Note that by using quarter-square triangles to create this unit, the bias edges are sewn together, leaving the straight grain along the outer edges.

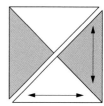

Illustration 11

Flying Geese Unit

Often used as a block, in sashing, and in borders, a Flying Geese unit is made of three 90° triangles in two different sizes (see Illustration 12, *below*). To keep the straight grain on the outer edges of this unit, the two smaller pieces are half-square triangles and the larger piece is a quarter-square triangle (see Chapter 5—Piecing for more information on making Flying Geese units).

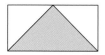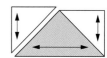

Illustration 12

Three-Triangle Unit

This versatile unit is made from a large 90° triangle and two smaller 90° triangles (see Illustration 13, *below*). To keep the straight grain on the outer edges of this unit, the two smaller triangles would be quarter-square triangles and the larger triangle would be a half-square triangle.

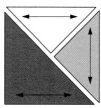

Illustration 13

Square-in-a-Square Unit

Four 90° half-square triangles sewn to a square produce the square-in-a-square unit (see Illustration 14, *below*).

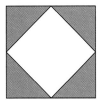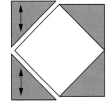

Illustration 14

Equilateral Triangles

With equal-length sides and equal angles of 60°, this triangle can be sewn into hexagon-shape blocks or into larger equilateral triangles (see Illustration 15, *below*). This shape is used for tessellating designs. The Pyramid block is made of four equilateral triangles. A Hexagon block is made from six equilateral triangles.

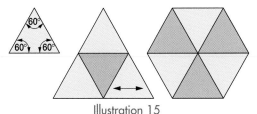

Illustration 15

Long Triangles

When a rectangle is cut in half diagonally, the result is two long triangles (see Illustration 16, *below*).

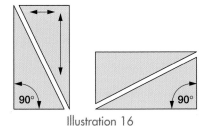

Illustration 16

Isosceles Triangles

With two equal-length sides, this triangle is half of a diamond shape (see Illustration 17, *below*).

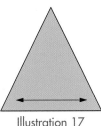

Illustration 17

Triangle-in-a-Square Unit

Add two long triangles to an isosceles triangle to produce a triangle-in-a-square unit (see Illustration 18, *below*).

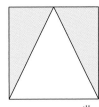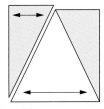

Illustration 18

Diamonds

The diamond shape, also called a parallelogram, can be used for one-shape quilt designs or to make stars. With careful color placement of the pieces, the diamond shape, when repeated multiple times, forms a mosaic and can create an optical illusion (see Illustration 19, *below*).

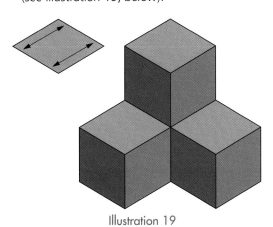

Illustration 19

The Tumbling Blocks quilt is made with only the diamond shape, yet has many design possibilities. Consistent value placement causes a cubelike pattern to emerge.

Diamond shapes combined with squares and 90° quarter-square triangles can be joined to make an Eight-Pointed Star block (see Illustration 20, *below*).

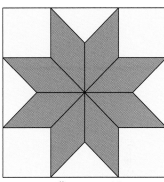

Illustration 20

Four long triangles can be joined to a diamond to create a pieced rectangle unit (see Illustration 21, *below*).

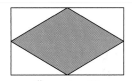

Illustration 21

Chapter 3 – Planning Your Quilt

Hexagons

With six sides, the hexagon can be pieced to other hexagons to form a tessellating design (see Illustration 22, *below*). English paper piecing is a popular technique used to join hexagon shapes (see Chapter 5—Piecing). These shapes are often pieced into a design called Grandmother's Flower Garden.

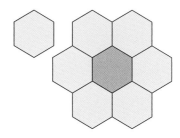

Illustration 22

Octagons

This eight-sided piece functions in quilt blocks just like a mosaic tile design (see Illustration 23, *below*). It appears most often in a block called Snowball.

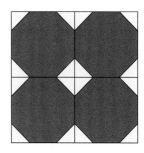

Illustration 23

Circles

Circles can be more difficult to piece than shapes with straight edges and are often appliquéd onto blocks (see Illustration 24, *below*). Sometimes one-fourth of a circle is pieced with a concave patch. When four such units are sewn together a complete circle is visible.

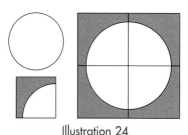

Illustration 24

THE GRID METHOD

Many blocks are based on a grid or can be broken down into one. Working with a grid organizes a design and makes cutting and piecing sequences easier to determine. Commonly used quilt making grids are detailed on the following pages.

2×2 Grid (Four-Patch)

A grid of four undivided or divided squares—a Four-Patch or 2×2 squares (see Illustration 25, *below*)—offers multiple design options.

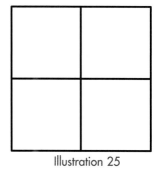

Illustration 25

Four three-triangle units on a grid of 2×2 squares form a Windmill block (see Illustration 26, *below*).

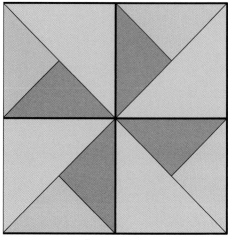

Illustration 26

A grid of 4×4 squares (see Illustration 27, *below*) allows more design opportunities.

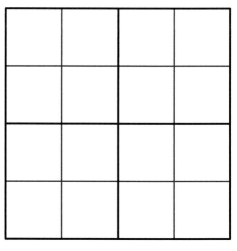

Illustration 27

Triangle-square units placed on a grid of 4×4 squares form a Broken Dishes block (see Illustration 28, *below*).

A grid of 8×8 squares yields a block of 64 squares in which many design possibilities exist (see Illustration 29, *below*).

Squares and triangle-square units on a grid of 8×8 squares form a Northumberland Star block (see Illustration 30, *below*).

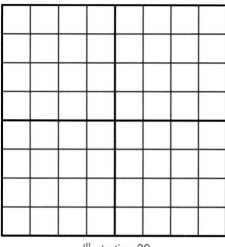

Illustration 28

Illustration 29

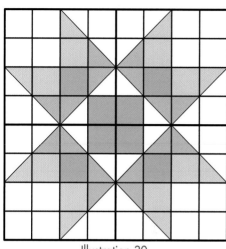

Illustration 30

Testing Unit Layouts

To determine your layout, make several of the same unit and experiment with various settings.

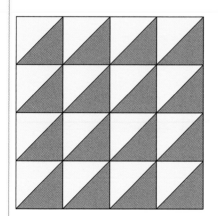

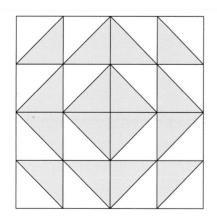

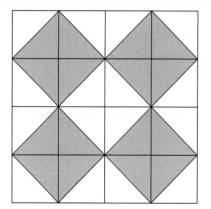

Changing the placement of a unit within a block causes different designs to appear. Changing the colors of fabric within the block expands the possibilities even further.

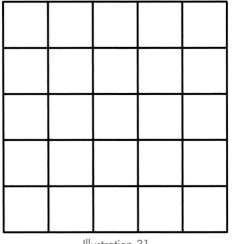

Illustration 31

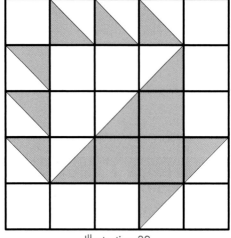

Illustration 32

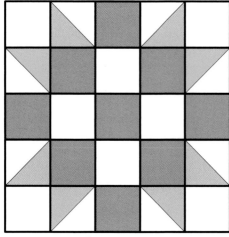

Illustration 33

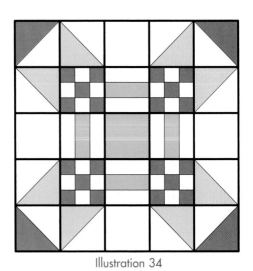

Illustration 34

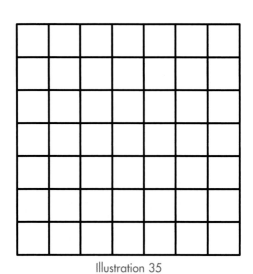

Illustration 35

5×5 Grid

Five squares along each edge give this block design versatility and a center point. Illustration 31, *far left, top,* shows a grid of 5×5 squares.

Triangle-squares and squares form a basket shape to make a Cake Stand block (see Illustration 32, *above left*).

The same pieces in a different layout create a Checkered Star block (see Illustration 33, *above*).

The New Mexico block, a variation on the Checkered Star, is formed with four Nine-Patch units and four three-bar units replacing the squares in the center (see Illustration 34, *far left*).

7×7 Grid

With 49 separate patches in this grid, many intricate designs are possible. Illustration 35, *left,* shows a grid of 7×7 squares.

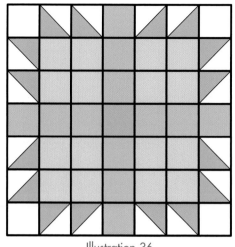

Illustration 36

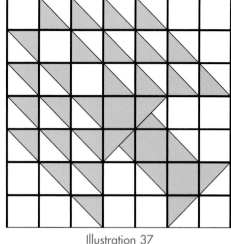

Illustration 37

Illustration 38

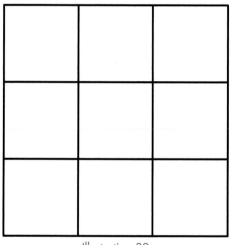

Illustration 39

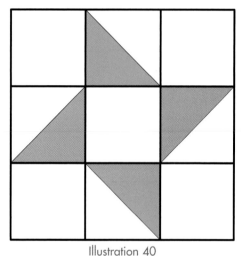

Illustration 40

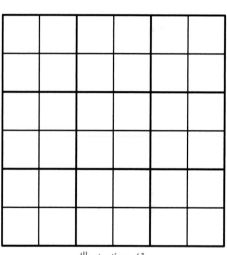

Illustration 41

Sashing separates the four Bear's Paw units in this Bear's Paw block (see Illustration 36, *above top*).

Triangle-squares and squares combine to form a Tree of Paradise block (see Illustration 37, *above right, top*).

The design of a question block radiates from the center (see Illustration 38, *top right*).

3×3 Grid (Nine-Patch)

A common block/unit in quiltmaking is the Nine-Patch. The Nine-Patch grid, like the Four-Patch, can vary in the number of squares it uses. In the case of a Nine-Patch, the number needs to be divisible by three. Illustration 39, *above left,* shows a grid of 3×3 squares (Nine-Patch).

Squares and triangle-square units compose a Friendship Star block on a grid of 3×3 squares (see Illustration 40, *above left*).

Illustration 41 *above* shows a grid of 6×6 squares.

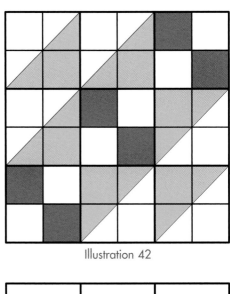

Illustration 42

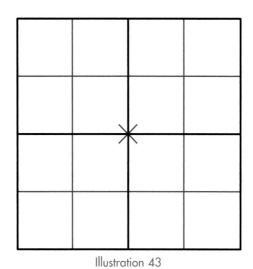

Illustration 43

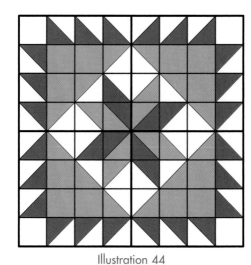

Illustration 44

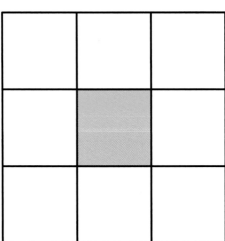

Illustration 45

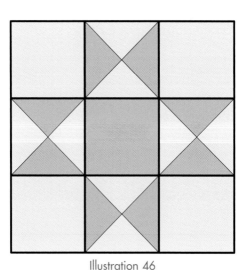

Illustration 46

Jacob's Ladder blocks combine into many different patterns when placed together (see Illustration 42, *far left, top*). Though based on the Nine-Patch grid, this block incorporates Four-Patch units.

Center Points

A Four-Patch grid has a center point where the corners of the units meet (see Illustration 43, *above left*).

Four pieced units combine to make a sawtooth and star block (see Illustration 44, *above*).

A Nine-Patch grid has a unit as its center point (see Illustration 45, *far left*).

The Ohio Star block is based on a Nine-Patch grid with the center of the star as its focal point (see Illustration 46, *left*).

DRAFTING BLOCKS

Drafting allows a quilter to copy a block in a quilt, develop an original design, or change the size of an existing block. Quilters need only a pencil and paper (or a computer design program, depending on personal preference) and a basic understanding of the grid method to draft blocks.

Reproducing a Block Design

When re-creating a block from an antique or heirloom quilt, identifying the block and grid can sometimes be difficult, especially with complex quilt tops. It is common for block designers to start with a base grid, such as the Nine-Patch, and further divide the patches into grids. For instance, the Double Nine-Patch block is based on the 3×3 Nine-Patch grid, but some of the squares have been divided into even smaller Nine-Patch units (see Illustration 47, below).

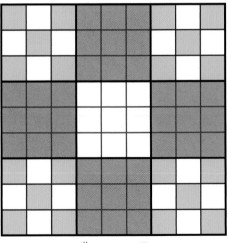

Illustration 47

Changing Block Sizes Using the Grid Method

For blocks based on the grid system, changing size is a matter of redrafting the block on the new grid size. For example, if a Nine-Patch grid makes a 6" finished block but a 9" finished block is needed, use this chart to determine the patch size needed for the larger block. The chart *below* shows that the new Nine-Patch grid would have 3" finished squares.
Note: *Where no number is listed, there is not an exact whole number or fractional number equivalent.*

Grid Size/Finished Block Sizes (inches)

Grid Size →

Block Size	2×2	4×4	8×8	5×5	7×7	3×3	6×6
	4-Patch	16-Patch	64-Patch	25-Patch	49-Patch	9-Patch	36-Patch
6"	3"	1½"	¾"			2"	1"
8"	4"	2"	1"				
9"	4½"	2¼"	1⅛"			3"	1½"
10"	5"	2½"	1¼"	2"			
12"	6"	3"	1½"			4"	2"
14"	7"				2"		
16"	8"	4"	2"				

৵Creative Tip

Turn your favorite quilt pattern into a potholder.

Stitch together a quilt block, add a pocket in the back, and

slip in recipe cards for favorite recipes.

—LANA, HARDLINES SUPERVISOR

Chapter 3 – Planning Your Quilt

To determine the units necessary to reproduce a favorite quilt block, follow these steps:

1. Isolate the block on the quilt.

2. Visualize a grid superimposed over the block. Look for a repeating pattern across the block and count the number of times the pattern repeats.

3. Measure the block to determine the finished size.

4. Using graph paper, rulers, and a pencil, draw out the block. Remember that the pieces drawn are finished size. Once the drafted block is complete, add ¼" seam allowances to all the edges before cutting. *Note: The finished size of a block is likely determined by the pattern being used. When designing an original quilt or modifying an existing pattern you can adjust the blocks to a specific finished size. Do keep in mind the grid for the block you've chosen when deciding on a finished size. For example, it is easier to cut the pieces for a 9" Nine-Patch block than it is to cut out a 10" Nine-Patch block.*

Photo 1A

When paper-piecing quilt squares, lightly shade the pattern pieces with colored pencils to remind you where the specific colors go in your design.

—COLLEEN, STORE ASSOCIATE

Original block design

Use the grid system to organize an original block design and to make it easier to figure out cutting and piecing. To practice, draw several miniature grids (see Photo 1A, *opposite*) and photocopy them. Draw lines throughout the grid to experiment with new block designs. Think about some of the basic units (see *pages 59–66*) and draw them in the grid squares. Keep doodle pads of grids handy, so you can design when inspiration strikes.

Computer programs

A number of computer programs are available for designing blocks and quilt tops. On a computer, multiple block options can be explored quickly and without drafting—a timesaver for doing a great deal of original design work. The programs allow flexibility in creating thousands of designs, adding color, and seeing how blocks will work together.

Advanced block design

Blocks designed with tight curves and unusual shapes may not work on the grid system. These designs can be executed with different techniques, such as appliqué (see Chapter 6—Appliqué Techniques) or foundation piecing (see Chapter 5—Piecing). Some blocks require multiple methods.

Test fabric choices

Finalize block design and fabric selections by mocking up a block (see Photo 1B, *below left*). Cut the fabric pieces to the finished size (leave off the seam allowances for this test only; these pieces will not be used in the finished project) and sketch the grid and block design on paper. Glue the fabric pieces in position on the paper to create a mock block. Place the mock block several feet away to view the design and color combination. If desired, make additional blocks to test alternate fabric choices.

To further test the color and layout, make color photocopies of the mock block. Use the copies to begin planning the quilt top, watching for secondary patterns to emerge and checking color placement in adjacent blocks (see Photo 1C, *below*). *Note: Although photocopies of block patterns are great for understanding the overall design, they are not good for using as accurate templates. Photocopiers can distort images. Before using any photocopies as templates for piecing, make a test copy of the block at 100%. Measure the original and photocopy to ensure they're exactly the same size. To ensure consistent reproduction quality, use the same copier when making additional photocopies. See the Reduction and Enlargement Percentage Chart on page 70 for more information on adjusting block size.*

Photo 1B

Photo 1C

Chapter 3 – Planning Your Quilt

69 ✂

Adjusting Block Size

Use a photocopier to see how a block will look when enlarged or reduced. The equations for determining the percentages shown in the chart are given below. It is necessary to know the original block size and the new block size before using the copier.

Note: Only blocks with whole number percentages have been listed:

(New Block Size ÷ Original Block Size) × 100 = Percent

Reduction and Enlargement Percentage Chart

New Size (Finished) →

Original Size (Finished) ↓

Original \ New	2"	3"	4"	5"	6"	7"	8"	9"	10"
2"	100%	150%	200%	250%	300%	350%	400%	450%	500%
3"		100%			200%			300%	
4"	50%	75%	100%	125%	150%	175%	200%	225%	250%
5"	40%	60%	80%	100%	120%	140%	160%	180%	200%
6"		50%			100%			150%	
7"						100%			
8"	25%		50%		75%		100%		125%
9"								100%	
10"	20%	30%	40%	50%	60%	70%	80%	90%	100%

Calculating Proportion

To figure dimensions on blocks that are not square, use these formulas.

Height Formula

If the desired width is known, use this formula to determine the block height:
- Desired Width ÷ Original Width = A (proportion factor)
- Original Height × A (proportion factor) = New Height

For example, if the original block is 5" high by 6" wide and it should be 12" wide, divide 12 by 6 to get 2 (proportion factor). Multiply the original height of 5" by 2 (proportion factor) to determine that the new finished height of the block is 10".

Width Formula

If the desired height is known, use this formula to determine the block width:
- Desired Height ÷ Original Height = B (proportion factor)
- Original Width × B (proportion factor) = New Width

For example, if the original block is 3" high by 7" wide and it should be be 4½" high, divide 4½ by 3 to get 1½ (proportion factor). Multiply the original width of 7" by 1½ (proportion factor) to determine that the new finished width of the block is 10½".

⟋Creative Tip

When beginning a quilt, make the first block out of scrap fabric to make sure you understand the instructions. If you've misread something, you haven't wasted any fabric from your project. If it is correct, you can use the block to begin another project or make a potholder or pillow to give as a gift.

—CHARLOTTE, STORE ASSOCIATE

Planning *Your Quilt Top*

Understanding how the elements of a quilt top work together makes it easier to plan a quilt successfully. In some cases, the size of a finished quilt is determined before the first piece of fabric is cut. At other times, the quilt is based on blocks that are already made or acquired (maybe via a block exchange, an inheritance, or an auction purchase) without a specific project in mind. If you find yourself in the latter category, use the following information to help plan block arrangements that make an attractive and functional quilt top. This information can also be used to alter a pattern and change its size or setting.

Measuring a Bed to Determine Quilt Size

Follow these instructions to measure a bed and determine the finished size of a quilt. When measuring, have the blankets, sheets, and pillows on the bed that will be used with the quilt. "Drop" is the part of the quilt that extends over the edge of the mattress. "Tuck" is the part of the quilt that folds under the pillows if the quilt is meant to cover them. The tuck can be shallow (10") or deep (20").
Note: *The amount of quilting done and the type of batting used can result in a 3 to 5% loss in the overall size of the quilt; plan accordingly.*

Width
Measure the mattress width and add twice the drop length. For a comforter-size finished project, measure from the top of the mattress to slightly past its lower edge to figure the drop length. For a coverlet, measure from the top of the mattress to slightly past the bottom of the bed rail. For a bedspread, measure from the top of the mattress to just above the floor.

Length
If the quilt is to cover the pillows, measure the mattress length, then add one drop length plus 10" to 20" for the pillow tuck. The exact amount to add will depend on the size and fullness of the pillows and the depth of the tuck. If the quilt is not to cover the pillows, measure the mattress length and add one drop length.

Shallow 10" tuck

Deep 20" tuck

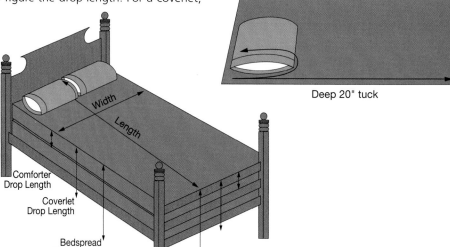

Width

Length

Comforter
Drop Length

Coverlet
Drop Length

Bedspread
Drop Length

DETERMINING QUILT SIZE

When using a pattern or kit and following the instructions exactly, the finished measurements of the quilt are predetermined. However, when modifying or designing a pattern to make a quilt that fits a specific bed or display area, the finished size of the project must be determined. The first step in the planning process is to decide on the desired finished size.

For a wall hanging, base the width and length on the space available for hanging the finished project. If the quilt is to hang from a special quilt rack or hanger, measure its width so the finished project will fit.

When making a throw, keep in mind who will be using it. Are they tall adults or small children? Will they want to lay it over their laps or wrap up in it? Usage conclusions should determine the optimum finished size.

For bed-size quilts, see Standard Bed and Batting Sizes, *top right*. For greater accuracy, measure the bed for which the quilt is to be made, since mattress heights vary (see Measuring a Bed to Determine Quilt Size, *opposite*). Consider whether the quilt is to fold under, then over the bed pillows or not and how far down on the bed it will hang (comforter, coverlet, or bedspread length).

ADJUSTING QUILT SIZE

Sometimes the quilt size is predetermined, but the chosen pattern is for a smaller or larger quilt. There are several ways to adjust the pattern. Keep in mind that altering some parts of a quilt may also change the proportions of the elements in relationship to one another. (See Border Proportions on *pages 77–78* for more information.) Sketch design ideas on graph paper first to see how the changes will affect the finished size and appearance of the quilt.

Standard Bed and Batting Sizes

Bed size	Mattress size W×L	Batting size* W×L
Crib	23×46"	45×60"
Twin	39×75"	72×90"
Double (or Full)	54×75"	81×96"
Queen	60×80"	90×108"
King	76×80"	120×120"
California King	72×84"	

Note: Batting sizes refer to commercially available, precut batts.

Sample Quilt Sizes

Drops are on three sides	Twin mattress 39×75" W×L	Double mattress 54×75" W×L	Queen mattress 60×80" W×L	King mattress 76×80" W×L
With 10" drop	59×85"	74×85"	80×90"	96×90"
And 10" tuck	59×95"	74×95"	80×100"	96×100"
With 12" drop	63×87"	78×87"	84×92"	100×92"
And 10" tuck	63×97"	78×97"	84×102"	100×102"
With 14" drop	67×89"	82×89"	88×94"	104×94"
And 10" tuck	67×99"	82×99"	88×104"	104×104"
With 16" drop	71×91"	86×91"	92×96"	108×96"
And 10" tuck	71×101"	86×101"	92×106"	108×106"
With 18" drop	75×93"	90×93"	96×98"	112×98"
And 10" tuck	75×103"	90×103"	96×108"	112×108"
With 20" drop	79×95"	94×95"	100×100"	116×100"
And 10" tuck	79×105"	94×105"	100×110"	116×110"

Sometimes there are too many—or too few—blocks to complete a quilt center. If the quilt top will be too large because there are too many blocks, rearrange the block layout. Or eliminate blocks by changing the number of blocks in a row or the number of rows. Use any extra blocks in the quilt backing (see Chapter 7—Assembling the Quilt Top and Backing for more information).

If removing blocks makes the quilt top too small, regain some of the inches by adding sashing between rows. If reducing the number of blocks is not an option, consider using narrower sashing.

If the quilt top will be too small because there are not enough blocks, make more blocks or add setting squares to spread out the blocks already made. Add or increase the width of the sashing between blocks, or try a diagonal (on point) block layout.

Or, in the planning stages of a project, consider changing the finished size of the blocks (see *page 70* for more information on changing block size).

If the finished size will be altered by adjusting the border, consider not only reducing or enlarging the border width but also creating an additional border. Again, keep the proportion of the borders to the finished quilt in mind.

ELEMENTS OF A QUILT TOP

All the elements of a quilt—blocks, borders, sashing, and binding—make a statement in the completed project. Whether that statement is subtle or bold is up to the quiltmaker.

Achieve different designs by changing the placement and colors of shapes and units within blocks. Many of those same techniques can be used when planning a quilt top.

Blocks are the main visual element in the quilt center. They most commonly are square but can also be other shapes, such as rectangular, triangular, or hexagonal. A single block style or several block styles may be used in a quilt top.

Setting squares or triangles are the secondary blocks or solid fabric pieces placed between the main blocks. They give the eye a place to rest, setting off the main blocks.

Sashing refers to strips of fabric (or strips and squares) between blocks that give the blocks definition. Not all quilt tops have sashing.

Borders frame the quilt center, visually holding in the design. Borders also give the eye a stopping point. Some quilt tops do not have borders.

Binding can blend in or contrast with the border or blocks, depending on the design statement you wish to make.

BLOCK SETTING OPTIONS

Setting refers to how the blocks are arranged on the quilt top. The possibilities for combining blocks are nearly endless. The following setting options offer ideas. (See Chapter 7—Assembling the Quilt Top and Backing for specific information on joining the pieces together.)

Straight Set, Block-to-Block
Lay out the blocks side by side in straight horizontal and vertical rows without sashing (see Illustration 48, *above right*).

Straight Set, Block-to-Block Variation
Change the direction of the asymmetrical blocks in a block-to-block layout and a new design will emerge (see Illustration 49, *opposite*).

Illustration 48

Straight Set with Alternate Squares or Blocks
Lay out blocks with alternating setting (plain) squares or contrasting blocks in straight horizontal and vertical rows without sashing, alternating types (see illustrations 50 and 51, *opposite*).

Straight Set with Continuous Sashing
Lay out the blocks in straight horizontal and vertical rows with strips for sashing between the blocks (see Illustration 52, *opposite*).

Straight Set with Sashing Strips and Squares (Cornerstones)
Lay out the blocks in straight horizontal and vertical rows with alternating strips and squares for sashing between the blocks (see Illustration 53, *opposite*).
Note: The blocks in the illustration are composed of four smaller blocks.

Diagonal Set with Alternate Squares or Blocks
Lay out the blocks and setting (plain) squares or contrasting blocks in diagonal rows without sashing, alternating types (see illustrations 54 and 55, *opposite*). Cut or piece side and corner setting triangles to fill out the set (see Chapter 4—Cutting Techniques for information on cutting side and corner setting triangles).

Illustration 49

Illustration 50

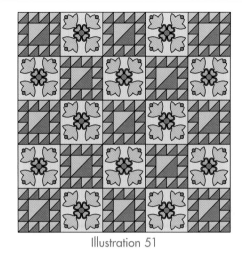

Illustration 51

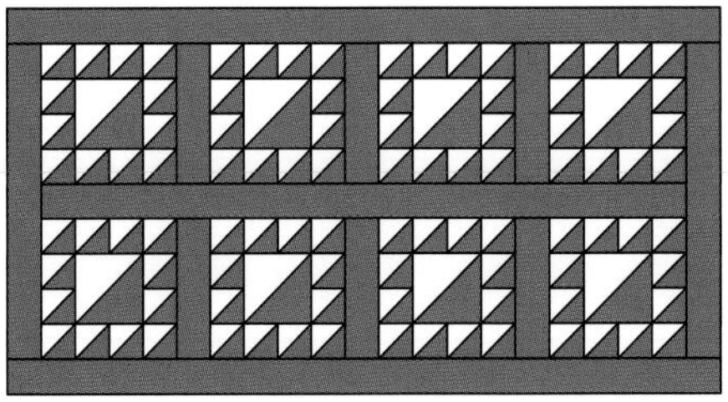

Illustration 52

Illustration 53

Illustration 54

Diagonal Set with Floating Blocks

Lay out the blocks and setting (plain) squares in diagonal rows (see Illustration 56, *far right*). To make it look as though the blocks are floating, cut the side and corner setting triangles up to 2" larger than the diagonal measurement of the block to fill out the set (see Chapter 4—Cutting Techniques for information on cutting side and corner setting triangles).

Illustration 55

Illustration 56

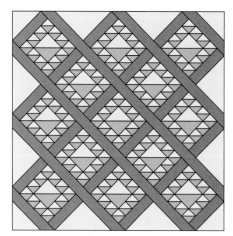

Illustration 57

Illustration 58

Illustration 59

Diagonal Set with Continuous Sashing

Lay out the blocks in diagonal rows with strips for sashing between the blocks (see Illustration 57, *left*). Cut or piece side and corner setting triangles to fill out the set (see Chapter 4—Cutting Techniques for information on cutting side and corner setting triangles).

Diagonal Set with Sashing Strips and Squares

Lay out the blocks in diagonal rows with alternating strips and squares for sashing between the blocks (see Illustration 58, *below left*). Cut or piece side and corner setting triangles to fill out the set.

Vertical or Zigzag Set

Lay out the blocks and setting triangles in diagonal rows for each vertical strip. For a zigzag set (see Illustration 59, *below left*), begin and end odd-numbered vertical rows with full blocks; begin and end even-numbered vertical rows with a trimmed block (a half block + seam allowance).

Note: Because each half block needs a seam allowance, it is not possible to get two half blocks from one block. First join the pieces in each vertical row, then join the rows together.

To expand the size of the quilt top, add sashing strips between the vertical rows.

Row-by-Row Set

Create a quilt top where each row is different from the others. Sashing can be added between the blocks and/or between the rows as desired (see Illustration 60, *below left*).

Framed Block Set

When beginning with a set of blocks that aren't all the same size, or when trying to unify blocks made in a variety of colors, consider framing the blocks with a single fabric (see Illustration 61, *below*). More frames in various widths can be added to each block to make them uniform. The blocks can then be organized in a straight block-to-block set (see *page 74*).

Illustration 60

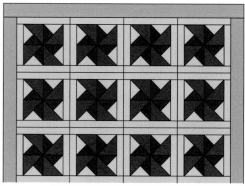

Illustration 61

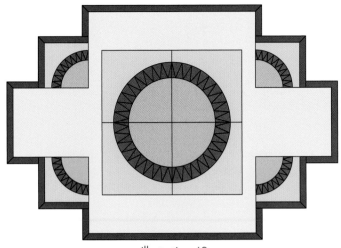

Illustration 62

Illustration 63

Illustration 64

Contemporary Set

Not all quilts are square or rectangular. And at times, even traditional blocks are set in unusual ways (see Illustration 62, *above*). Blocks may vary in size and/or be staggered in creative arrangements. If a nontraditional setting is the goal, first sketch the design onto graph paper to determine the positions of blocks and sashing.

Single-Shape Set

Create a quilt primarily from a single shape. The Lone Star (see Illustration 63, *above right*) and Grandmother's Flower Garden (see Illustration 64, *right*) designs are two examples.

BORDER OPTIONS

Borders frame a quilt center and can be as simple as single strips of complementary or contrasting fabric. A border also can be intricately pieced or elaborately appliquéd. When using a large-scale print in the quilt center's blocks, bring unity to the quilt by repeating it in the border.

Border Proportions

Borders should be in proportion to the size of the finished quilt. Generally, a small wall hanging should have a border of less than 6", whereas a quilt for a king-size bed could handle a 12–14" border. Borders that are too small can make a quilt seem out of balance. Borders that are too wide diminish the quilt center design. To decide how wide to make a border, begin with the finished block size. If the quilt center is made of 4" blocks, try a 4"-wide border.

If the quilt top needs to be enlarged, consider adding sashing, pieced borders, or multiple borders. Unless the difference is minimal, avoid adjusting only the border; for instance, widening it can make the quilt look out of proportion.

When trying to determine what type of border to add to a quilt center, look at quilting books and magazines for appealing border and block combinations. Study the proportion of the border to the block size and the amount of piecing or detail in the border as compared to the blocks. (See Chapter 7—Assembling the Quilt Top and Backing for specific information on measuring and assembling the border elements.)

Straight Borders

The simplest border uses a single fabric in strips around all four sides of the quilt center (see Illustration 65, *below left*). Add the border strips in pairs to opposite edges. For example, first sew strips to the side edges, then add them to the top and bottom edges.

For added interest, inset rectangles at the center of each edge (see Illustration 66, *below*).

Or add a solid square to each end of the top and bottom border strips before sewing the strips to the quilt center (see Illustration 67, *below*).

Using pieced blocks instead of solid squares adds interest (see Illustration 68, *bottom, far left*).

Mitered Borders

Mitering the corners of a straight border is another possible variation (see Illustration 69, *below left, bottom*). Decide whether to use this method before cutting the border strips, as mitering requires extra length.

Multiple border strips may be added to a quilt top (see Illustration 70, *below bottom*). They may be added one at a time or first joined into a unit that is then sewn to the

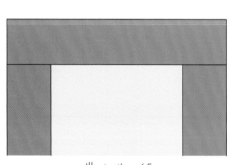

Illustration 65

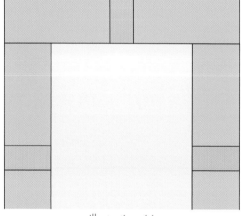

Illustration 66

Illustration 67

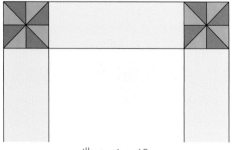

Illustration 68

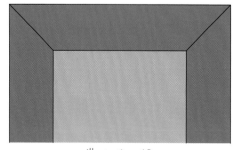

Illustration 69

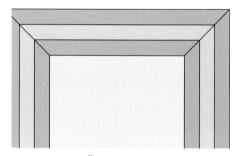

Illustration 70

quilt center. When mitering the corners, joining the strips into a single unit first works best.

Appliqué Borders

The appliqué work on a border, whether by hand or machine, may be done before or after the border strips are joined to the quilt center (see Illustration 71, *below*).

Cut the border strips slightly larger than needed, and trim them after the appliqué work is complete, to give yourself room to work. Any appliqué pieces that cross over a seam will need to be sewn in place after the border strips are added to the quilt center.

Plan how the design will turn the corners by sketching out the complete border design before appliquéing.

Scalloped Borders

A scalloped border edge softens the look of a quilt and adds another element of interest (see Illustration 72, *below*).

Mark scallops on borders after the border strips are sewn to the quilt center, then cut the scallops after the hand or machine quilting is complete. Determine an appropriate width for the scallops so they will fit evenly along the edges and around the corners.

Illustration 71

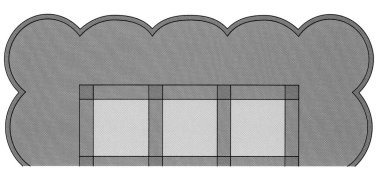

Illustration 72

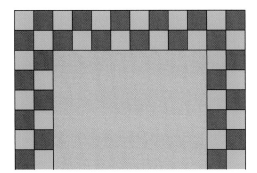

Illustration 73

Illustration 74

Illustration 75

Pieced Borders with Straight-Set Blocks

From a strip of pieced rectangles to a checkerboard of Four-Patch blocks, the options for pieced borders are many (see Illustration 73, *above*).

Pay special attention to the layout of the pieced blocks and, if the units are directional, how they turn the corners. It is best to have all four corners match (see Illustration 74, *above right*).

If this isn't possible, plan to use corner squares to avoid taking the focus off the center of the quilt (see Illustration 75, *above far right*).

Make sure that the finished size of the block divides evenly into the finished measurement of the quilt center's edges. This will prevent the need for partial blocks in the border.

In cases when the block size cannot be divided evenly into the quilt center's edge measurements, alteration options include resizing the pieced border blocks to fit, adding a spacer border (see Spacer Borders, *opposite*), or, if the difference is not too large, insetting a rectangle at the center of each border strip (see Illustration 76, *opposite*).

Pieced Borders with Diagonally Set Blocks

Borders that contain blocks or units set diagonally, or on point, are easiest to use on a plain quilt center or a quilt center with blocks set on point (see Illustration 77, *opposite*). Refer to the Diagonal Measurements of Squares chart in Chapter 4—Cutting Techniques for mathematical help in planning a diagonally set border.

Make sure that the finished diagonal measurement of the block divides evenly into the finished measurements of the quilt

center's edges. This will prevent the need for partial blocks in the border. If the block size cannot be evenly divided into the quilt center's edge measurements, add a spacer border, as described *opposite*.

Directional Borders

Directional borders are those that have designs running in a particular sequence or order (such as triangle-squares combining into a sawtooth border). Because it is best for a border to appear to be the same along all four sides, plan carefully in order to turn corners smoothly (see Illustration 78, *opposite*). Sketch the border on paper before proceeding with assembly.

Occasionally directional borders require a special corner unit or block to make the transition from side to side with visual ease. Again, draw the border on paper before proceeding with assembly to determine how and where the corner units will need to be rotated.

Illustration 76

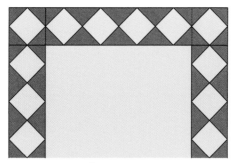

Illustration 77

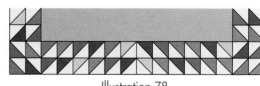

Illustration 78

Unbalanced Borders

For contemporary designs try borders of differing sizes along each side of the quilt center. For an asymmetrical look, sew border strips to only two or three sides of the quilt center.

Spacer Borders

Spacer borders are plain borders that are sewn between the quilt center and outer pieced borders (see Illustration 79, *above right*). Think of a spacer border as a mat on a framed picture. They are a good solution when the dimensions of the pieced border and the quilt center are not compatible or whenever there is a need for some visual "breathing room" between the pieced or appliquéd quilt center and the outer border.

Spacer borders can be the same width along all quilt center edges or they can be one width along the sides and another along the top and bottom.

Illustration 79

When the same fabric is used for the pieced quilt center and a spacer border, the center blocks appear to float within the outer border (see Illustration 80, *above right*).

A spacer border of contrasting fabric calls attention to the separation between the quilt center and the outer border (see Illustration 81, *right*).

Illustration 80

Illustration 81

Chapter 3 – Planning Your Quilt

Chapter 4

CUTTING
TECHNIQUES

Mastering a variety of cutting techniques will

make your quilting experience more enjoyable—

and more successful.

CUT GLASS DISH

In the 1930s, quilters preferred quilts with a scrappy look. Among the favorites were Grandmother's Flower Garden, Double Wedding Ring, Dresden Plate, and other designs that were attractively made with solid and print pastels. Cut Glass Dish, meant to resemble the facets of sparkling crystal, is also effective in scraps. Difficult to see, a Cut Glass Dish block has three large squares set on the diagonal—two white and one print. The squares are surrounded by small print and white triangles, making the block a Nine-Patch. The pattern is also called Winged Square. This quilt is edged with triangles in nile green and lavender, a popular color combination during the Depression.

Cutting *Techniques*

A successful quilt requires precise cutting. With accurately cut pieces, even a beginning quiltmaker can assemble a quilt with ease. Knowing which cutting technique to use when can make all the difference in your quiltmaking experience.

CUTTING TOOLS

For a review of both traditional and rotary cutting tools, see Chapter 1—Tools and Materials.

FABRIC GRAIN

Always consider the fabric grain before cutting. The arrow on the pattern piece or template indicates which direction the fabric grain should run. Because one or more straight sides of every fabric piece should follow the lengthwise or crosswise grain, it is important to have the line on the pattern or template run parallel to the grain.

The lengthwise grain runs parallel to the tightly woven finished edge, or selvage, and is sometimes referred to as the straight grain. It has the least amount of stretch and is the strongest and smoothest grain. Do not use the selvage edge in a quilt. When washed, the selvage, because it is so tightly woven, may shrink more than the rest of the fabric.

The crosswise grain runs perpendicular to the selvage (see Illustration 1, *below left*). It is sometimes referred to as the cross grain. The crosswise grain is usually looser and has slightly more stretch than the lengthwise grain.

True bias intersects the lengthwise grain and crosswise grain at a 45° angle, but any line that runs diagonally between the two grain lines is called the bias. It has more stretch and flexibility than either the crosswise or lengthwise grain.

When the lengthwise grain and the crosswise grain intersect at a perfect right angle (see Illustration 2, *below right*), the fabric is said to be on grain, or grain perfect. If the grains don't intersect at a perfect right angle, they are considered off grain and the threads are distorted.

A fabric that is slightly off grain is still usable. However, significantly off-grain fabric will require careful handling during assembly and heavy quilting to stabilize it in a finished quilt.

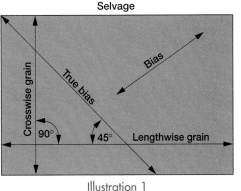

Illustration 1

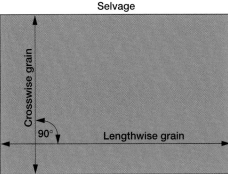

Illustration 2

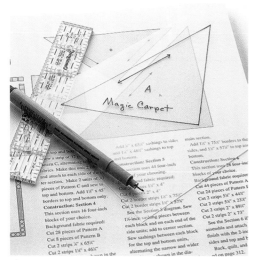

Photo 1A

Photo 1B

Photo 1C

MARKING WITH TEMPLATES

A template is a thin, firm pattern that aids quilters as they cut the various fabric pieces needed for patchwork and appliqué work. The centuries-old process of cutting patchwork or appliqué pieces employs scissors and templates. Using a template may still be the best way to mark and cut curved or irregular-shape pieces, and many quilters use templates for traditional shapes, too. Commercially available acrylic templates are helpful for quick rotary cutting of specialty shapes and patterns, especially those that need to be cut in large multiples.

This section addresses templates made for both hand and machine piecing. For information on cutting appliqué templates, see Chapter 6—Appliqué Techniques.

Templates can be made from different materials; the selection depends on how often they will be used. Make sure that the template material will hold up to the wear that it receives from multiple tracings without wearing away at the edges.

Sturdy, durable material such as template plastic, available at your Jo-Ann Store, is suitable for making permanent templates for scissors-cut pieces.

Making Templates for Hand Piecing

For information on appliqué templates, see Chapter 6—Appliqué Techniques.

1. Lay template plastic over a printed quilt pattern and trace the pattern onto the plastic using a permanent marker and straightedge (see Photo 1A, *above left*). Because it is for hand piecing, make the template the exact size of the finished piece; do not include seam allowances. Mark the template with its letter designation, grain line, and block name.

2. Cut out the template and check it against the original pattern for accuracy (see Photo 1B, *above*).

Using Templates in Hand Piecing

1. Place the template facedown on the wrong side of the fabric and trace around outside edges with a pencil, chalk, or special quilt marker that makes a thin, accurate line (see Photo 1C, *above*).

Note: Place 220-grit sandpaper beneath the fabric to prevent stretching it as you trace around the template. Position tracings at least ½" apart. The lines drawn on the fabric are the sewing lines.

2. Mark cutting lines ¼" away from the sewing lines or estimate by eye a ¼" seam allowance around each piece as you cut out the fabric shapes with sharp scissors (see Photo 1D, *opposite*).

Making Templates for Machine Piecing

1. Lay template plastic over a printed quilt pattern and trace the pattern onto the plastic using a permanent marker and straightedge (see Photo 1E, *opposite*). Because it is for machine piecing, make the template the exact size of the finished piece plus the ¼" seam allowance. Mark the template with its block name, letter designation, grain line, and the matching point of each corner on the seam line.

Photo 1D

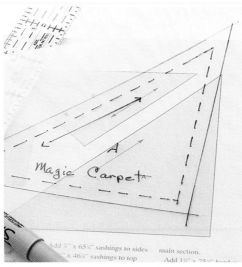

Photo 1E

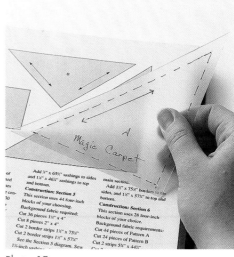

Photo 1F

Photo 1G

Photo 1H

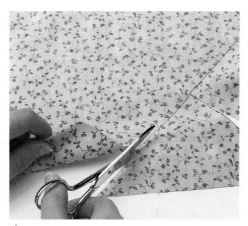

Photo 1I

2. Cut out the template. Check the template against the original pattern for accuracy (see Photo 1F, *top right*).

3. Using a pushpin, make a hole in the template at each corner matching point (see Photo 1G, *above*). The hole must be large enough for the point of a pencil or marking pen to mark through.

Using Templates in Machine Piecing

1. Place the template facedown on the wrong side of the fabric and trace around outside edges with a pencil, chalk, or special quilt marker that makes a thin, accurate line (see Photo 1H, *above*). *Note: Place 220-grit sandpaper beneath the fabric to prevent stretching it as you trace around the template.* Mark the corner matching points through the holes in the

template; they should be right on the seam line. Position tracings without space between them as the lines drawn on the fabric are the cutting lines.

2. Using sharp scissors or a rotary cutter and ruler, cut precisely on the drawn lines (see Photo 1I, *above*).

Photo 1J

Photo 1K

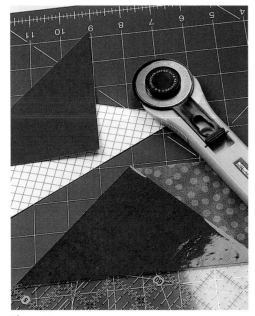

Photo 1L

Photo 1M

Using Templates for Rotary Cutting

Premade templates of thick plastic or acrylic material are often available at fabric stores and quilt shops in a variety of commonly used shapes. These templates are durable enough to be used with a rotary cutter, which speeds the cutting process.

1. Place the template faceup on the right side of an appropriately sized fabric strip.

2. Cut precisely around edges of template with a rotary cutter (see Photo 1J, *far left*).

Other Template Types
Printed Paper Patterns

To eliminate the tracing step, sandwich a printed paper pattern between two pieces of template plastic, or one piece of template plastic and tag board or sandpaper (see Photo 1K, *above left*). Use rubber cement or a glue stick to adhere the template plastic to the top of the pattern piece and the template plastic, tag board, or sandpaper to the back of the pattern piece. Let the adhesive dry before cutting through all layers at once to make an accurate template.

Flexible, See-Through Plastic Sheeting

Available at quilt shops, this special-purpose, colored plastic uses static electricity to stick to the rotary-cutting ruler (see Photo 1L, *far left*). It is used for do-it-yourself rotary-cutting template making. Cut the plastic to size and place on the rotary-cutting ruler as an aid in speedy cutting.

Graph Paper Templates

Use the printed lines on graph paper to draw a pattern piece (see Photo 1M, *left*). Glue the graph-paper pattern to template plastic, tag board, or cardboard. Allow the adhesive to dry before cutting through all layers at once to make an accurate template.

What About Dog-Ears?

Long points that will extend beyond the seam allowance line after the pieces are stitched together—"dog-ears" in quilter's terms—can be eliminated when making a template. This can make it far easier to align the pieces for sewing.

As a general rule, blunt points of less than 90° at the ¼" seam line so they will match neighboring pieces. Trim points from templates on regularly shaped pieces when the right side of the piece is the same as the left side.

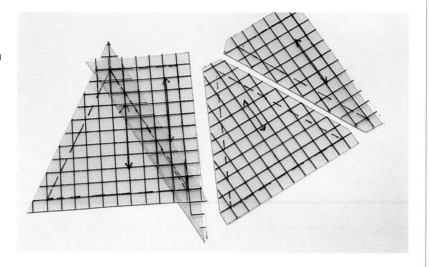

Angles other than 90° are trickier. When in doubt as to when and where to trim a template point, make templates with the points left on. Then match the seam lines of adjoining pieces and decide whether to remove any points that stick out beyond both layers.

The untrimmed templates shown in the photo *above* overlap on the seam lines as they would if sewn together. The top and side points of the bottom triangle extend beyond both layers, so they could be trimmed off. Likewise, the left and bottom points of the upper triangle extend beyond both layers, so they, too, could be trimmed off. The trimmed, ready-for-use templates are shown to the right.

⸙Creative Tip

Keep a second pair of scissors handy for

cutting batting and paper patterns so the

scissors you use for cutting fabric won't become dull.

—CHRISTIE, SALES ASSOCIATE

Photo 1N

Photo 1O

Photo 1P

Photo 1Q

Rotary Cutting

With a rotary cutter it is possible to make accurate cuts through multiple layers of fabric. One of the strongest appeals of rotary cutting is the precision and speed with which multiple strips, squares, triangles, and diamonds can be cut. It speeds the quiltmaking process and makes it more enjoyable for many quiltmakers.

As with many techniques, the more you practice the easier and more natural the process will become. Practice rotary cutting on fabric scraps until you develop confidence in your cutting accuracy.

Tool Basics

Three basic pieces of equipment are needed to rotary-cut fabrics: a rotary cutter, an acrylic ruler, and a cutting mat.

A rotary cutter should always be used with a cutting mat designed specifically for rotary cutting. The mat protects the cutting surface and keeps the fabric from shifting while it's being cut.

Cutting mats usually have one side printed with a grid and one side that's plain. To avoid confusion when lining up fabric with the lines printed on the ruler, some quilters prefer to use the plain side of the mat. Others prefer to use the grid on the mat.

The round blade of a rotary cutter is razor sharp. Because of this, be sure to use a cutter with a safety guard and keep the guard over the blade whenever the cutter is not in use. Rotary cutters are commonly available in three sizes; a good all-purpose blade is a 45 mm.
Note: *For more information on the tools needed for rotary cutting and their care, see Chapter 1—Tools and Materials.*

Squaring Up the Fabric Edge
Before rotary-cutting fabric into strips, it is imperative that one edge of the fabric be straightened, or squared up. Because the accuracy of all subsequent cuts depends on this first cut, squaring up the fabric edge is critical. There are several ways to square up fabric; the two most common are the single-ruler technique and the double-ruler technique shown here. The following instructions are for right-handed cutting; reverse them for left-handed cutting.

Squaring Up with the Single-Ruler Technique
This method requires just one ruler. Turn the mat or move to the opposite side of the cutting surface after squaring up the fabric before cutting strips.

1. Lay the fabric right side down on the cutting mat with one selvage edge away from you (see Photo 1N, *top left*).

2. Fold the fabric in half with the wrong side inside and selvages together (see Photo 1O, *middle left*).

3. Fold the fabric in half again, aligning the folded edge with the selvage edges. Lightly hand-crease all folds (see Photo 1P, *far left*).

4. Position the folded fabric on the cutting mat with selvage edges away from you and the bulk of the fabric to your left (see Photo 1Q, *opposite*).

5. With the ruler on top of the fabric, align a horizontal grid line on the ruler with the lower folded fabric edge, leaving about 1" of fabric exposed along the right-hand edge of ruler (see Photo 1R, *right*).

Do not try to align the uneven raw edges along the other side of the fabric. If the grid lines on the cutting mat interfere with your ability to focus on the ruler grid lines, turn the cutting mat over and work on the unmarked side.

6. Hold the ruler firmly in place with your left hand, spreading your fingers apart slightly and keeping them away from the right-hand edge of the ruler (see Photo 1S, *far right, top*). Apply pressure to the ruler with fingertips. (Some quilters keep their little finger just off the ruler edge, pressing it on the cutting mat to stabilize the ruler.) With the ruler firmly in place, hold the rotary cutter with the handle at an angle to the cutting mat and the blade abutted against the ruler's right-hand edge. Roll the blade along the ruler's edge, starting the cut just off the folded edge and pushing the cutter away from you, toward the selvage edges.

7. The fabric strip to the right of the ruler's edge should be cut cleanly away, leaving a straight edge from which all subsequent cuts can be measured. Do not pick up the fabric once the edge has been squared; instead, turn the cutting mat to rotate the fabric (see Photo 1T, *above right*).

8. Begin cutting strips, measuring from the cut edge (see Photo 1U, *above, far right*).

Photo 1R

Photo 1S

Photo 1T

Photo IU

Chapter 4 – Cutting Techniques

❧Creative Tip

When you're rotary cutting large quantities of strips at one time, place
self-sticking notes on the back of your see-through ruler
to mark the increments you need. This provides a visible guide
and makes the process faster.

—THELMA, STORE ASSOCIATE

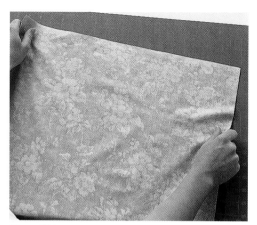

Photo 1V

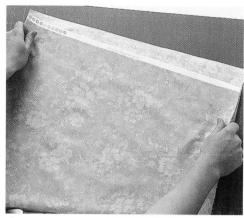

Photo 1W

Photo 1X

Photo 1Y

Squaring Up with the Double-Ruler Technique

This method requires two rulers. Begin cutting strips as soon as the fabric is squared up; turning the mat is not necessary.

1. Lay the fabric right side down on the cutting mat with one selvage edge away from you (see Photo 1V, *above*).

2. Fold the fabric in half with the wrong side inside and selvages together (see Photo 1W, *above right*).

3. Fold the fabric in half again, aligning the folded edge with the selvage edges. Lightly hand-crease all the folds (see Photo 1X, *above, far right*).

4. Position the folded fabric on the cutting mat with selvage edges away from you and the bulk of the fabric to your right (see Photo 1Y, *right*).

5. With a large square ruler on top of the fabric, align a horizontal grid line on the ruler with the lower folded fabric edge (see Photo 1Z, *opposite*). Leave a small amount of fabric exposed along the left-hand edge of the ruler. Abut a rectangular ruler against the square ruler along left-hand edge.

6. Carefully remove the large square ruler, leaving the rectangular ruler in place (see Photo 2A, *opposite*).

7. Trim away the edge of the fabric to square up fabric (see Photo 2B, *opposite*). Do not pick up the fabric once the edge has been squared.

8. Reposition the rectangular ruler and begin cutting strips, measuring from the cut edge without rotating the cutting mat (see Photo 2C, *opposite*).

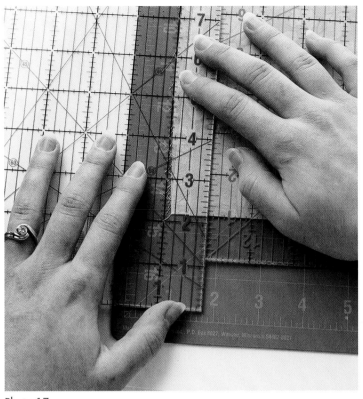

Photo 1Z

Photo 2A

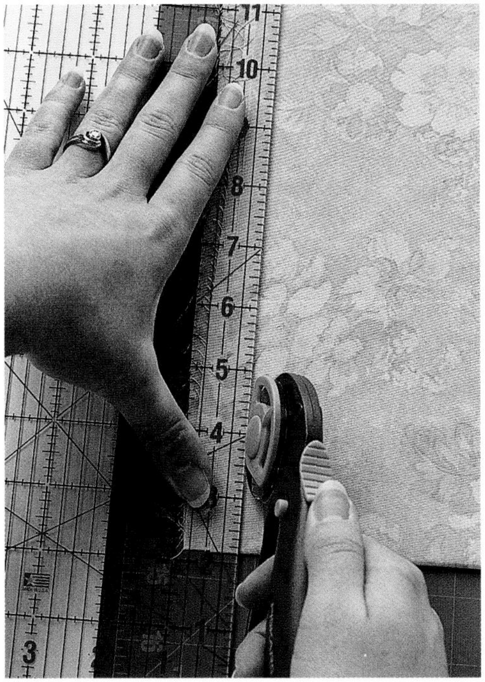

Photo 2B

Photo 2C

Photo 2D

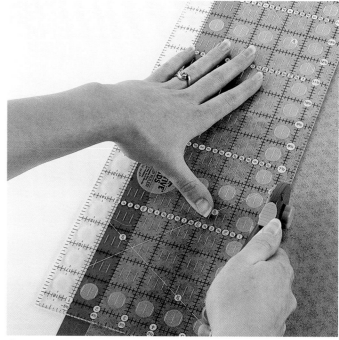

Photo 2E

Cutting Fabric Wider Than the Ruler

Occasionally it is necessary to cut fabric that is wider than the ruler is long. Cutting border strips from the lengthwise grain is one example.

1. After squaring up the fabric, align the ruler and cut to the end of the ruler (see Photo 2D, *above*; refer to *page 90* for instructions on squaring up the fabric edge).

2. Leaving the rotary cutter in place on the fabric, slide the ruler ahead to the uncut area (see Photo 2E, *above right*). Align the ruler edge with the cut edge of the fabric.

3. Continue cutting and moving the ruler ahead as needed until the desired length of fabric has been cut.

Rotary-Cutter Troubleshooting

Is the cutter not cutting through all the layers? Check the following:

- Is the blade dull? If so, replace it and carefully dispose of the used one. Some blades may be successfully sharpened with a special tool.

- Is there a nick in the blade? Evenly spaced uncut threads indicate that a blade section is not touching the fabric during each rotation. Replace the blade. In the future, avoid cutting over pins and/or dropping the rotary cutter.

- Did you use enough pressure? If the blade is sharp but there are still large areas where fabric layers weren't cut through cleanly, or where only the uppermost layers were cut, you may not be putting enough muscle behind the cutter. If the problem persists, try cutting fewer fabric layers at a time.

- Is the mat worn out? With extended use, grooves can be worn into a cutting mat, leaving the blade with not enough resistance to make clear cuts through the fabric.

YARDAGE ESTIMATOR: Squares from Strips

Use this chart to determine the number of squares that can be cut from various yardages. The figures on this chart are mathematically accurate. It may be wise to purchase extra fabric to allow for errors.

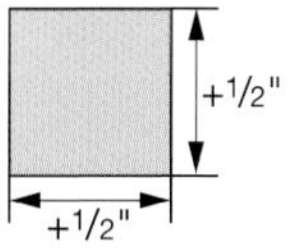

Yardage figures include ¼" seam allowances and are based on 42"-long strips.

SIZE OF SQUARE		YARDAGE (44/45"-WIDE FABRIC)							
Finished	Cut Strip Width	¼	½	¾	1	1¼	1½	1¾	2
1"	1½"	168	336	504	672	840	1008	1176	1344
1½"	2"	84	189	273	378	462	567	651	756
2"	2½"	48	112	160	224	288	336	400	448
2½"	3"	42	84	126	168	210	252	294	336
3"	3½"	24	60	84	120	144	180	216	240
3½"	4"	20	40	60	90	110	130	150	180
4"	4½"	18	36	54	72	90	108	126	144
4½"	5"	8	24	40	56	72	80	96	112
5"	5½"	7	21	28	42	56	63	77	91
5½"	6"	7	21	28	42	49	63	70	84
6"	6½"	6	12	24	30	36	48	54	66
6½"	7"	6	12	18	30	36	42	54	60
7"	7½"	5	10	15	20	30	35	40	45
7½"	8"	5	10	15	20	25	30	35	45
8"	8½"	4	8	12	16	20	24	28	32
8½"	9"	4	8	12	16	20	24	28	32
9"	9½"	-	4	8	12	16	20	24	28
9½"	10"	-	4	8	12	16	20	24	28
10"	10½"	-	4	8	12	16	20	24	24
10½"	11"	-	3	6	9	12	12	15	18
11"	11½"	-	3	6	9	9	12	15	18
11½"	12"	-	3	6	9	9	12	15	18
12"	12½"	-	3	6	6	9	12	15	15
12½"	13"	-	3	6	6	9	12	12	15
13"	13½"	-	3	6	6	9	12	12	15
13½"	14"	-	3	3	6	9	9	12	15
14"	14½"	-	2	2	4	6	6	8	8
14½"	15"	-	2	2	4	6	6	8	8
15"	15½"	-	2	2	4	4	6	8	8
15½"	16"	-	2	2	4	4	6	6	8
16"	16½"	-	2	2	4	4	6	6	8
16½"	17"	-	2	2	4	4	6	6	8
17"	17½"	-	2	2	4	4	6	6	8
18"	18½"	-	-	2	2	4	4	6	6

Cutting Squares or Rectangles from Strips

Use a rotary cutter and strips of fabric to cut multiple squares and rectangles accurately and quickly. Refer to the charts on *pages 95 and 97* for specific measurements.

1. To cut squares, cut fabric strips that are the desired finished measurement of the square, plus ½" for seam allowances. For example, for 3" finished squares, cut 3½"-wide fabric strips (see Photo 2F, *right*).

2. Square up one end of each strip (see Photo 2G, *below right*; refer to *page 90* for instructions).

3. Using a ruler, align a vertical grid line with the cut edge of a fabric strip (see Photo 2H, *below, far right*). Align the top and bottom edges of the fabric strip with horizontal lines on the ruler.

To cut squares, cut fabric into lengths equal to the strip width. For example, for 3" finished squares, cut the 3½"-wide fabric strips into 3½"-long pieces.

4. To cut rectangles, cut fabric strips that are the desired finished length, plus ½" for seam allowances. For example, for 3×5" finished rectangles, cut 3½"-wide fabric strips into 5½" lengths.

Photo 2F

Photo 2G

Photo 2I

Cutting a Single Square Or Rectangle

1. Align a ruler in a fabric corner. Make two cuts along the ruler's edges to separate the section from the remainder of the fabric (see Photo 2I, *bottom left*). Make sure the section is slightly larger than the square or rectangle you need.

2. Rotate the section of fabric and align the cut edges of the fabric with the desired measurements on the ruler (see Photo 2J, *bottom*). Make two more cuts along the ruler's edges to complete the square or rectangle.

Photo 2H

Photo 2J

YARDAGE ESTIMATOR: Rectangles from Strips

Use this chart to determine the number of rectangles that can be cut from various yardages (see the note below on cutting strip width for rectangles).

Yardage figures include ¼" seam allowances and are based on 42"-long strips.

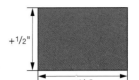

+½"

+½"

SIZE OF RECTANGLE		YARDAGE (44/45"-WIDE FABRIC)							
Finished	Cut Strip Width	¼	½	¾	1	1¼	1½	1¾	2
1×2"	1½×2½"	96	*196	288	*392	*504	*588	*700	*784
1×3"	1½×3½"	72	144	216	288	360	432	504	576
1½×3"	2×3½"	48	108	156	216	264	324	*378	432
1½×4½"	2×5"	32	72	*105	*147	*189	216	*252	*294
1½×8"	2×8½"	*21	*42	*63	*84	*105	*126	*147	*168
1½×9"	2×9½"	16	36	52	72	88	108	*126	*147
1½×10"	2×10½"	16	36	52	72	88	108	*126	144
1½×12"	2×12½"	12	27	*42	54	66	*84	*105	108
2×4"	2½×4½"	*32	*64	*96	*128	162	*192	225	*256
2×6"	2½×6½"	18	42	*64	84	108	*128	150	*176
2×8"	2½×8½"	*16	*32	*48	*64	*80	*96	*112	*128
2×9"	2½×9½"	12	28	40	56	72	84	100	112
2×10"	2½×10½"	12	28	40	56	72	84	100	112
2×12"	2½×12½"	9	21	*32	42	54	*64	*80	84
2½×5"	3×5½"	21	42	63	84	*112	126	*154	*182
2½×7½"	3×8"	15	30	45	60	75	90	105	*126
2½×8"	3×8½"	*14	*28	*42	*56	*70	*84	*98	*112
2½×9"	3×9½"	12	24	36	48	60	72	84	*98
2½×10"	3×10½"	12	24	36	48	60	72	84	96
2½×12"	3×12½"	9	18	*28	36	45	*56	*70	72
3×6"	3½×6½"	12	30	*48	60	72	*96	108	*132
3×8"	3½×8½"	*12	*24	*36	*48	*60	*72	*84	*96
3×9"	3½×9½"	8	20	28	40	48	60	72	*84
3×10"	3½×10½"	8	20	28	40	48	60	72	80
3×12"	3½×12½"	6	15	*24	30	36	*48	*60	60

Note: *Unless otherwise noted, always cut the initial strip from the smallest width of the rectangle. Sometimes more pieces can be cut from yardage if the first strip is cut at the larger width. These exceptions have been denoted with an asterisk (*). For example, follow the line to the right of "Finished 1×2", Cut Strip Width 1½×2½"." With ½ yard of fabric, more rectangles can be cut if the strips are first cut 2½", then cross-cut into 1½" segments.*

YARDAGE ESTIMATOR: Flying Geese and Squares from Strips

When using the one rectangle and two squares method of making Flying Geese units, use this chart to determine the number of rectangles and squares that can be cut from various yardages (see note below on cutting strip width for rectangles). For more information, see Flying Geese Method 1 in Chapter 5—Piecing.

Yardage figures include ¼" seam allowances and are based on 42"-long strips.

SIZE OF RECTANGLES AND SQUARES				YARDAGE (44/45"-WIDE FABRIC)							
Finished Unit Size	Rectangle Size	Square Size	Cut Strip Width	¼	½	¾	1	1¼	1½	1¾	2
½x1"	1x1½"		1"*	252	504	756	1,008	1,260	1,512	1,764	2,016
		1"	1"	378	756	1,134	1,512	1,890	2,268	2,646	3,024
¾x1½"	1¼x2"		1¼"*	147	*297	441	*594	756	903	1,050	1,197
		1¼"	1¼"	231	462	693	924	1,188	1,419	1,650	1,881
1x2"	1½x2½"		1½"*	96	*196	288	*392	480	*588	*700	*784
		1½"	1½"	168	336	504	672	840	1,008	1,176	1,344
1¼x2½"	1¾x3"		1¾"*	*72	*144	*216	*288	*360	*432	504	*576
		1¾"	1¾"	120	240	360	480	600	720	864	984
1½x3"	2x3½"		2"*	48	108	156	216	264	324	*378	432
		2"	2"	84	189	273	378	462	567	651	756
1¾x3½"	2¼x4"		2¼"*	40	80	120	*162	200	240	280	*324
		2¼"	2¼"	72	144	216	288	360	432	504	576
2x4"	2½x4½"		2½"*	*32	*64	*96	*128	162	*192	225	*256
		2½"	2½"	48	112	160	224	288	336	400	448
2¼x4½"	2¾x5"		2¾"*	24	48	*75	*105	*135	152	*180	*210
		2¾"	2¾"	45	90	135	195	240	285	330	390
2½x5"	3x5½"		3"*	21	42	63	84	*112	126	*154	*182
		3"	3"	42	84	126	168	210	252	294	336
2¾x5½"	3¼x6"		3¼"*	14	*36	56	77	91	112	133	154
		3¼"	3¼"	24	60	96	132	156	192	228	264
3x6"	3½x6½"		3½"*	12	30	*48	60	72	*96	108	*132
		3½"	3½"	24	60	84	120	144	180	216	240
3¼x6½"	3¾x7"		3¾"*	12	24	42	*55	72	84	*99	114
		3¾"	3¾"	22	44	77	99	132	154	176	209
3½x7"	4x7½"		4"*	10	20	30	45	*60	*70	*80	90
		4"	4"	20	40	60	90	110	130	150	180
3¾x7½"	4¼x8"		4¼"*	10	20	30	40	50	60	70	*81
		4¼"	4¼"	18	36	54	72	90	108	126	144
4x8"	4½x8½"		4½"*	8	*18	*27	*36	*45	*54	*63	*72
		4½"	4½"	18	36	54	72	90	108	126	144

Note: *Unless otherwise noted, always cut the initial strip from the smallest width of the rectangle. Sometimes more pieces can be cut from yardage if the first strip is cut at the larger width. These exceptions are denoted with an asterisk (*). For example, follow the line to the right of "Finished Unit Size 1x2", Rectangle Size 1½x2½", Cut Strip Width 1½"." With ½ yard of fabric, more rectangles can be cut if the strips are first cut 2½", then cross-cut into 1½" segments.*

Cutting Half-Square Triangles

Referring to the chart on *page 100* for specific measurements, follow these instructions to rotary cut half-square triangles (see Illustration 3, *right*).

1. Square up the fabric (see *page 90* for instructions).

2. Cut the fabric in strips as wide as the desired finished width of the triangle-squares, plus ⅞" for seam allowances (see Photo 2K, *right*). For example, for a 3" finished half-square triangle, cut a 3⅞"-wide fabric strip.

3. Square up one end of each strip (see Photo 2L, *below*).

4. Using a ruler, cut the strip into lengths equal to the strip's width (see Photo 2M, *below right*). In this example, the strip would be cut into 3⅞"-long pieces.

5. Position the ruler diagonally across a square and cut the square in half to make two equal-size right triangles (see Photo 2N, *below, far right*).

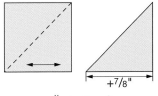

Illustration 3

Photo 2K

Photo 2L

Photo 2M

Photo 2N

Chapter 4 – Cutting Techniques

YARDAGE ESTIMATOR: Half-Square (Right) Triangles from Strips

Use this chart to determine the number of half-square triangles that can be cut from various yardages.

Yardage figures include ¼" seam allowances and are based on 42"-long strips.

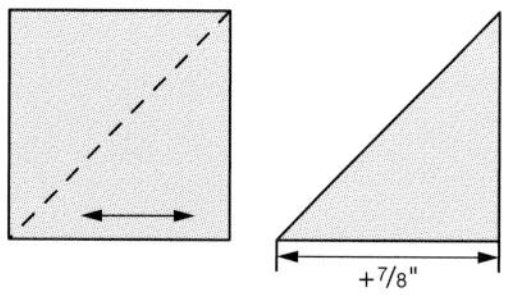

Illustration 4

SIZE OF TRIANGLE		YARDAGE (44/45"-WIDE FABRIC)							
Finished	Cut Strip Width	¼	½	¾	1	1¼	1½	1¾	2
1"	1⅞"	176	396	616	836	1056	1232	1452	1672
1½"	2⅜"	102	238	374	510	612	748	884	1020
2"	2⅞"	84	168	252	336	420	504	588	700
2½"	3⅜"	48	120	192	240	312	384	432	504
3"	3⅞"	40	80	120	180	220	260	320	360
3½"	4⅜"	36	72	108	144	180	216	252	288
4"	4⅞"	16	48	80	112	144	176	192	224
4½"	5⅜"	14	42	70	84	112	140	154	182
5"	5⅞"	14	42	56	84	98	126	140	168
5½"	6⅜"	12	24	48	60	84	96	108	132
6"	6⅞"	12	24	36	60	72	84	108	120
6½"	7⅜"	10	20	30	40	60	70	80	90
7"	7⅞"	10	20	30	40	50	60	80	90
7½"	8⅜"	10	20	30	40	50	60	70	80
8"	8⅞"	8	16	24	32	40	48	56	64
8½"	9⅜"	-	8	16	24	32	40	48	56
9"	9⅞"	-	8	16	24	32	40	48	56
9½"	10⅜"	-	8	16	24	32	40	48	48
10"	10⅞"	-	6	12	18	24	24	30	36
10½"	11⅜"	-	6	12	18	18	24	30	36
11"	11⅞"	-	6	12	18	18	24	30	36
11½"	12⅜"	-	6	12	12	18	24	30	30
12"	12⅞"	-	6	12	12	18	24	24	30
12½"	13⅜"	-	6	12	12	18	24	24	30
13"	13⅞"	-	6	6	12	18	18	24	30
13½"	14⅜"	-	4	4	8	12	12	16	20
14"	14⅞"	-	4	4	8	12	12	16	16
14½"	15⅜"	-	4	4	8	8	12	16	16
15"	15⅞"	-	4	4	8	8	12	12	16
15½"	16⅜"	-	4	4	8	8	12	12	16
16"	16⅞"	-	4	4	8	8	12	12	16
16½"	17⅜"	-	4	4	8	8	12	12	16
17"	17⅞"	-	4	4	8	8	12	12	16
17½"	18⅜"	-	-	4	4	8	8	12	12
18"	18⅞"	-	-	4	4	8	8	12	12

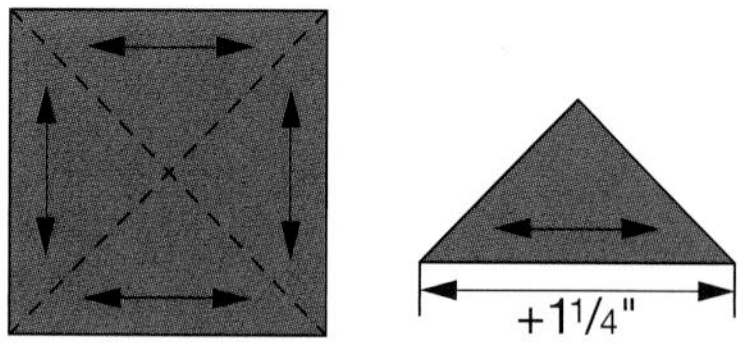

Cutting Quarter-Square Triangles

Referring to the chart on *page 102* for specific measurements, follow these instructions to rotary cut quarter-square triangles (see Illustration 4, *above*).

1. Square up the fabric (see *page 90* for instructions).

2. Cut the fabric in strips as wide as the desired finished width of the quarter-square triangle, plus 1¼" for seam allowances (see Photo 2O, *opposite*). For example, for a 3" finished quarter-square triangle, cut a 4¼"-wide fabric strip.

3. Square up one end of each strip (see Photo 2P, *opposite*).

4. Using a ruler, cut the strip into lengths equal to the strip's width (see Photo 2Q, *opposite*). In this example, the strip would be cut into 4¼"-long pieces.

5. Position the ruler diagonally across the square and cut the square in half to make two equal-size right triangles (see Photo 2R, *opposite*). Do not move or pick up the triangles.

6. Position the ruler diagonally across the cut square in the opposite direction and cut the square in half again to make a total of four equal-size triangles (see Photo 2S, *opposite*).

Photo 2O

Photo 2P

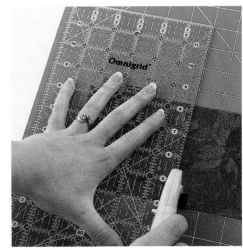

Photo 2Q

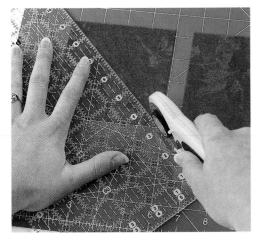

Photo 2R

Photo 2S

YARDAGE ESTIMATOR: Quarter-Square (Right) Triangles from Strips

Use this chart to determine the number of quarter-square triangles that can be cut from various yardages.

Yardage figures include ¼" seam allowances and are based on 42"-long strips.

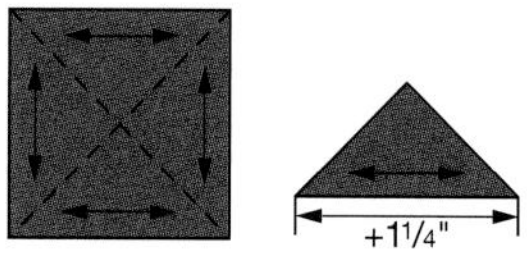

SIZE OF TRIANGLE		YARDAGE (44/45"-WIDE FABRIC)							
Finished	Cut Strip Width	¼	½	¾	1	1¼	1½	1¾	2
1"	2¼"	288	576	864	1,152	1,440	1,728	2,016	2,304
1½"	2¾"	180	360	540	780	960	1,140	1,320	1,560
2"	3¼"	96	240	384	528	624	768	912	1,056
2½"	3¾"	88	176	308	396	528	616	704	836
3"	4¼"	72	144	216	288	360	432	504	576
3½"	4¾"	32	96	160	224	288	352	416	480
4"	5¼"	32	96	160	192	256	320	384	416
4½"	5¾"	28	84	112	168	196	252	280	336
5"	6¼"	24	48	96	120	168	192	240	264
5½"	6¾"	24	48	96	120	144	192	216	240
6"	7¼"	20	40	60	80	120	140	160	180
6½"	7¾"	20	40	60	80	100	120	160	180
7"	8¼"	20	40	60	80	100	120	140	160
7½"	8¾"	16	32	48	64	80	96	112	128
8"	9¼"	-	16	32	48	64	80	96	112
8½"	9¾"	-	16	32	48	64	80	96	112
9"	10¼"	-	16	32	48	64	80	96	112
9½"	10¾"	-	12	24	36	48	60	60	72
10"	11¼"	-	12	24	36	48	48	60	72
10½"	11¾"	-	12	24	36	36	48	60	72
11"	12¼"	-	12	24	24	36	48	60	60
11½"	12¾"	-	12	24	24	36	48	48	60
12"	13¼"	-	12	24	24	36	48	48	60
12½"	13¾"	-	12	12	24	36	36	48	60
13"	14¼"	-	8	8	16	24	24	32	40
13½"	14¾"	-	8	8	16	24	24	32	32
14"	15¼"	-	8	8	16	16	24	32	32
14½"	15¾"	-	8	8	16	16	24	32	32
15"	16¼"	-	8	8	16	16	24	24	32
15½"	16¾"	-	8	8	16	16	24	24	32
16"	17¼"	-	8	8	16	16	24	24	32
16½"	17¾"	-	8	8	16	16	24	24	32
17"	18¼"	-	-	8	8	16	16	24	24
18"	19¼"	-	-	8	8	16	16	24	24

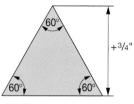

Illustration 5

Cutting 60° Equilateral Triangles

Referring to the chart *below right* for specific measurements, follow these instructions to rotary cut 60° equilateral triangles (see Illustration 5, *above*).

1. Square up the fabric (see *page 90* for instructions).

2. Cut the fabric in strips as wide as the desired finished height of the triangle, plus ¾" for seam allowances (see Photo 2T, *above right*). For example, to make a finished equilateral triangle that is 3" high, cut a 3¾"-wide fabric strip.

3. Align a ruler's 60° line with the long, lower edge of the strip and cut (see Photo 2U, *above, far right*).

4. Rotate the ruler so the opposing 60° line is aligned with the same long, lower edge of the strip and cut (see Photo 2V, *above right*).

5. Repeat steps 3 and 4, working across the fabric strip, to cut additional equilateral triangles (see Photo 2W, *above, far right*).

Photo 2T

Photo 2U

Photo 2V

Photo 2W

YARDAGE ESTIMATOR: 60° Equilateral Triangles from Strips

Use this chart to determine the number of 60° equilateral triangles that can be cut from various yardages.

Yardage figures include ¼" seam allowances and are based on 42"-long strips.

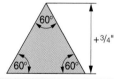

SIZE OF TRIANGLE		YARDAGE (44/45"-WIDE FABRIC)							
Finished	Cut Strip Width	¼	½	¾	1	1¼	1½	1¾	2
1"	1¾"	180	360	540	720	900	1,080	1,296	1,476
1½"	2¼"	120	240	360	480	600	720	840	960
2"	2¾"	66	132	198	286	352	418	484	572
2½"	3¼"	36	90	144	198	234	288	342	396
3"	3¾"	32	64	112	144	192	224	256	304
3½"	4¼"	28	56	84	112	140	168	196	224
4"	4¾"	12	36	60	84	108	132	156	180

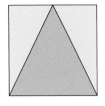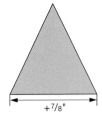

Illustration 6

Cutting Center Triangles for Isosceles Triangle-in-a-Square Blocks

The center triangle in a triangle-in-a-square block is an isosceles triangle, which means it has two sides of equal length (see Illustration 6, *above*).

1. Square up the fabric (see *page 90* for instructions).

2. Cut the fabric in strips as wide as the desired finished width of the triangle, plus ⅞" (see Photo 2X, *above right*). For example, to make an isosceles triangle for a 3" finished triangle-in-a-square, cut a 3⅞"-wide fabric strip.

3. Square up one end of each strip (see Photo 2Y, *above, far right*).

4. Position the ruler over the strip and cut a square (see Photo 2Z, *right*). In this example, cut a 3⅞" square from the 3⅞"-wide strip.

5. Fold the square in half to find top center and lightly finger-crease (see Photo 3A, *above, far right*).

6. Position the ruler diagonally across the square from a bottom corner to the creased top center mark and cut. Do not pick up the fabric pieces (see Photo 3B, *right*).

7. Rotate the ruler only and align it diagonally from the other bottom corner to the creased top center mark and cut (see Photo 3C, *far right*).

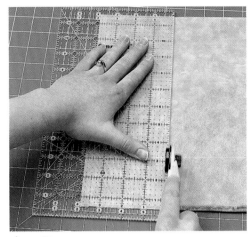

Photo 2X

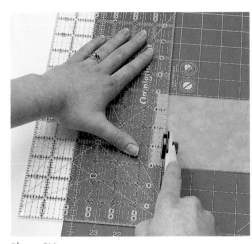

Photo 2Y

Photo 2Z

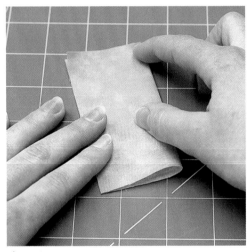

Photo 3A

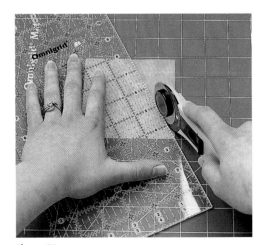

Photo 3B

Photo 3C

Cutting Side Triangles for Isosceles Triangle-in-a-Square Blocks

The side triangles in a triangle-in-a-square block are long triangles with a 90° corner (see Illustration 7, *right*).

1. Square up the fabric (see *page 90* for instructions).

2. Cut the fabric in strips as wide as the desired finished width of the side triangle plus ¾". For example, for a 3" finished triangle-in-a-square, the finished width of the side triangle is 1½", so you would cut a 2¼"-wide fabric strip (1½" + ¾").

3. Position two layers of strips, stacked with like sides together, parallel to one of the mat's grid lines and square up one end (see Photo 3D, *right*).

4. Position the ruler over the stacked strips and measure the desired finished height of the side triangle, plus 1¼" for seam allowances, and cut the rectangle (see Photo 3E, *right*). In this example, make one cut in the stacked 2¼"-wide strips to make two rectangles each 2¼×4¼".
Note: The isosceles triangle-in-a-square has two side triangles that are mirror images of each other. Always cut in double layers to make the mirror-image shapes. Two rectangles yield two left-hand side triangles and two right-hand side triangles.

5. Position the ruler diagonally across the stacked rectangles and cut the rectangles in half to make two each of the left-hand and right-hand side triangles (see Photo 3F, *far right*).

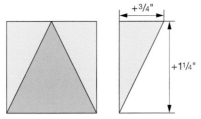

+¾"

+1¼"

Illustration 7

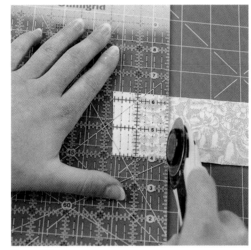

Photo 3D

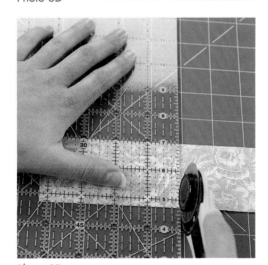

Photo 3E

Photo 3F

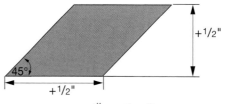

Illustration 8

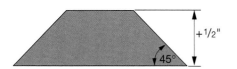

Illustration 9

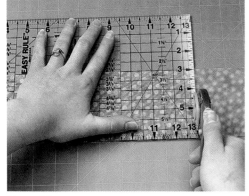

Photo 3G

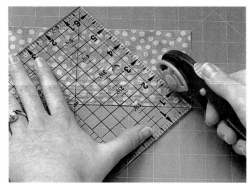

Photo 3H

Photo 3I

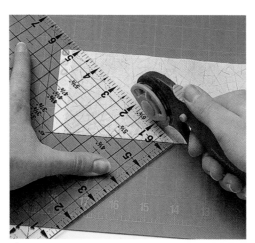

Photo 3J

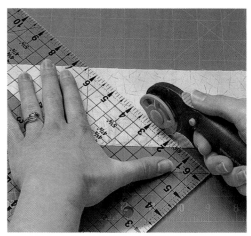

Photo 3K

Cutting 45° Trapezoids

Follow these instructions to rotary cut 45° trapezoids (see Illustration 8, *above left*).

1. Square up the fabric (see *page 90* for instructions).

2. Cut the fabric in strips as wide as the desired finished height of the trapezoid, plus ½" for seam allowances. For example, for a 3"-high trapezoid, cut a 3½"-wide fabric strip.

3. Square up one end of each strip.

4. Position the ruler over a strip and measure the desired finished length of the trapezoid, plus 1¼" for seam allowances; cut a rectangle (see Photo 3G, *above left*). For example, for a 10¼"-long finished trapezoid, cut an 11½" length from the strip to make a 3½×11½" rectangle.

5. Align a ruler's 45° line with the horizontal edge of the rectangle (see Photo 3H, *left*).

Cut a 45° angle from the bottom corner to the top edge. Do not pick up the fabric rectangle.

6. Pick up and rotate the ruler only (see Photo 3I, *below left*). Position it on the opposite rectangle end and align the 45° line with the opposite edge of the fabric. Cut a 45° angle from the bottom corner to the top edge.

Cutting 45° Diamonds

Follow these instructions to rotary cut 45° diamonds (see Illustration 9, *above left*).

1. Square up the fabric (see *page 90* for instructions).

2. Cut the fabric in strips as wide as the desired finished width of the diamond, plus ½" for seam allowances. For example, for a 3"-wide diamond, cut a 3½"-wide fabric strip.

3. Square up one end of each strip.

4. Position the ruler on the strip, aligning the 45° line with the horizontal edge of the strip (see Photo 3J, *below left*). Cut a 45° angle from the bottom edge to the top edge.

5. Aligning the ruler with the first cut edge, reposition the ruler on the strip at the desired width measurement, plus ½" for seam allowances (see Photo 3K, *opposite*). Cut a second 45° angle parallel to the first from the bottom edge to the top edge.

Fussy Cutting

Isolating and cutting out a specific print or pattern is referred to as fussy cutting.

1. Trace the finished-size shape on a piece of frosted template plastic that is at least 2" larger on all sides than the desired shape (see Photo 3L, *below*).

2. Using a crafts knife and ruler, cut away the interior of the shape to make a viewing window (see Photo 3M, *bottom left*).

3. Move the viewing window over the fabric to isolate the desired portion of the print (see Photo 3N, *below*). Mark the position with pins or chalk.

4. Remove the viewing window and re-mark as needed. Add seam allowances and cut out the print portion with scissors or a rotary cutter and ruler.

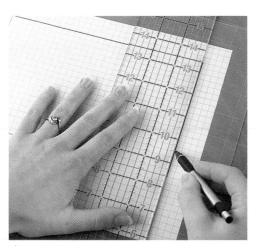

Photo 3L

Photo 3M

Photo 3N

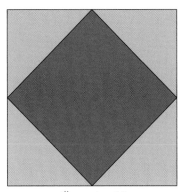

Illustration 10

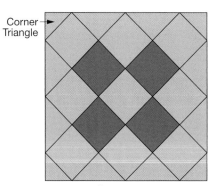

Side Triangle

Illustration 11

Cutting Setting Triangles and Blocks

Quilt blocks set on the diagonal (or "on point") may require setting triangles to fill out the design (see Illustration 10, *far left*). These setting triangles are often called filler triangles. When quilt blocks are turned on the diagonal it often means that the straight grain of the block is on the diagonal also (for more information see Chapter 7— Assembling the Quilt Top and Backing).

To stabilize the fabric and control its natural tendency to sag, it is critical that the setting triangles are cut so that the straight grain runs up and down.

Some quilters prefer to cut triangles ½ to 1" larger than required and trim away the excess fabric after piecing the top. The measurements given in the chart on *page 110* are mathematically correct and do not allow for any excess fabric.

Note: To "float" the blocks in a diagonal set, cut the side and corner setting triangles up to 2" larger than the diagonal measurement of the block (see Chapter 3—Planning Your Quilt for more information on a Diagonal Set with Floating Blocks).

Side Triangles

Side setting triangles are quarter-square triangles (see Illustration 11, *above left, top*); one square produces four side triangles.

To calculate the size to cut a square for setting triangles, multiply the finished block size by 1.414 and add 1¼" for seam allowances. (For example, 10" block × 1.414 = 14.14 + 1.25" = 15.39"; rounded up the measurement would be 15½".)

Side triangle measurements for several standard block sizes are shown in the chart on *page 110*.

Corner Triangle

Illustration 12

Setting Square

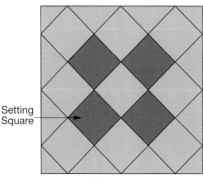

Illustration 13

Ruler and Calculator Equivalents

To convert a calculated yardage or measurement into the nearest ruler equivalent, use this at-a-glance reference chart.

Ruler Fraction	Calculator Decimal
1/64	.016
1/32	.031
1/16	.0625
1/8	.125
3/16	.1875
1/4	.25
5/16	.3125
3/8	.375
7/16	.4375
1/2	.50
9/16	.5625
5/8	.625
11/16	.6875
3/4	.75
13/16	.8125
7/8	.875
15/16	.9375

Corner Triangles

Corner triangles are half-square triangles (see Illustration 12, *opposite*); one square yields two corner triangles.

To calculate the size to cut a square for corner setting triangles, divide the finished block size by 1.414 and add .875" for seam allowances. (For example, 10" block divided by 1.414 = 7.07 + .875" = 7.945"; rounded up the measurement would be 8".) See *page 110* for corner triangle measurements for several standard block sizes.

Setting Squares

Setting squares are generally solid squares cut to place between pieced or appliquéd blocks to set off a design (see Illustration 13, *opposite*).

To calculate the size to cut a square for setting squares, add ½" to the finished block size to allow for seam allowances. (For example, 10" block + ½" = 10½".) See *page 110* for setting square measurements for several standard block sizes.

Magic Numbers for Rotary Cutting

To determine the cutting size of a variety of shapes when rotary-cutting, use this chart. All measurements assume a ¼" seam allowance is being used.

STRIP
Cut finished width + ½".

SQUARE AND RECTANGLE
Cut finished size + ½".

HALF-SQUARE TRIANGLE
Cut finished width + ⅞".

QUARTER-SQUARE TRIANGLE
Cut finished width + 1¼".

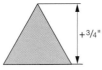
EQUILATERAL TRIANGLE
Cut finished height + ¾".

ISOSCELES TRIANGLE-IN-A-SQUARE CENTER TRIANGLE
Cut finished width + ⅞".

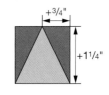
ISOSCELES TRIANGLE-IN-A-SQUARE SIDE TRIANGLE
Cut finished width + ¾", finished height + 1¼" (must be made in mirror images).

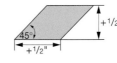
45° DIAMOND
Cut finished height + ½", finished width + ½".

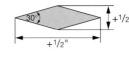
30° DIAMOND
Cut finished height + ½", finished width + ½".

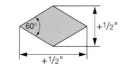
60° DIAMOND
Cut finished height + ½", finished width + ½".

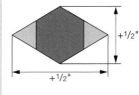
HEXAGON
From a 60° diamond, cut finished height + ½", finished width + ½".

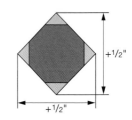
OCTAGON
From a square, cut finished height + ½", finished width + ½".

Setting Triangles and Setting Squares

• Formula A—To calculate the size to cut a square for side setting triangles, multiply the finished block size by 1.414 and add 1.25" for seam allowances. (For example, 10" block × 1.414 = 14.14 + 1.25" = 15.39"; rounded up the measurement would be 15½".)

• Formula B—To calculate the size to cut a square for corner setting triangles, divide the finished block size by 1.414 and add .875" for seam allowances. (For example, 10" block divided by 1.414 = 7.07 + .875" = 7.945"; rounded up the measurement would be 8".)

• Formula C—To calculate the size to cut a setting square, add ½" to the finished block size to allow for seam allowances. (For example, 10" block + ½" = 10½".)

Use this chart to determine the correct size to cut side and corner setting triangles and setting squares based on the size of your finished block.

FINISHED BLOCK SIZE	FORMULA A: SIZE TO CUT SQUARE FOR SIDE SETTING TRIANGLES 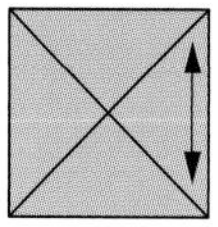	FORMULA B: SIZE TO CUT SQUARE FOR CORNER SETTING TRIANGLES 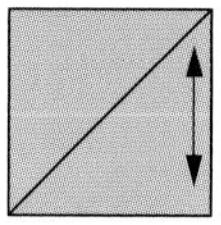	FORMULA C: SIZE TO CUT SETTING SQUARES 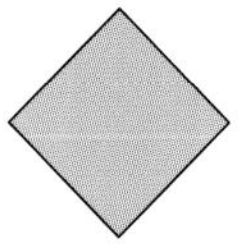
1"	2¾"	1⅝"	1½"
2"	4⅛"	2⅜"	2½"
3"	5½"	3"	3½"
4"	7"	3¾"	4½"
5"	8⅜"	4½"	5½"
6"	9¾"	5⅛"	6½"
7"	11¼"	5⅞"	7½"
8"	12⅝"	6⅝"	8½"
9"	14"	7¼"	9½"
10"	15½"	8"	10½"
11"	16⅞"	8¾"	11½"
12"	18¼"	9⅜"	12½"
13"	19¾"	10⅛"	13½"
14"	21⅛"	10⅞"	14½"
15"	22½"	11½"	15½"
16"	23⅞"	12¼"	16½"
17"	25⅜"	13"	17½"
18"	26¾"	13⅝"	18½"
19"	28⅛"	14⅜"	19½"
20"	29⅝"	15⅛"	20½"

Diagonal Measurements of Squares

Use this chart to determine quilt center size of a diagonally set quilt. For example, 12" finished blocks are set on point, quilt center size = (17" × number of blocks horizontally) + (17" × number of blocks vertically).

To calculate the finished diagonal measurement of a block, multiply the finished block measurement (without seam allowances) by 1.414.

Shown below are diagonal measurements for several standard block sizes. Figures are rounded up to the nearest ⅛" (.125").

FINISHED BLOCK SIZE	FINISHED DIAGONAL MEASUREMENT	DECIMAL EQUIVALENT OF DIAGONAL MEASUREMENT
1"	1½"	1.5"
1½"	2⅛"	2.125"
2"	2⅞"	2.875"
2½"	3⅝"	3.625"
3"	4¼"	4.25"
3½"	5"	5.0"
4"	5⅝"	5.625"
4½"	6⅜"	6.375"
5"	7⅛"	7.125"
5½"	7⅞"	7.875"
6"	8½"	8.5"
6½"	9¼"	9.25"
7"	10"	10.0"
7½"	10⅝"	10.625"
8"	11⅜"	11.375"
8½"	12⅛"	12.125"
9"	12¾"	12.75"
9½"	13½"	13.5"
10"	14¼"	14.25"
10½"	14⅞"	14.875"
11"	15⅝"	15.625"
11½"	16⅜"	16.375"
12"	17"	17.0"
12½"	17¾"	17.75"
13"	18½"	18.5"
14"	19⅞"	19.875"
15"	21¼"	21.25"
16"	22⅝"	22.625"
17"	24⅛"	24.125"
18"	25½"	25.5"
19"	26⅞"	26.875"
20"	28⅜"	28.375"

Yardage and Metric Equivalents

To convert a pattern's units of measurement, use this chart to determine the quantities needed. Equivalents are for inches, yardage in fractions and decimals, and meters.

INCHES	YARDS (fractions)	YARDS (decimals)	METERS	INCHES	YARDS (fractions)	YARDS (decimals)	METERS
4½"	⅛ yd.	.125 yd.	.144 m	157½"	4⅜ yd.	4.375 yd.	4.001 m
9"	¼ yd.	.25 yd.	.229 m	162"	4½ yd.	4.5 yd.	4.115 m
12"	⅓ yd.	.333 yd.	.304 m	166½"	4⅝ yd.	4.625 yd.	4.229 m
13½"	⅜ yd.	.375 yd.	.343 m	171"	4¾ yd.	4.75 yd.	4.343 m
18"	½ yd.	.5 yd.	.457 m	180"	5 yd.	5.0 yd.	4.572 m
22½"	⅝ yd.	.625 yd.	.572 m	184½"	5⅛ yd.	5.125 yd.	4.686 m
24"	⅔ yd.	.667 yd.	.610 m	189"	5¼ yd.	5.25 yd.	4.801 m
27"	¾ yd.	.75 yd.	.686 m	193½"	5⅜ yd.	5.375 yd.	4.915 m
31½"	⅞ yd.	.875 yd.	.8 m	198"	5½ yd.	5.5 yd.	5.029 m
36"	1 yd.	1.0 yd.	.914 m	202½"	5⅝ yd.	5.625 yd.	5.144 m
40½"	1⅛ yd.	1.125 yd.	1.029 m	207"	5¾ yd.	5.75 yd.	5.258 m
45"	1¼ yd.	1.25 yd.	1.143 m	216"	6 yd.	6.0 yd.	5.486 m
48"	1⅓ yd.	1.333 yd.	1.219 m	220½"	6⅛ yd.	6.125 yd.	5.601 m
49½"	1⅜ yd.	1.375 yd.	1.257 m	225"	6¼ yd.	6.25 yd.	5.715 m
54"	1½ yd.	1.5 yd.	1.372 m	229½"	6⅜ yd.	6.375 yd.	5.829 m
58½"	1⅝ yd.	1.625 yd.	1.486 m	234"	6½ yd.	6.5 yd.	5.944 m
60"	1⅔ yd.	1.667 yd.	1.524 m	238½"	6⅝ yd.	6.625 yd.	6.058 m
63"	1¾ yd.	1.75 yd.	1.6 m	243"	6¾ yd.	6.75 yd.	6.172 m
67½"	1⅞ yd.	1.875 yd.	1.715 m	252"	7 yd.	7.0 yd.	6.401 m
72"	2 yd.	2.0 yd.	1.829 m	256½"	7⅛ yd.	7.125 yd.	6.515 m
76½"	2⅛ yd.	2.125 yd.	1.943 m	261"	7¼ yd.	7.25 yd.	6.629 m
81"	2¼ yd.	2.25 yd.	2.057 m	265½"	7⅜ yd.	7.375 yd.	6.744 m
84"	2⅓ yd.	2.333 yd.	2.134 m	270"	7½ yd.	7.5 yd.	6.858 m
85½"	2⅜ yd.	2.375 yd.	2.172 m	274½"	7⅝ yd.	7.625 yd.	6.972 m
90"	2½ yd.	2.5 yd.	2.286 m	279"	7¾ yd.	7.75 yd.	7.087 m
94½"	2⅝ yd.	2.625 yd.	2.4 m	288"	8 yd.	8.0 yd.	7.315 m
96"	2⅔ yd.	2.667 yd.	2.438 m	292½"	8⅛ yd.	8.125 yd.	7.43 m
99"	2¾ yd.	2.75 yd.	2.515 m	297"	8¼ yd.	8.25 yd.	7.544 m
108"	3 yd.	3.0 yd.	2.743 m	301½"	8⅜ yd.	8.375 yd.	7.658 m
112½"	3⅛ yd.	3.125 yd.	2.858 m	306"	8½ yd.	8.5 yd.	7.772 m
117"	3¼ yd.	3.25 yd.	2.972 m	310½"	8⅝ yd.	8.625 yd.	7.887 m
120"	3⅓ yd.	3.333 yd.	3.048 m	315"	8¾ yd.	8.75 yd.	8.001 m
121½"	3⅜ yd.	3.375 yd.	3.086 m	324"	9 yd.	9.0 yd.	8.23 m
126"	3½ yd.	3.5 yd.	3.2 m	328½"	9⅛ yd.	9.125 yd.	8.344 m
130½"	3⅝ yd.	3.625 yd.	3.315 m	333"	9¼ yd.	9.25 yd.	8.458 m
132"	3⅔ yd.	3.667 yd.	3.353 m	337½"	9⅜ yd.	9.375 yd.	8.573 m
135"	3¾ yd.	3.75 yd.	3.429 m	342"	9½ yd.	9.5 yd.	8.687 m
144"	4 yd.	4.0 yd.	3.658 m	346½"	9⅝ yd.	9.625 yd.	8.801 m
148½"	4⅛ yd.	4.125 yd.	3.772 m	351"	9¾ yd.	9.75 yd.	8.915 m
153"	4¼ yd.	4.25 yd.	3.886 m	360"	10 yd.	10.0 yd.	9.144 m

Yardage Width Conversions

If the width of the fabric is different than what the pattern calls for, use this chart to determine the yardage needed. Yardage conversions are from 44/45"-wide fabric to 36"- or 58/60"-wide fabrics.

44/45"-WIDE	36"-WIDE	58/60"-WIDE	44/45"-WIDE	36"-WIDE	58/60"-WIDE
⅛ yd.	¼ yd.	⅛ yd.	4⅜ yd.	5½ yd.	3⅓ yd.
¼ yd.	⅓ yd.	¼ yd.	4½ yd.	5⅝ yd.	3½ yd.
⅓ yd.	½ yd.	⅓ yd.	4⅝ yd.	5⅞ yd.	3⅝ yd.
⅜ yd.	½ yd.	⅓ yd.	4¾ yd.	6 yd.	3⅝ yd.
½ yd.	⅝ yd.	½ yd.	5 yd.	6¼ yd.	3⅞ yd.
⅝ yd.	⅞ yd.	½ yd.	5⅛ yd.	6½ yd.	4 yd.
⅔ yd.	⅞ yd.	⅝ yd.	5¼ yd.	6⅝ yd.	4 yd.
¾ yd.	1 yd.	⅝ yd.	5⅜ yd.	6¾ yd.	4⅛ yd.
⅞ yd.	1⅛ yd.	⅔ yd.	5½ yd.	6⅞ yd.	4¼ yd.
1 yd.	1¼ yd.	⅞ yd.	5⅝ yd.	7⅛ yd.	4⅓ yd.
1⅛ yd.	1½ yd.	⅞ yd.	5¾ yd.	7¼ yd.	4⅜ yd.
1¼ yd.	1⅝ yd.	1 yd.	6 yd.	7½ yd.	4⅝ yd.
1⅓ yd.	1⅔ yd.	1⅛ yd.	6⅛ yd.	7⅔ yd.	4¾ yd.
1⅜ yd.	1¾ yd.	1⅛ yd.	6¼ yd.	7¾ yd.	4⅞ yd.
1½ yd.	1⅞ yd.	1¼ yd.	6⅜ yd.	8 yd.	4⅞ yd.
1⅝ yd.	2⅛ yd.	1¼ yd.	6½ yd.	8⅛ yd.	5 yd.
1⅔ yd.	2⅛ yd.	1⅓ yd.	6⅝ yd.	8⅓ yd.	5⅛ yd.
1¾ yd.	2¼ yd.	1⅓ yd.	6¾ yd.	8½ yd.	5⅛ yd.
1⅞ yd.	2⅜ yd.	1½ yd.	7 yd.	8¾ yd.	5⅓ yd.
2 yd.	2½ yd.	1⅝ yd.	7⅛ yd.	9 yd.	5½ yd.
2⅛ yd.	2⅔ yd.	1⅝ yd.	7¼ yd.	9⅛ yd.	5½ yd.
2¼ yd.	2⅞ yd.	1¾ yd.	7⅜ yd.	9¼ yd.	5⅝ yd.
2⅓ yd.	3 yd.	1⅞ yd.	7½ yd.	9⅜ yd.	5¾ yd.
2⅜ yd.	3 yd.	1⅞ yd.	7⅝ yd.	9⅝ yd.	5⅞ yd.
2½ yd.	3⅛ yd.	2 yd.	7¾ yd.	9¾ yd.	6 yd.
2⅝ yd.	3¼ yd.	2 yd.	8 yd.	10 yd.	6⅛ yd.
2⅔ yd.	3⅓ yd.	2⅛ yd.	8⅛ yd.	10¼ yd.	6¼ yd.
2¾ yd.	3½ yd.	2⅛ yd.	8¼ yd.	10⅓ yd.	6⅓ yd.
2⅞ yd.	3⅝ yd.	2¼ yd.	8⅜ yd.	10½ yd.	6⅜ yd.
3 yd.	3¾ yd.	2⅓ yd.	8½ yd.	10⅝ yd.	6½ yd.
3⅛ yd.	4 yd.	2⅜ yd.	8⅝ yd.	10⅞ yd.	6⅝ yd.
3¼ yd.	4⅛ yd.	2½ yd.	8¾ yd.	11 yd.	6¾ yd.
3⅜ yd.	4¼ yd.	2⅝ yd.	9 yd.	11¼ yd.	6⅞ yd.
3½ yd.	4⅜ yd.	2⅔ yd.	9⅛ yd.	11½ yd.	7 yd.
3⅝ yd.	4⅝ yd.	2¾ yd.	9¼ yd.	11⅝ yd.	7⅛ yd.
3¾ yd.	4¾ yd.	2⅞ yd.	9⅜ yd.	11¾ yd.	7⅛ yd.
3⅞ yd.	4⅞ yd.	3 yd.	9½ yd.	11⅞ yd.	7¼ yd.
4 yd.	5 yd.	3⅛ yd.	9⅝ yd.	12 yd.	7⅓ yd.
4⅛ yd.	5¼ yd.	3¼ yd.	9¾ yd.	12¼ yd.	7½ yd.
4¼ yd.	5⅓ yd.	3¼ yd.	10 yd.	12½ yd.	7⅝ yd.

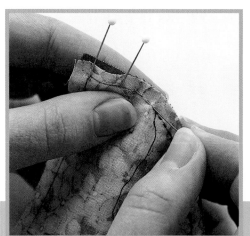
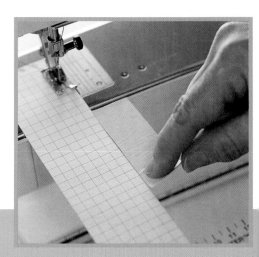

Chapter 5

PIECING

Whether you piece by hand or by machine, one of the greatest joys of quilting is creating a beautiful quilt top. Learn these piecing techniques, then quilt as your heart desires either by hand or with a sewing machine.

ODD FELLOWS/FLYING STAR

Patriotic colors are commonly seen in quilts made during wars and other periods of national togetherness. This Odd Fellows/ Flying Star variation by Ohio quilter Chloe Hoffert Wolfe was made around the time of the Spanish-American War (1898) when the battleship Maine was sunk near Cuba. The war that followed was only a few months long, but many Americans served in Cuba and the Philippines. The circular blocks are intricate; each one contains 96 pieces and is set into a red print background.

Piecing *By Hand*

Traditional hand piecing produces seams with "soft," or rounded, edges because the seam allowances are not sewn so can be pressed in any direction. Many quilters enjoy the relaxing, portable technique because they find that they have more control than when machine sewing.

THE IMPORTANCE OF ACCURATE SEAMS

Quilting depends upon accuracy in workmanship at every step. It's especially important to hand-sew along accurately marked lines throughout quilt construction to make certain all the patchwork pieces fit together smoothly and accurately.

Make certain to use a template that is the exact desired size. Test a template periodically during use to be sure all fabric pieces and blocks are the correct size. Even a slight deviation from the marked seam line will multiply quickly considering the number of pieces that are sewn together to make a quilt top (see Chapter 4—Cutting Techniques for more information on making templates).

Supplies

See Chapter 1—Tools and Materials for complete information on marking tools, thread choices, and needle options for hand piecing. The following items are the basic necessities to get started.

Marking Pencil Use a sharp quilter's pencil to draw around templates onto fabric. (Place 220-grit sandpaper beneath your fabric pieces to prevent stretching them as you mark lines.)

Thread Use high-quality 100% cotton or cotton-wrapped polyester thread for hand piecing. Don't be tempted to purchase bargain-basement thread. These short-staple threads fray easily and are difficult to needle. Economize elsewhere, but splurge on the best available thread to make hand-piecing an enjoyable process.

Use a neutral-color thread, such as gray, taupe, or beige, throughout assembly if the fabrics have many colors; otherwise, match the thread to the lighter fabric. Because relatively short lengths of thread are used when hand piecing, colors can be changed with ease.

Needles Invest in a new packet of "sharps" or "betweens" needles with each new project. These thin, sharp, all-purpose needles glide in and out of fabrics with ease. The size and type used depends on personal preference and comfort. Start with a multisize packet, trying the size 10 needle first. Replace needles as needed. A blunt needle will weaken the fabric and an older needle with a burr may snag it.

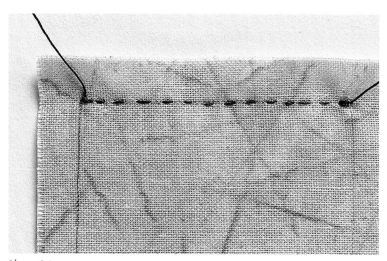

Photo 1A

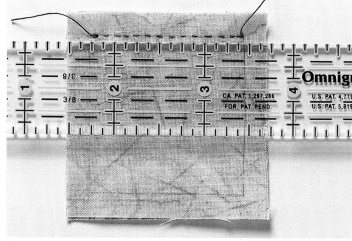

Photo 1B

Stitch Length

Experienced hand piecers use ⅛"-long stitches (or eight stitches per inch) as their goal. Begin and end a row of stitching at the indicated matching points with a knot or a few backstitches (see Photo 1A, *above*).

Stitch Consistency

More important than achieving a set number of stitches per inch is achieving consistency in stitch length and spacing (see Photo 1B, *above right*). Six uniform stitches per inch spaced an equal distance apart will result in a more desirable finished appearance than eight uneven stitches per inch. Rather than focusing on the quantity of stitches per inch, focus on the quality of your stitching.

PINNING

Because the seam lines of patchwork pieces must line up perfectly, it is important to pin before sewing. Use extra-fine pins, as large-diameter pins can leave holes in the fabric and distort seaming. Use as many pins as needed to hold the fabric pieces securely (see Photo 1C, *above right*).

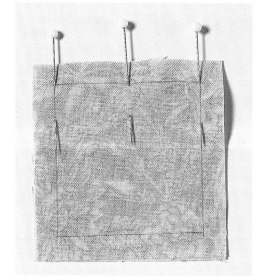

Photo 1C

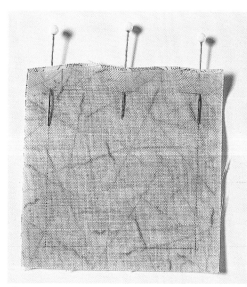

Photo 1D

With right sides together, align the seam lines of two pieces.

Note: *Seam lines should be marked on the wrong side of both pieces. See Chapter 4—Cutting Techniques for information on marking your fabric pieces.*

Push a pin through both fabric layers at each matching point, first at the ends, then at the center. Add pins along the length of the seam line as needed (see Photo 1D, *above right*).

Photo 1E

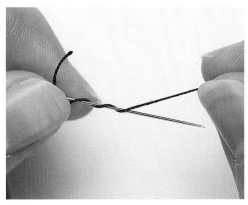

Photo 1F

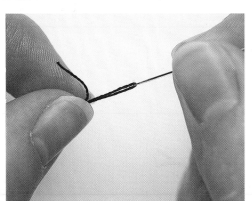

Photo 1G

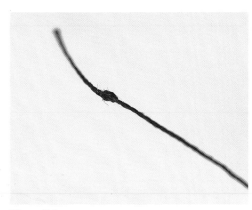

Photo 1H

 ## Creative Tip

When hand-sewing or hand-quilting, put water balloons on your

thumb and forefinger. This helps you grip the needle better.

—*WENDY, SALES ASSOCIATE*

KNOTS TO KNOW

When hand piecing, it is smart to use more than a backstitch to secure a thread tail. Below are the steps for tying three different knots—knot on the needle, two-loop backstitch knot, and one-loop backstitch knot.

The knot on the needle, also known as the quilter's knot, is a good knot for most hand sewing, including hand piecing, appliqué, and quilting.

The two-loop backstitch knot and the one-loop backstitch knot are good choices to end a line of sewing.

Choose the knot that works best for each particular situation.

Knot On the Needle

1. With the needle threaded, hold the thread tail on top of the needle, extending it about ½" above (see Photo 1E, *top, far left*).

2. Holding the thread tail against the needle with one hand, use your other hand to wrap the thread around the needle clockwise three times (see Photo 1F, *above left, top*).

3. Pinching the thread tail and thread wraps with your thumb and forefinger, grasp the needle near the point and gently pull it through the thread wraps (see Photo 1G, *above, far left*).

4. Continue pinching the thread wraps until the thread is pulled completely through and forms a small, firm knot near the end of the thread tail (see Photo 1H, *above left*).

Chapter 5 – Piecing

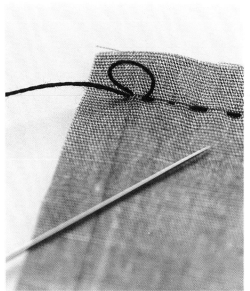

Photo 1I

Photo 1J

Two-Loop Backstitch Knot

1. Take a small backstitch close to where the last stitch ended, making a loop (see Photo 1I, *far left*).

2. Draw the needle through the loop, making a second loop (see Photo 1J, *left*).

3. Then draw the needle through the second loop (see Photo 1K, *below left*).

4. Pull gently on the needle to make a figure eight (see Photo 1L, *below*).

5. Pull the thread up tightly to close the figure eight and make a knot (see Photo 1M, *bottom*). Clip the thread end.

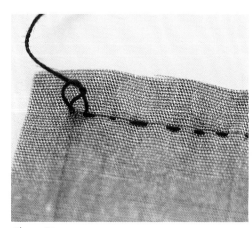

Photo 1L

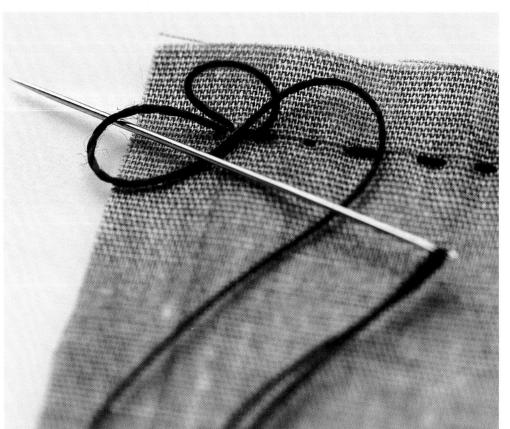

Photo 1K

Photo 1M

Photo 1N

One-Loop Backstitch Knot

1. Take a small backstitch on top of the last stitch, making a small loop (see Photo 1N, *left*).

2. Draw the needle through the loop (see Photo 1O, *below left*).

3. Pull the thread tightly to close the loop and make a knot (see Photo 1P, *below*).

4. Make a second knot, if necessary. Clip the thread end.

Photo 1O

Photo 1P

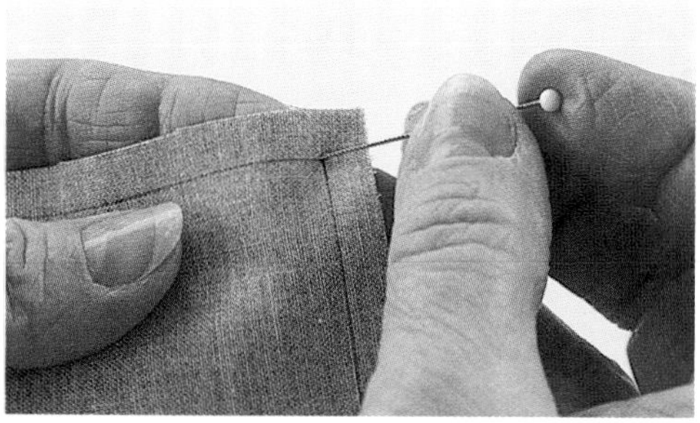

Photo 1Q

SEWING A STRAIGHT SEAM

1. With right sides together, align the seam lines of two pieces.
Note: Seam lines should be marked on the wrong side of both pieces (see Chapter 4—Cutting Techniques for information on marking fabric pieces).

Push a pin through both fabric layers at each matching point, first at the ends, then at the center (see Photo 1Q, *above left*). Add pins along the seam line as needed.

2. To begin sewing, remove the pin at one end and insert the needle through both layers of fabric at the matching points (see Photo 1R, *left*). Make a backstitch or two, leaving a 1" tail.

Or, make a small knot at the end of the thread and insert the needle through both layers of fabric at the matching points (see Photo 1S, *below left*).

Note: Keep seam allowances free of stitching. They are not sewn down as they are in machine piecing.

3. Weave the needle in and out of the fabrics along the seam line using a short running stitch. Take four to six stitches before pulling the thread taut (see Photo 1T, *below left*). To add stability to the seam, take a backstitch every ¾ to 1" along the length of the seam.

4. Remove pins as you sew, and turn the piece over frequently to make certain the stitches are on the marked seam line of the underside piece. Do not sew past the matching points at the other end where the future seams will intersect (see Photo 1U, *bottom, far left*).

5. At the opposite matching points, remove the final pin and take a final stitch. Make a backstitch or two at the matching points (see Photo 1V, *bottom left*). Trim the thread, leaving a short tail.

Joining Rows of Patchwork

1. With right sides together, align the seam lines of two pieces (see Photo 1W, *opposite*).
Note: Seam lines should be marked on the wrong side of both pieces. See Chapter 4—Cutting Techniques for information on marking fabric pieces.

Push a pin through both fabric layers at each matching point, first at the ends, then at the center. Add pins along the length of the seam line as needed.

2. Remove the pin at one end and insert the needle through both layers of fabric at the matching points. Make a backstitch or two, leaving a 1" tail (see Photo 1X, *opposite*). Or make a small knot at the end of the thread and insert the needle through both layers of fabric at the matching points.

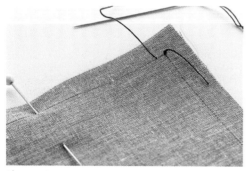
Photo 1R

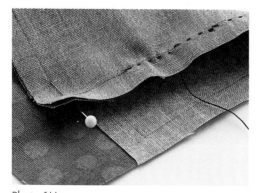
Photo 1S

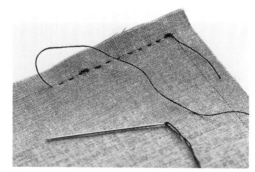
Photo 1T

Photo 1U

Photo 1V

Photo 1W

Photo 1X

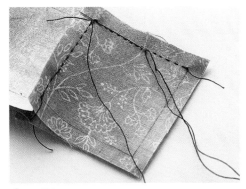
Photo 1Y

Photo 1Z

Photo 2A

Photo 2B

Note: Keep seam allowances free of stitching. They are not sewn down as they are in machine piecing.

3. Weave the needle in and out of the fabrics along the seam line using a short running stitch (see Photo 1Y, *top, far right*). At each seam allowance, take a backstitch.

4. Insert the needle at the matching points, coming out on the opposite side (see Photo 1Z, *above*).
Note: The seam allowance itself should be free from stitching.

5. Take a stitch, then a backstitch (see Photo 2A, *above right*).

6. Remove the pins as you sew, and turn the pieces over frequently to check that the stitches are on the marked seam line of the underside piece (see Photo 2B, *above middle, far right*).

Photo 2C

Photo 2D

7. Continue sewing to the end of the patchwork row, joining at the seams and backstitching at the final matching points to complete the seam (see Photo 2C, *above*). Leave a short thread tail.

8. Press the seams to one side as they are completed using your finger, a hardwood hand ironing tool, mini iron, or iron (see Photo 2D, *above*).

Photo 2E

Photo 2F

Sewing Diamond Shapes

Because diamond shapes have at least two sides cut on the bias grain, they can be tricky to handle. (Remember that bias means stretch.) Handle bias-cut pieces carefully as they can easily stretch out of shape.

To control the stretchiness of diamond shapes, cut them facing the same direction on the fabric with the straight of grain along two edges. As with other hand piecing, do not stitch into the seam allowances.

1. With right sides together, align the seam lines of two pieces.
Note: Seam lines should be marked on the wrong side of both pieces. See Chapter 4— Cutting Techniques for information on marking fabric pieces.

Push a pin through both fabric layers at each matching point, first at the ends, then at the center (see Photo 2E, *far left*). Add pins along the seam line as needed.

2. To begin sewing, remove the pin at one end and insert the needle through both layers of fabric at the matching points. Make a backstitch or two, leaving a 1" tail (see Photo 2F, *above left*).
Note: Keep seam allowances free of stitching. They are not sewn down as they are in machine piecing.

3. Weave the needle in and out of the fabrics along the seam line using a short running stitch. Take four to six stitches before pulling the thread taut. To add stability to the seam, take a backstitch every ¾ to 1" along the length of the seam (see Photo 2G, *far left*). Remove pins as you sew.

4. Turn the piece over frequently to make certain the stitches are on the marked seam line of the underside piece.

5. Sew to the opposite matching point; do not sew past it, where future seams will intersect. Make a backstitch or two at the matching points. Trim the thread, leaving a short tail (see Photo 2H, *above left*).

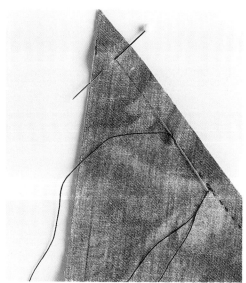

Photo 2G

Photo 2H

⚜Creative Tip

Tape a yardstick to the edge of your crafting table to use as

a quick reference when measuring fabric.

—CYNTHIA, SALES ASSOCIATE

Photo 2I

Photo 2J

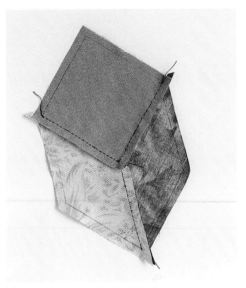
Photo 2K

SET-IN SEAMS

Blocks composed of diamond shapes frequently contain set-in squares and triangles. Setting in such pieces requires negotiating multiple seam allowances. The following instructions describe a square being set into the opening left by two pieced-together diamonds.

1. With right sides together, pin one edge of the diamond unit to one edge of the square, aligning matching points. Hand-stitch the seam from the open end of the diamond into the corner, beginning and ending at the matching points and removing pins as you sew. Backstitch at the inside corner to secure, but do not cut the thread (see Photo 2I, *above*).
Note: *Keep seam allowances free of stitching. They are not sewn down as they are in machine piecing.*

2. Bring the adjacent edge of the square up and align it with the adjacent edge of the diamond unit. Insert a pin at aligned matching points, then pin the remainder of the seam line. Hand-stitch the seam from the corner to the open end of the angle, removing pins as you sew (see Photo 2J, *above*). Do not sew past the matching points at the end. Backstitch to secure the seam. Leave a short thread tail.

3. Press both seam allowances of the set-in square toward the diamonds; press the diamonds' joining seam to one side (see Photo 2K, *above right*).

Sew a set-in triangle in the same manner as a set-in square.

Photo 2L

Photo 2M

Photo 2N

Photo 2O

Photo 2P

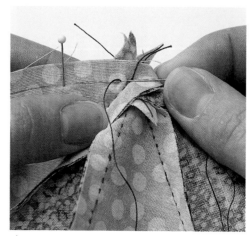

Photo 2Q

Photo 2R

DIAMONDS AND CENTER-INTERSECTING BLOCKS

The eight-pointed star represents one of the more challenging quilt blocks because it's tricky to achieve a smooth, unpuckered center. Understanding the direction to sew and press these multiple seams can make a big difference in a finished block.

1. Lay out eight diamonds in a star shape (see Photo 2L, *top left*).

2. Layer the diamonds in pairs with right sides together. Align marked seam lines and matching points exactly; pin together (see Photo 2M, *top middle*). Sew from matching point to matching point, backstitching at each seam end as described in Sewing Diamond Shapes on *page 124*.
Note: *Keep seam allowances free of stitching. They are not sewn down as they are in machine piecing.*

3. Finger-press the seam allowances to one side, pressing all seams in the same direction (clockwise or counterclockwise), as shown in Photo 2N, *above*.

4. Layer two diamond pairs with right sides together (see Photo 2O, *opposite*). Where the points intersect, push pins straight down. Beginning at the outer corner with a backstitch, stitch toward the intersection, adjusting the stitch length as needed for the needle to come up at the matching points pinhole; backstitch to make a star half. Repeat to make a second star half.

5. Pin the star halves with right sides together, aligning the matching points at each end. Secure the center point by positioning a pin straight down through the intersection as shown in Photo 2P, *opposite*). Add pins as needed to keep the star halves aligned.

6. Beginning at the outer matching points with a backstitch, sew up to the intersection (see Photo 2Q, *opposite*). Adjust the stitch length as necessary for the needle to come up at the center matching points pinhole; backstitch.

7. Stitching through the top seam allowance only, nudge the seam allowance to the right (see Photo 2R, *opposite*). Make a backstitch on the opposite side of the seam. Carefully align the points on both sides of the seam as you sew to the opposite outer matching points.

8. At the end of the seam, remove the final pin and stitch in the matching points pinhole; make a backstitch or two.

9. Press the seam allowances to one side in a circular fashion as shown in Photo 2S, *above right*. This causes the seams to swirl neatly in the center, which reduces the bulk where the star points are joined (see Photo 2T, *right*).

Photo 2S

Photo 2T

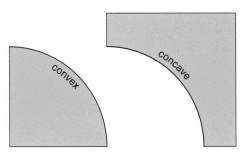

Illustration 1

CURVED SEAMS

Curved shapes add gentle ease and a sense of motion to pieced designs. Many quilters find it easier to stitch curves by hand than by machine because it is easier to maintain precise control of the fabric pieces.

Typically curved pieces are made by joining two separate shapes: a convex curve with a concave curve (see Illustration 1, *above*).

As with other hand piecing, transfer the seam lines, matching points, and center points from the templates to the fabric pieces; do not stitch into seam allowances.

The following example shows the piecing sequence of curved pieces.

1. Trace around the templates, making sure the seam lines, matching points, and center points are clearly marked on the wrong side.

2. If the template doesn't have a center mark, fold the concave piece in half and gently finger-crease the center of the curved edge (see Photo 2U, *above right*). Repeat folding and creasing the convex piece.

3. Layer the pieces with right sides together and center points aligned; the convex piece should be facing you. Pin the pieces together perpendicular to the seam line at the center points.

Photo 2U

4. Pinning perpendicular to the seam line and curling the pieces around your thumb, insert a pin at each end matching point, aligning the seam lines. Add pins about every ½" between the ends and the center (see Photo 2V, *opposite*). Keeping the convex piece against your thumbs and gently curling the fabric over them makes it possible to ease in any excess fabric without creating folds or tucks.

5. To begin sewing, remove the pin at one end and insert the needle through both layers of fabric at the matching points. Make a backstitch or two, leaving a 1" tail. *Note: Keep seam allowances free of stitching. They are not sewn down as they are in machine piecing.*

6. Weave the needle in and out of the fabrics along the seam line using a short running stitch. Take four to six stitches

before pulling the thread taut. To add stability to the seam, take a backstitch every ¾ to 1" along the length of the seam.

7. Remove pins as you sew and ease the fabric into the curves, gently curving the pieces around your thumb to keep the seam lines aligned (see Photo 2W, *opposite*). Turn the piece over frequently to make certain the stitches are on the marked seam line.

It is not necessary to clip seam allowances when hand-piecing. Simply ease the fabric into the curves as you stitch (see Photo 2X, *opposite*).

8. Stop sewing at the opposite matching points and make a backstitch or two. Trim the thread, leaving a short tail.

9. Press the seam allowance toward the convex piece (see Photo 2Y, *opposite*).

Photo 2V

Photo 2W

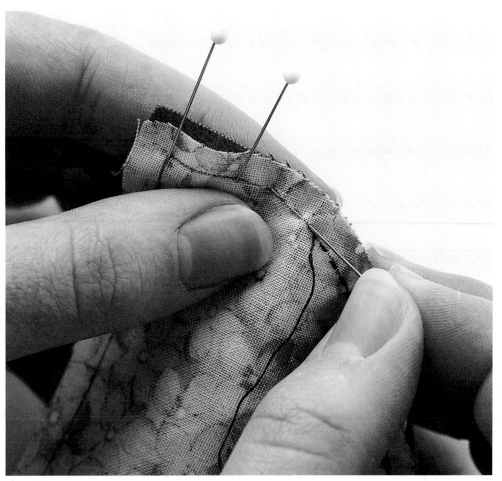

Photo 2X

Photo 2Y

✖Creative Tip

*Finger pressing should be used on fabrics
where a permanent crease may not come out.
If you must press, use a steam iron and lightly
press so the crease won't show.*
—ROBYN, STORE ASSOCIATE

Photo 2Z

Photo 3A

Photo 3B

Photo 3C

Photo 3D

Photo 3E

Photo 3F

Photo 3G

Photo 3H

ENGLISH PAPER PIECING

This technique of stabilizing fabric with a paper template is a sure way to guarantee accuracy. English paper piecing is most effective for designs that don't have long straight sides but do have numerous set-in corners, such as the hexagon shapes in a Grandmother's Flower Garden quilt.

Many precut paper templates are available through quilt shops and by mail order. To make templates, trace the pattern on a sturdy paper multiple times and cut out carefully and accurately.

1. Pin a paper template to one or more layers of fabric. Cut out around the template with a ¼" seam allowance (see Photo 2Z, *opposite*). The seam allowance does not have to be exact because the template will be an accurate guide.

2. Place a template right side down on the wrong side of a fabric piece and fold the seam allowance over one edge. Beginning with a knot on the right side of the fabric, baste the seam allowance in place; stitch through the fabric and the paper template with ¼"-long stitches (see Photo 3A, *opposite*). Finger-press the basted edge.

3. Near the corner, fold the seam allowance of the next edge over the template and continue stitching (see Photo 3B, *opposite*). Stitch all edges in the same manner. Don't knot the thread; leave a thread tail of about ½" or so on the right side of the fabric.

4. Repeat steps 2 and 3 until all fabric pieces have been basted to paper templates.

5. Place two fabric-covered templates with right sides together, aligning the edges to be joined. Pin the pieces together at the center as shown in Photo 3C, *opposite*.

6. With a single strand of quilting thread, begin stitching about ⅛" from one corner using tiny whipstitches and catching a thread of both fabric folds (see Photo 3D, *opposite*). The paper templates can be felt with the needle, but do not stitch through them.

7. Referring to Photo 3E, *opposite*, backstitch to the nearest corner.

8. At the corner, reverse the stitching direction and sew across the edges to the opposite corner (see Photo 3F, *opposite*). Take a backstitch, and knot the thread with the knot in the fabric using a one-loop backstitch knot (see *page 121*).

9. Lightly press open the joined pieces and check the seam from the right side (see Photo 3G, *opposite*). Stitches should not show. If they do, remove the seam and resew it, taking smaller whipstitches through less of the fabric folds.

10. To set in a piece, pin and sew the seam on one side. Reposition the stitched pieces so the next seam is aligned and continue sewing (see Photo 3H, *opposite*).

11. When all edges of a piece have been stitched to adjoining pieces, remove the paper template as shown in Photo 3I, *below, far left*. Pull the basting threads and templates out from the back (see Photo 3J, *below left*).

Photo 3I

Photo 3J

131

Piecing *By Machine*

Piecing by machine can speed the patchwork process, making it possible to complete a large patchwork quilt in far less time than it would take by hand. And for some quilters, machine piecing also allows for greater accuracy in joining individual pieces, larger units, and blocks.

THE IMPORTANCE OF PRECISE ¼" SEAMS

Quilting depends upon precise accuracy in workmanship at every step. Use exact ¼" seams throughout quilt construction to make certain all the pieces fit together smoothly and accurately. Once you've selected a seam guide, test it to make sure the seams will be precisely ¼" wide. Even a slight deviation will multiply quickly considering the number of pieces that are sewn together to make a quilt top.

Choosing a Seam Guide
¼" Presser Foot
On many machines the distance between the needle and the right edge of the presser foot is ¼". If this is not the case with your machine, consider purchasing a special ¼" presser foot for use in patchwork and quilting.

Most sewing machine companies offer this specialty foot for their machines. In addition, several generic ¼" feet are available for use on a variety of models, as shown in Photo 3K, *opposite*. Be sure to note what type of shank or by what means the presser foot is attached to the machine before purchasing a specialty presser foot.

Masking Tape or Adhesive Moleskin
As shown in Photo 3L, *opposite*, layers of masking tape or moleskin placed on a sewing machine bed in front of the throat plate act as a guide for the fabric, feeding it straight into the presser foot and needle.

Testing Your Presser Foot
Test your presser foot by aligning the raw fabric edges with the right edge of the presser foot and sewing a sample seam. Measure the resulting seam allowance using a ruler or graph paper that has a ¼" grid as a guide (see Photo 3M, *opposite*).

On some sewing machines, the needle can be moved to the left or right to create a perfect ¼" seam allowance. If so, record the original needle position in the machine's manual or on a self-stick note placed near the machine. Then the machine can be quickly reset for patchwork.

If the presser foot is not a perfect ¼" and the needle cannot be repositioned, mark a ¼" seam guide on the throat plate with masking tape or moleskin using ¼" graph paper as a measuring tool, as shown in Photo 3N, *opposite*.

Carefully trim the graph paper along a grid line. Place the graph paper under the needle. Slowly lower the needle into the grid one line from the newly trimmed edge. Use masking tape or moleskin to mark the new seam guide's location ahead of the needle.

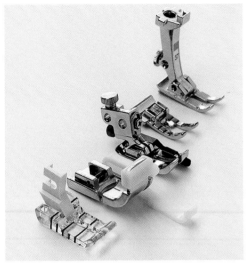

Photo 3K

❧Creative Tip

I found the fusible grid-block method of quilting to be very helpful in teaching a beginner to join squares. The grid helps with the layout and design for watercolor quilts, and it is easy to sew straight ¼" seams by following the marked lines on the back. Pressing after sewing each row is critical, however.

—SUE, EDUCATION/MARKETING CONTENT SPECIALIST

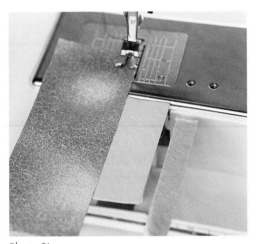

Photo 3L

Photo 3N

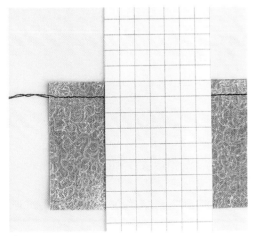

Photo 3M

133 ❧

Photo 3O

Photo 3P

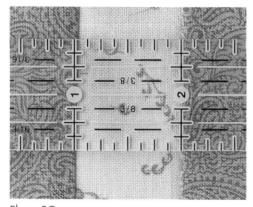

Photo 3Q

Photo 3R

Practice Sewing Exact ¼" Seams

1. Cut three 1½"-wide strips of fabric, using fabrics with contrasting colors.

2. Sew together two of the strips using a ¼" seam allowance as shown in Photo 3O, *above*. Join the third strip to the first two, again using a ¼" seam allowance.

3. Press the seam allowances away from the center strip (see Photo 3P, *left*).

4. On the right side of the fabric, measure the width of the center strip. If the seam allowances are ¼", the center strip should measure 1" wide, as shown in Photo 3Q, *left*.

If the center strip is not 1" wide, the seam allowance is not an exact ¼". Take the seam out and repeat steps 1 through 4 until the center strip is 1" wide. Retest the seam guide as necessary.

SUPPLIES

Thread Use top-quality, 100% cotton or cotton-wrapped polyester thread for best results. It's tempting to purchase cheap thread because large quantities are needed for patchwork and quilting. However, substandard threads break and fray, adding unnecessary frustration to an otherwise enjoyable experience. ***Note:*** *Many seasoned quilters keep just three shades of thread for sewing patchwork: light (beige, light gray), medium (taupe, gray, gray-green), and dark (navy, black, dark green).*

When piecing with high-contrast fabrics, use two different colors of thread—one in the needle and one in the bobbin. Match thread colors to fabric colors, as shown in Photo 3R, *above*. Use threads of the same type and weight.

If the quilt has fabrics in many colors, use thread in a neutral color, such as gray, taupe, or beige, throughout the assembly.

Needles Begin every project with a new sewing machine needle. Change it after every eight hours of sewing, as a blunt needle will weaken fabric; a needle with a burr may snag the fabric. Most often, a sharp point 75/11 or 80/12 needle is best for machine piecing (use a 90/14 needle for flannel). Often if stitches are not forming correctly or are uneven, the problem can be corrected by simply changing the sewing machine needle.

PINNING

The seam lines of patchwork pieces must line up perfectly. At times, it's unnecessary to pin the pieces together before sewing. For instance, pins aren't needed for sewing together long strips in a strip-piecing project (see Strip Piecing on *page 146*).

Other situations, such as piecing complicated blocks, are much easier when the pieces are pinned together before sewing. Some pinning guidelines follow.

Use extra-fine pins. Do not use pins labeled "quilting" as they often are thick and long and can leave holes in the fabric and distort the seams you're trying to match. Some quilters prefer glass-head pins, which are easy to see and stand up to the heat of an iron. Avoid plastic-head pins as they may melt when ironed. (See Chapter 1—Tools and Materials for additional information.)

Abut seams when possible. When aligning two pieced units, press the seam allowances in opposite directions and place them with right sides together. First insert a pin through both layers at the seam intersection to hold the pieces in place, as shown in Photo 3S, *above right*. Then bring the pin back up through the seam intersection from the opposite side.

Pin the pieces together with the pins no more than ⅛" away from either side of the seam (see Photo 3T, *top, right*).

Place pins perpendicular to the seam with heads toward the right edge for easy removal (left-handed quilters may want to place pins with heads facing left).

Photo 3S

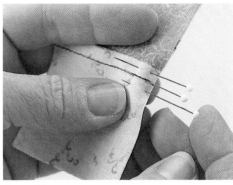

Photo 3T

Photo 3U

An alternative to this method is to place a single pin diagonally through the pieces, catching both the top and bottom seam allowances, as shown in Photo 3U, *right*.

Use as many pins as needed to get the job done. Three pins can hold some pieced blocks together. Others require more. Pin longer pieces at the ends first, then at the center; pin along the length as needed.

Avoid sewing over pins. Remove each pin just before the machine needle gets to it so the pinhole can be filled by the machine needle, and so that the machine needle doesn't strike a pin (see Photo 3V, *right*).

When a machine needle hits a pin it can, at best, nick, bend, or break the needle. Worse, it can alter the timing of the machine. If so, refer to the sewing machine manufacturer's manual for instructions on replacing the needle or resetting the timing.

Photo 3V

Photo 3W

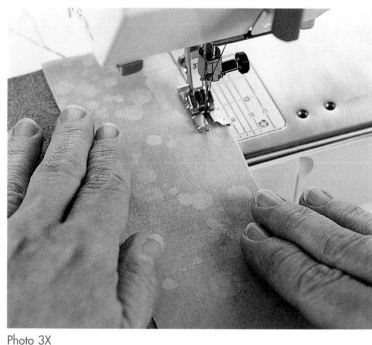
Photo 3X

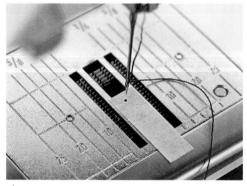
Photo 3Y

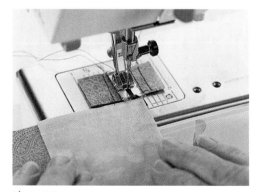
Photo 3Z

SEWING A STRAIGHT SEAM THAT WILL BE INTERSECTED

It is not necessary to backstitch the beginning of a seam that will be intersected with another seam later in the quiltmaking process.

Begin stitching at the edge of the fabric. Hold the top and bobbin threads together in your left hand as you begin a seam to avoid catching the threads in the stitching (see Photo 3W, *above left*). Stitch slowly and evenly.

Guide the fabric with one hand on the fabric in front of the presser foot and the other hand on the fabric to the left of the presser foot, as shown in Photo 3X, *above right*. Let the machine walk the fabric through to the opposite edge. Pushing or pulling the fabric will result in uneven, puckered seams.

If the fabric is "swallowed" by the machine, replace the throat plate with a small-holed, straight-stitch throat plate, as shown in Photo 3Y, *left*.

Or cover the hole with masking tape. The needle will pierce a hole of the needed size in the tape as it goes up and down. ***Note:*** *Make sure the masking tape does not cover the feed dogs.*

Another option is to sew on a small fabric scrap to begin the seam. Stitch on the fabric scrap first, then feed in patchwork fabrics (see Photo 3Z, *left*). End the seam with a small scrap, too. Then, snip off the stitched scrap.

This technique is particularly useful for joining small pieces. It helps prevent the patchwork seam from puckering at the beginning and assures complete, even stitches at both the beginning and end of each seam.

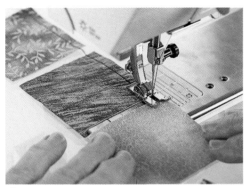

Photo 4A

Chain Piecing

Patchwork pieces that are sewn together from edge to edge without backstitching can be sewn together in a single long chain to save time and thread. To chain-piece, feed pairs of pieces under the machine needle without lifting the presser foot or clipping the threads (see Photo 4A, *above*). Short lengths of thread will link the stitched pairs, as shown in Photo 4B, *right*.

Blocks and rows of blocks can be chain-pieced also. Feed the pairs of blocks or rows under the machine needle to join them, as shown in Photo 4C, *top, far right*. Pay attention to the direction of the seam allowances, alternating them whenever possible (see Photo 4D, *far right*).

SEWING A STRAIGHT SEAM THAT WILL NOT BE INTERSECTED

It is important to secure seams that will not be sewn across again (such as those in border units) and seams that are not sewn to the edge of the fabric (as with inset seams). Simply add a few backstitches on top of previous stitching at both the beginning and the end of these seams, as shown in Illustration 2, *right*.

Photo 4B

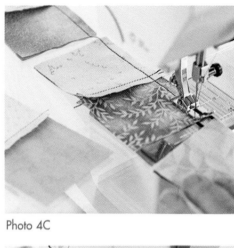

Photo 4C

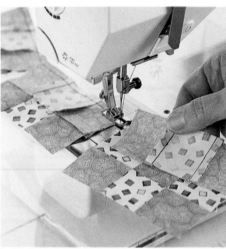

Photo 4D

Illustration 2

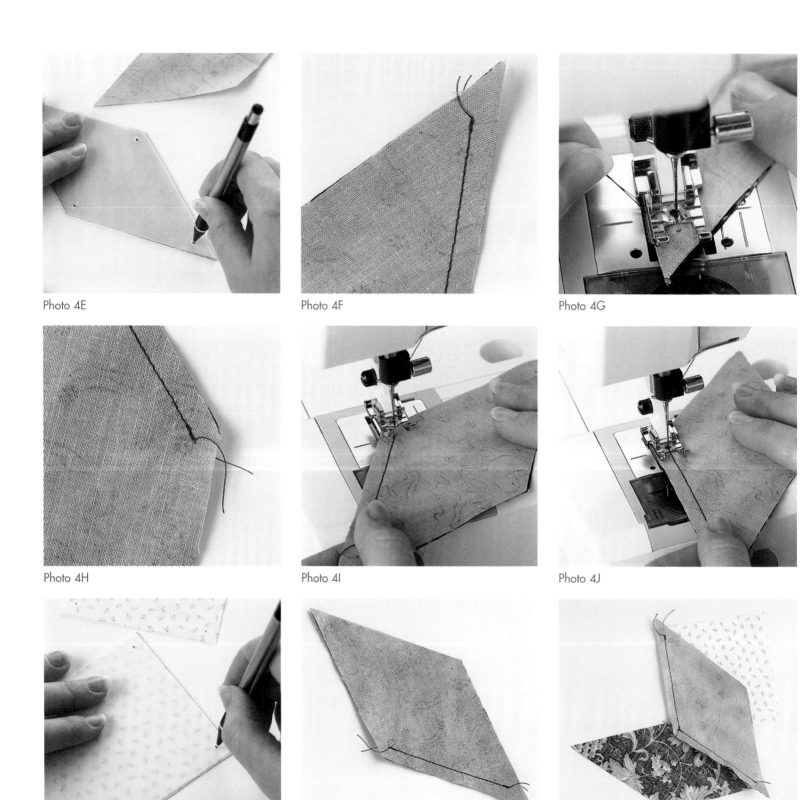

Photo 4E

Photo 4F

Photo 4G

Photo 4H

Photo 4I

Photo 4J

Photo 4K

Photo 4L

Photo 4M

Set-In Seams

Set-in seams are used to construct blocks that cannot be successfully assembled with continuous straight seams. The piece to be added is stitched into the unit in two steps. Diamond blocks frequently contain set-in squares and triangles. Joining stitches for these pieces run from marked dot to marked dot and do not extend into seam allowances.

Transferring Dots to Fabric Pieces

To ensure that the pieces fit together accurately, the pattern templates should have dots marked on the ¼" seam line at the outer and inner corners. To transfer those dots to the fabric pieces, first pierce a small hole through the dots on the template with a large needle or awl. Make sure the hole is just large enough for the point of a marking pen or pencil. Then align the template over the wrong side of the fabric piece and mark through the holes (see Photo 4E, *opposite*).

Starting a Set-In Seam

Seams that begin away from the fabric edge need to be secured with a few backstitches.

Method 1

Begin sewing forward at the dot for a couple of stitches, take a couple of backstitches, and continue sewing to the opposite edge or dot. Avoid the urge to backstitch too far; too many layers of thread will add unnecessary bulk to the finished seam. Backstitch only to the starting point. Stitching forward, backstitching, and stitching forward again gives the beginning part of the seam three layers of thread, as shown in Photo 4F, *opposite*.

Method 2

1. Turn the fabric so the starting dot is ¼" in front of the needle. Stitch forward to the dot (see Photo 4G, *opposite*).

2. Leaving the needle in the fabric, pivot the work 180° and continue sewing the seam. With this method, there are only two layers of thread in the beginning part of the seam.

Ending a Set-In Seam

Seams that end away from the fabric edge need to be secured with a few backstitches.

Method 1

End sewing forward at the dot and take a few backstitches (see Photo 4H, *opposite*).

Method 2

1. End sewing forward at the dot. Leave the needle in the fabric at the dot, pivot the work 180°, as shown in Photo 4I, *opposite*.

2. Take a couple of stitches forward on top of the previous stitching (see Photo 4J, *opposite*.

Assembling a Set-In Seam

1. As shown in Photo 4K, *opposite*, mark dots at the ¼" seam lines on the wrong side of pieces at the outer and inner corners.

2. Pin and sew together the first two pieces, starting and stopping at the dots (see Photo 4L, *opposite*). Press the pieces open.

3. Match the corners and dots of the first and third pieces; pin together (see Photo 4M, *opposite*). Sew from the dot at the inside corner to the dot at the outer edge.

4. Bring the edge of the second piece up and align it with the adjacent edge of the third piece, matching corners and dots (see Photo 4N, *below left*). Sew from the dot at the inside corner to the dot at the outer edge.

5. Press the unit open (see Photo 4O, *below middle*).

Sew a set-in triangle in the same manner as a set-in square (see Photo 4P, *below)*.

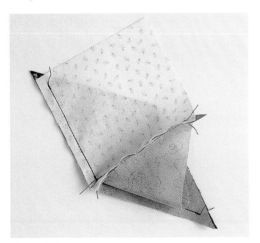

Photo 4N

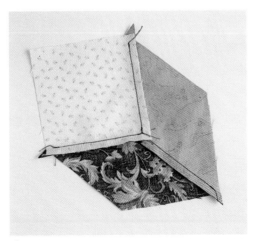

Photo 4O

Photo 4P

Diamonds and Center-Intersecting Blocks

An eight-pointed star represents one of the more challenging blocks because it's tricky to assemble with a smooth, unpuckered center. Directional stitching from joining dot to joining dot and directional pressing make the difference.

1. Mark joining dots at the ¼" seam lines on the wrong side of each diamond-shape piece in all corners (see Photo 4Q, *left*).

2. Lay out the eight diamond shapes as they will be assembled, as shown in Photo 4R, *below left*.

3. With right sides together, pin the diamond shapes together in pairs along the adjoining seam, matching dots exactly (see Photo 4S, *below middle*). Sew from the center dots to the outer dots, backstitching at each end as described in Set-In Seams on *page 139*.

4. Press the seam allowances to one side (see Photo 4T, *below*). Press them all in the same direction, either clockwise or counterclockwise.

Photo 4Q

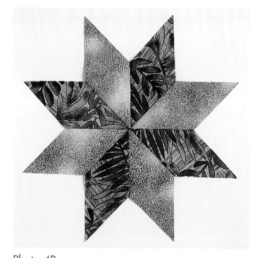

Photo 4R

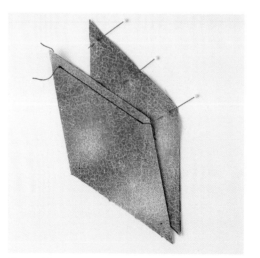

Photo 4S

Photo 4T

Photo 4U

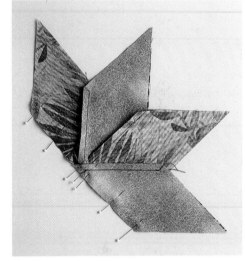

Photo 4V

5. Join the diamond pairs to make two star halves, sewing from the center dots to the outer dots. Trim fabric dog-ears that extend beyond the raw edges, as shown in Photo 4U, *above*.

6. Pin the two star halves together. Secure the center point and add pins as needed to keep the star halves aligned (see Photo 4V, *above, far right*).

7. Stitch from the outer dot to the opposite outer dot to join the two star halves. Press the seam allowance to one side (see photos 4W and 4X, *right*).

8. Set in any remaining pieces as described in Set-In Seams on *page 139*.

Photo 4W

Photo 4X

141

PARTIAL SEAMS

Some blocks have pieces surrounding a center shape that extend unequally beyond the center. These blocks can be constructed with a seam that appears to be set-in but is actually made in two steps. The key is to sew a partial seam.

1. As shown in Photo 4Y, *below,* sew part of the first seam (about half the distance).

2. Determine the sequence for adding the remaining pieces (see Photo 4Z, *below*).

3. Pin and complete the stitching of the first, or partial, seam, as shown in Photo 5A, *bottom left*. Work your way around the block, adding each piece in this manner.

4. Press seam allowances toward the outer strips (see Photo 5B, *below bottom*) for a smooth, even block, as shown in Photo 5C, *bottom right*.

CURVED SEAMS

Joining pieces with curved edges presents challenges. Cutting a small notch in the center of a curved edge, as shown in Photo 5D, *opposite*, makes it easier.

1. With right sides together match the center notches of curved edges. Pin together at the center point, at seam ends, and liberally in between, gently easing the edges as needed to align (see Photo 5E, *opposite*).

2. Sew together the curved edges. Clip into the seam allowance of the edge that curves in (concave) as needed, as shown in Photo 5F, *opposite*. Do not cut into or beyond the seam lines; do not clip the convex edge.

3. Press the seam allowance toward the piece that has the inner (concave) curve, as shown in Photo 5G, *opposite*.

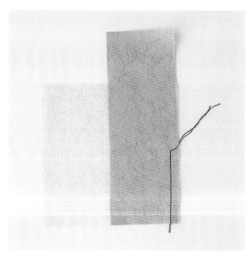

Photo 4Y

Photo 4Z

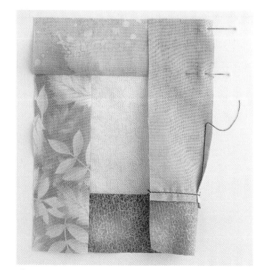

Photo 5A

Photo 5B

Photo 5C

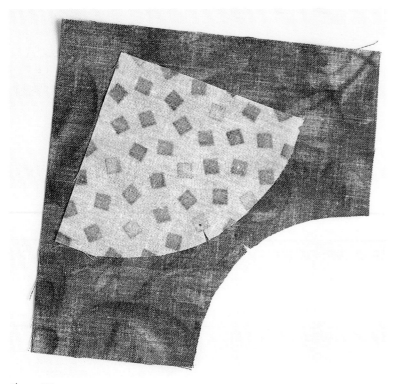

Photo 5D

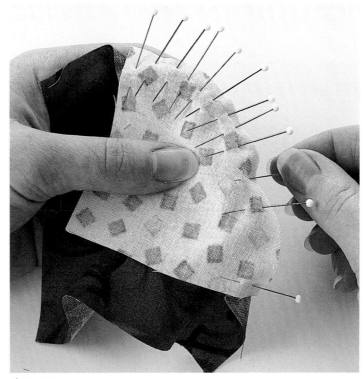

Photo 5E

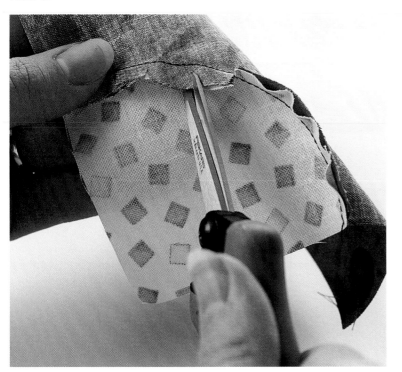

Photo 5F

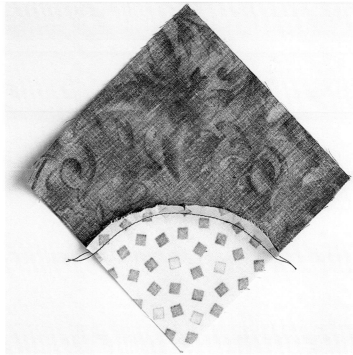

Photo 5G

Photo 5H

Photo 5I

Photo 5J

Photo 5K

Photo 5L

Photo 5M

Photo 5N

PRESSING

Good pressing is essential for accurate piecing (see Chapter 1—Tools and Materials for information on pressing equipment). In general, every seam needs to be pressed before another unit is added, and most seam allowances are pressed to one side.

Press with an iron set on a temperature appropriate to the fabric on a flat, firm surface. (An ironing board or pad with a heat-resistant cushion and cotton cover is fine. Avoid a nonstick-coated, heat-reflective ironing board cover. This coating reflects heat and steam upward, not allowing them to pass completely through the fabrics.) To avoid distorting the quilt pieces, press only after pieces are stitched together.

Pressing Straight Seams

Straight seams should be pressed with the iron parallel to the straight grain of the fabric.

1. First press the stitching flat with right sides together and the darker fabric on top (see Photo 5H, *top, far left*). "Setting the seam" is the term for this critical first step that locks the threads together, smooths out any puckers, and evens out minor thread tension differences.

2. Beginning at one end of the seam, lift up the top piece and position the tip of the iron on the lighter color fabric. Glide the iron along the seam edge with the tip moving from the lighter color piece to the darker color piece (see Photo 5I, *opposite*). This method will both open up the unit and press the seam to one side in a single step. Pressing the unit from the right side helps avoid pressing tucks and pleats into the seams.

3. Some quilt patterns specify which direction to press the seam allowances. When in doubt, press seam allowances toward the darker fabric. This avoids creating a shadow on the lighter fabric. If pressing toward the lighter fabric is a must, trim the darker fabric seam allowance by 1/16" after the seam is sewn to prevent any shadows.

4. If a seam allowance has been pressed the wrong way, return it to its original unpressed state and press the unit flat to remove the crease. Allow the fabric to cool, then press the seam allowance in the desired direction.

Pressing Bias Seams
A bias seam should be pressed with the iron at a 45° angle to the seam and along the straight grain to avoid distortion (see Photo 5J, *opposite*).

Finger-Pressing
As a temporary measure, press short seam allowances with your finger.

1. Place a pieced unit on a hard surface. From the wrong side, spread the unit apart with the seam allowance folded toward the darker fabric. Press with your fingers along the length of the seam allowance (see Photo 5K, *opposite*).

2. Turning the unit right side up with the seam allowance still facing the darker side, finger-press again (see Photo 5L, *opposite*).

Finger-pressing isn't a substitute for using an iron, but it does temporarily press seam allowances in one direction or another. It's a good method to use if you're unsure which way seams will eventually need to be pressed.

Opposing Seams
When two seams will be joined together, press the seam allowances in opposite directions as shown in Photo 5M, *opposite*. This helps distribute the bulk of the seam allowances evenly and ensures that the seam allowances can abut one another.

When to Press Seams Open
Seam allowances are pressed open when multiple seams come together in one area. This helps distribute the fabric bulk evenly in a small area, eliminating lumps and making the seam easier to quilt through.

When pressing seams open, press first from the wrong side of the fabric. Use your fingernail or a hardwood hand ironing tool to open up the seam ahead of the iron (see Photo 5N, *opposite*).

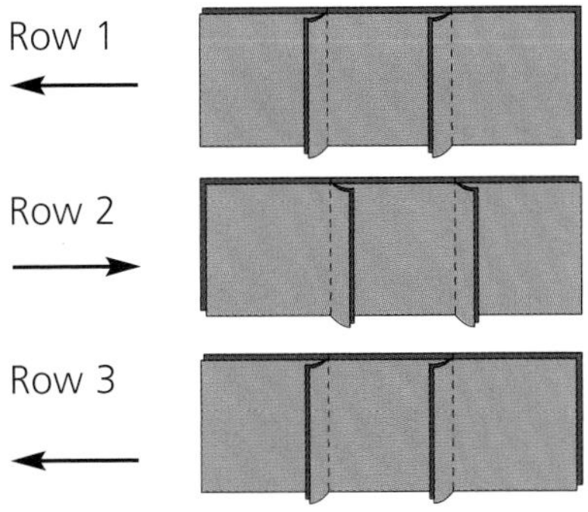

Planning to Press
Eliminate ironing-board guesswork by developing a plan for pressing. Start by studying a practice block that represents the block or blocks in the project. Divide the block into rows or units. Observe which seams will abut and know that the seam allowances in adjoining rows will be pressed in opposing directions using one of the following two methods.

Method 1
Press seam allowances in odd-numbered rows in one direction and those in even-numbered rows in the opposite direction, as shown in Illustration 3, *below left*.

Method 2
Press seam allowances in odd-numbered rows to the outside of the block and those in even-numbered rows to the inside of the block, as shown in Illustration 4, *below*.

Choose a method based on how the blocks are set together. If pieced blocks are to be alternated with plain blocks, the direction of the seam allowances on outer edges will be of little consequence. If pieced blocks are to be positioned next to other pieced blocks, the direction to press the seams on alternating blocks may need to change from the original plan.

Row 1
Row 2
Row 3

Illustration 3

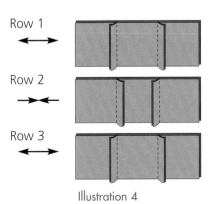

Row 1
Row 2
Row 3

Illustration 4

Photo 5O

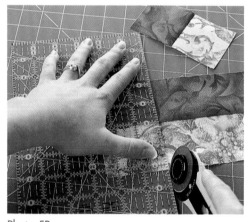

Photo 5P

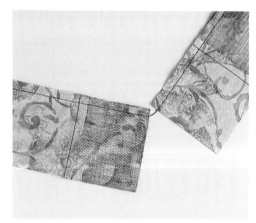

Photo 5Q

Photo 5R

STRIP PIECING

This fast machine-piecing technique involves sewing together long fabric strips that then are cut into segments, which are sewn together into blocks.

Four-Patch Strip Piecing

1. You need same-size strips of two different fabrics. With right sides together, sew together the two strips along a long edge to make a strip set. Press the seam allowance toward the darker fabric (see Photo 5O, *left*).

2. Use a ruler and rotary cutter to cut the strip set into segments that are the same width as a single strip before stitching, as shown in Photo 5P, *far left*. (For example, if the individual strips were 2½×42", cut the strip set into 2½"-wide segments.) Align the ruler's cross line with the seam line of the strip to be sure each cut is straight.

3. Rotate a segment 180°, pair it with another segment, match the seam lines, and sew together to make a Four-Patch block. Chain-piecing can be used if you wish to assemble multiple Four-Patch blocks (see Photo 5Q, *left*). For instructions, refer to Chain Piecing on *page 137.*

4. Press each Four-Patch block open, pressing the seam allowance to one side. Repeat with the remaining segments to make as many Four-Patch blocks as you need (see Photo 5R, *left*).

Photo 5S

Nine-Patch Strip Piecing

1. Start with three same-size strips each of two different fabrics. With right sides together, sew the strips together lengthwise in sets of three, alternating fabrics, to make two strip sets. Press the seam allowances toward the darker fabrics (see Photo 5S, *above*).

2. Use a ruler and rotary cutter to cut the strip sets into segments that are the same width as a single strip, as shown in Photo 5T, *above right*. (For example, if the strips were 2×42", cut the strip sets into 2"-wide segments.) Align the ruler's cross line with the seam line of the strip to be sure each cut is straight.

3. Sew together two segments from one strip set and one segment from the other strip set to make a Nine-Patch block (see Photo 5U, *right*).

4. Press the Nine-Patch block open, pressing the seam allowances away from the center strip as shown in Photo 5V, *far right*. Repeat with the remaining segments to make as many Nine-Patch blocks as needed.

Photo 5T

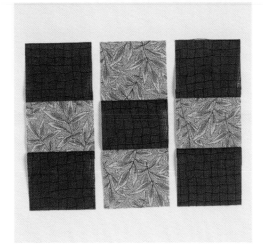

Photo 5U

Photo 5V

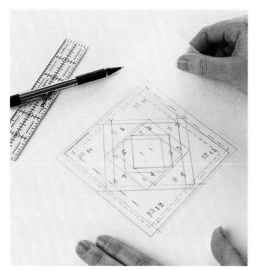

Photo 5W

Photo 5X

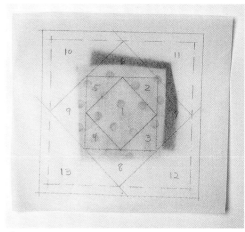

Photo 5Y

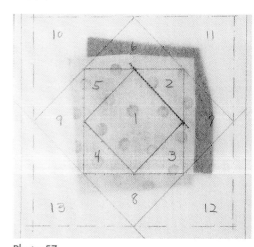

Photo 5Z

FOUNDATION PIECING

To make precisely pieced, intricate blocks, sew together fabric scraps on a paper pattern, or foundation. Some quilters find this technique to be freeing because precise cutting isn't required and grain line direction is not a worry. However, because fabric is added from the reverse (underneath) side of the paper, this method of piecing requires a different approach.

1. Trace the desired pattern onto tissue paper, including all numbers and lines to make a paper foundation (see Photo 5W, *above*).

Repeat the tracing step for each block, or make multiple templates at once: Staple the traced paper foundation onto multiple layers of tracing tissue paper. With no thread in the needle and a medium to long stitch length, sew precisely on the lines of the traced pattern (see Photo 5X, *above right*). The needle will pierce holes in the tissue layers that will exactly match the pattern lines.

2. Cut out the traced or needle-pierced paper foundations beyond the outer lines.

3. Set the machine's stitch length to a short setting (18 to 20 stitches per inch). This will perforate the foundation, making it easier to remove once the block is completed.

4. Cut fabric pieces at least ¼" larger on all sides than the areas they are to cover. Cutting generous fabric pieces will reduce the chance for assembly errors.

The fabric pieces are sewn directly to the foundation patterns. There is no need to consider grain lines when cutting fabric pieces, because the foundation patterns provide support. The fabric pieces don't have to be cut perfectly, as the excess will be trimmed away after each fabric piece is stitched to the paper foundation.

5. Layer the fabric pieces for areas 1 and 2, right sides together.

6. With the right side of the paper foundation facing up, place the layered fabric pieces under area 1, as shown in Photo 5Y, *above top*. The fabric for piece 1 should be next to the paper foundation.

To check fabric placement, pin through the foundation and the two layers of fabric at the seam line (the line where areas 1 and 2 join) and flip open fabric piece 2. It should completely cover area 2 on the paper foundation and extend at least ¼" beyond it. If it doesn't, reposition the fabric and check again.

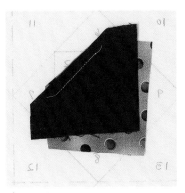
Photo 6A

Photo 6B

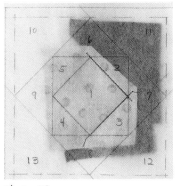
Photo 6C

Photo 6D

Photo 6E

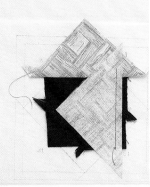
Photo 6F

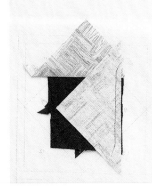
Photo 6G

Photo 6H

7. With the paper foundation still on top, stitch through the paper and the fabric on the shared line where pieces 1 and 2 join (see Photo 5Z, *opposite*). Begin stitching ¼" before the seam line and continue sewing, staying precisely on the line until ¼" after it ends.

8. Trim the seam allowance to ¼". Be careful to trim away only the fabric, not the paper foundation (see Photo 6A, *above, top*).

9. Press open piece 2 from the fabric side, as shown in Photo 6B, *top, middle left*.

10. Add piece 3, following the same procedure and joining it on the shared line between areas 2 and 3, as shown in Photo 6C, *top, middle right*. Press open from the fabric side (see Photo 6D, *top, far right*).

11. Join the remaining fabric pieces in numerical order. Trim and press after each addition, as shown in photos 6E, 6F, 6G, and 6H, *above*.

12. Trim on the outer foundation lines, leaving a ¼" seam allowance on all sides. It is not necessary to sew the seam allowance on the outer edges of the block to the foundation. Join the paper-pieced blocks together before removing the paper foundations (see Photo 6I, *right*).

Photo 6I

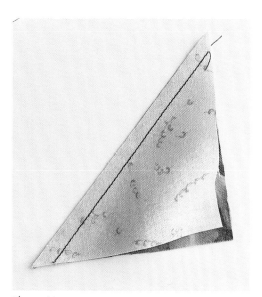

Photo 6J

Photo 6K

Photo 6L

PIECING BASIC QUILT BLOCK UNITS

Triangle-Square

The triangle-square is a basic unit used in making many quilts. Use this simply pieced unit on its own or as a part of a larger, more elaborately pieced quilt block. Four different methods of making triangle-squares are outlined here. Choose the method that works best for you.

Method 1: Using Two Same-Size Triangles of Contrasting Fabric
This method eliminates waste, but requires careful handling of the fabric to avoid distortion as the bias edges are joined. To determine what size half-square triangles to cut, add ⅞" to the desired finished size of the triangle-square. For example, for a 2" finished triangle-square, cut a 2⅞" square diagonally in half to yield two triangles.

1. With right sides together, sew the triangles together along the long edges using a ¼" seam allowance (see Photo 6J, *above, far left*).

2. Press the seam allowance toward the darker fabric to make one triangle-square, as shown in Photo 6K, *above left*.
Note: *If the seam allowance must be pressed toward the lighter fabric, trim the edge of the darker seam by ¹/₁₆" so it won't show through on the right side of the block.*

3. Trim the dog-ears of the seam allowance (the fabric that extends beyond the block edges) to make a square (see Photo 6L, *left*).

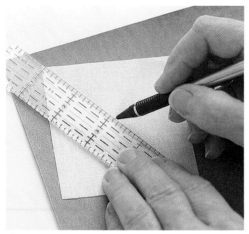

Photo 6M

Photo 6N

Photo 6O

Method 2: Using Two Same-Size Squares of Contrasting Fabrics to Make Two Triangle-Squares

This method eliminates fabric waste but requires precise marking and stitching. To determine what size squares to cut, add $7/8$" to the desired finished size of the triangle-square. For example, for a 3" finished triangle-square, cut $3\frac{7}{8}$" squares.

1. Use a quilter's pencil to mark a diagonal line on the wrong side of one square (see Photo 6M, *above*). To prevent the fabric from stretching as you draw the lines, place 220-grit sandpaper under the square.

2. Layer the marked square atop the second square. Sew the squares together with two seams, stitching ¼" on each side of the drawn line as shown in Photo 6N, *top middle*.

3. Cut the squares apart on the drawn line to make two triangle units (see Photo 6O, *top right*).

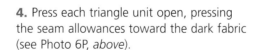

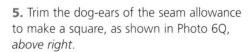

Photo 6P

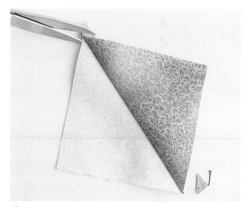

Photo 6Q

4. Press each triangle unit open, pressing the seam allowances toward the dark fabric (see Photo 6P, *above*).

5. Trim the dog-ears of the seam allowance to make a square, as shown in Photo 6Q, *above right*.

Photo 6R

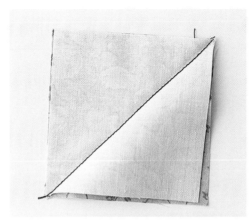

Photo 6S

Method 3: Using Two Same-Size Squares of Contrasting Fabrics to Make One Triangle-Square

With this method there is some waste as excess fabric is trimmed; however, it is not necessary to mark directly onto the fabric. To determine what size squares to cut, add ½" to the desired finished size of the triangle-square. For example, for a 3" finished triangle-square, cut 3½" squares.

1. Using an iron, press one square in half diagonally with the wrong side inside, as shown in Photo 6R, *far left*.

2. Open up the pressed square; layer it atop the second square with right sides together. Sew the squares together with one seam, stitching on the pressed crease line (see Photo 6S, *above left*).

3. Align a ruler with the ¼" mark on top of the stitched seam line. Trim away the excess fabric, as shown in Photo 6T, *left*.

4. Press the triangle unit open to make a triangle-square.

5. Trim the dog-ears of the seam allowance to make a square.

Photo 6T

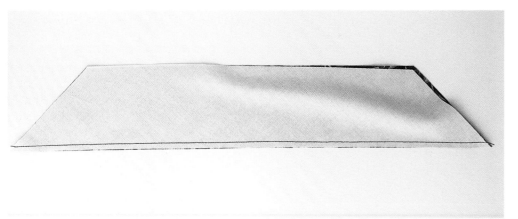

Photo 6U

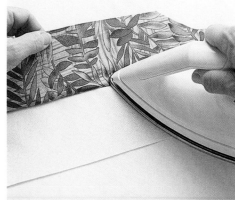

Photo 6V

Method 4: Using Two Bias Strips of Contrasting Fabrics to Make Multiple Triangle-Squares

1. Cut bias strips 1" wider than the desired finished size of the triangle-squares.

2. With right sides together and ends matching, join two contrasting strips along the long edges with a ¼" seam allowance (see Photo 6U, *above*). To get the most cuts from pieced bias strips, sew the strips together with a V at one end.

3. Press the seam allowance toward the darker fabric, as shown in Photo 6V, *above right*.

4. Using a square ruler marked with a 6" grid and a rotary cutter, cut squares ½" larger than the desired finished size of the triangle-squares (see Photo 6W, *right*). For example, for a 2½" finished triangle-square, cut the triangle-square at 3". Keep the diagonal line of the gridded square and the seam line of the sewn strips aligned.

Photo 6W

Flying Geese
Method 1: Using a Rectangle of One Fabric and Two Squares of a Contrasting Fabric

To determine what size rectangle to cut, add ½" to the finished height and width of the Flying Geese unit. Cut two squares the same size as the height of the cut rectangle. For example, for a 1½×3" finished Flying Geese unit, cut a 2×3½" rectangle and two 2" squares.

1. Use a quilter's pencil to mark a diagonal line on the wrong side of each square (see Photo 6X, *left*). To prevent the fabric from stretching as you draw the lines, place 220-grit sandpaper under the square. *Note: Instead of drawing a line, press the squares in half diagonally as described in Method 3 of Triangle-Squares on page 152.*

2. With right sides together, align a marked square with one end of a rectangle; note the placement of the marked diagonal line. Stitch on the marked line (see Photo 6Y, *below, far left*).

3. Trim the seam allowance to ¼", as shown in Photo 6Z, *below left*.

4. Press the attached triangle open, as shown in Photo 7A, *below*.

5. Align a second marked square with the opposite end of the rectangle, again noting the placement of the marked diagonal line; pin in place (see Photo 7B, *bottom, far left*). Stitch on the marked line; trim as before.

6. Press the attached triangle open to make a Flying Geese unit as shown in Photo 7C, *bottom left*.

Photo 6X

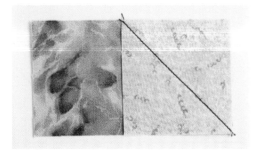

Photo 6Y

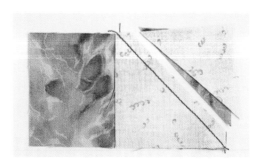

Photo 6Z

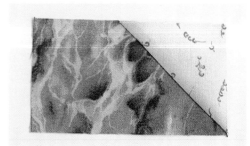

Photo 7A

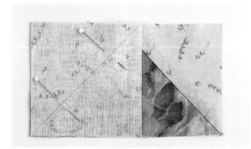

Photo 7B

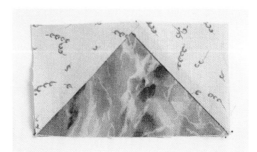

Photo 7C

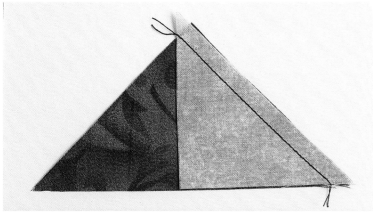

Photo 7D

Photo 7E

Photo 7F

Photo 7G

Method 2: Using One Large Triangle of One Fabric and Two Small Triangles of a Contrasting Fabric

To determine what size of quarter-square triangle to cut for the center of the Flying Geese unit, add 1¼" to the desired finished width of the Flying Geese unit. To determine what size half-square triangles to cut for the small triangles, add ⅞" to the desired finished height of the Flying Geese unit. For example, for a 1½×3" finished Flying Geese unit, cut a 4¼" square diagonally twice in an X to yield four large triangles. Cut a 2⅜" square, cutting it diagonally in half to yield two small triangles.

1. With right sides together, sew a small triangle to a short edge of the large triangle using a ¼" seam allowance (see Photo 7D, *top left*).
Note: *The corners of the small triangle will extend ¼" beyond each end of the large triangle.*

2. Press the attached small triangle open, pressing the seam allowance toward the small triangle (see Photo 7E, *top right*).

3. In the same manner, join the remaining small triangle to the large triangle as shown in Photo 7F, *above left*.

4. Press the small triangle open to make a Flying Geese unit (see Photo 7G, *above right*).

5. Trim fabric dog-ears that extend beyond the raw edges (see *page 150*).

155

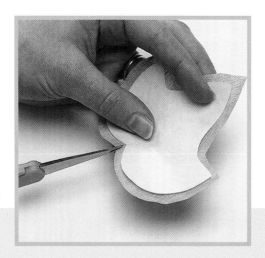
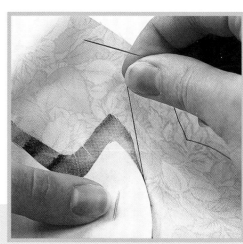

Chapter 6

APPLIQUÉ
TECHNIQUES

Appliqué offers unlimited quilt design options, with

styles ranging from simple to intricate and from

primitive to elegant.

1855 QUAKER WEDDING QUILT

In the middle of the 19th century, some quilters reserved their best work for a showy appliquéd bedcover done in red, green, and gold with touches of blue and pink. During this time, balanced designs were important, leading quilters to use blocks that could be evenly divided. The "Honey Bee" variation shown here has groups of four blocks, and each block can be divided into four segments. Around the quilt top's borders are matching sets of arcs with flowers. The buds and fleurs-de-lis (lilies) in the border are carefully arranged in alternating colors. In one corner of the quilt, the makers have quilted a hand with a heart in its palm; there are two sets of initials inside the heart, suggesting that this was a wedding gift. Also in the corner, the quilters added their initials and the year, a common practice in quilts of yesteryear.

Appliqué *Techniques*

The time-honored tradition of appliqué—adding fabric motifs to a fabric foundation—allows freedom in design not always available with piecing. Numerous appliqué methods have been developed, giving quiltmakers a wide variety of choices in finished appearance.

TEMPLATES

An appliqué template is a pattern used to trace the appliqué shape onto fabric. The template's material depends on how often the template will be used. Make sure that the template will hold up to the wear that it receives from multiple tracings without deteriorating at the edges. A sturdy, durable material such as template plastic, available at quilt and crafts supply stores, is suitable

Photo 1A

for making permanent templates for scissors-cut appliqué pieces. (For information on cutting templates for piecing, see Chapter 4—Cutting Techniques.)

Making Appliqué Templates

1. For most appliqué techniques, the templates should be the exact size of the finished pieces with no seam allowances (the allowances are added when the pieces are cut). Trace the patterns onto template plastic using a permanent marker (see Photo 1A, *left*). Use a ruler for any straight lines.

2. Mark each appliqué template with its letter designation, grain line (if indicated), block name, and appliqué sequence order. (See Stitching Sequence, page 160, for more information.) Mark an X on edges that do not need to be turned under and transfer the X's to the fabric shapes when you trace around the templates, as shown in Photo 1B, *below left*.

3. Cut out each template, then verify the accuracy of each piece by placing it over its printed pattern (see Photo 1C, *below*).

Photo 1B

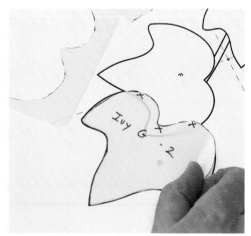

Photo 1C

159

Using Appliqué Templates

1. Choose a marking tool to trace around the templates on fabric. As shown in Photo 1D, *below right*, a pencil works well on light-color fabric; a white, silver, or yellow dressmaker's pencil is a good choice on dark-color fabric. (See Chapter 1—Tools and Materials for complete information on marking tools.)

Note: Keep the pencil point sharp to ensure accuracy. Do not use a ballpoint or ink pen; it may bleed when washed. Test all marking tools on a fabric scrap before using them.

⤳Creative Tip

To appliqué with tissue lamé, use sewable Heat 'n Bond (the lower heat requirement is tolerated by the fabric), a ball-point needle, and Fray Check to stop raveling.

—Christie, Sales Associate

2. Place templates on the fabric, positioning them at least ½" apart. Whether the templates are placed faceup or facedown on the fabric's right or wrong side depends on the appliqué method used.

3. Trace around each template (see Photo 1E, *below bottom*). The drawn lines represent the sewing lines. The appliqué technique will dictate how much, if any, seam allowance to leave when cutting the shape out of the fabric.

Photo 1D

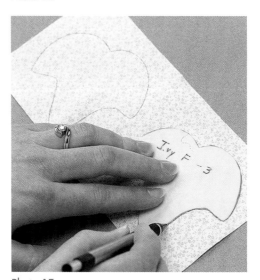

Photo 1E

4. Cut out the appliqué shapes, including seam allowances necessary for the chosen appliqué method.

Stitching Sequence

The edges of appliqué pieces that will be covered by other pieces do not need to be turned under before they are appliquéd. Prepare all of the appliqué pieces at once, and plan for overlaps. This will save stitching time and considerable bulk in the finished project.

If the pattern does not indicate a numerical stitching sequence, observe which piece is closest to the foundation fabric and farthest from you (see Photo 1F, *below*). Appliqué that piece to the foundation first. Working from that bottom layer to the top, appliqué the rest of the pieces to the foundation.

PREPARING APPLIQUÉ PIECES

Prepare the appliqué pieces according to the needs of the chosen appliqué method. Preparation options include basting, freezer paper, double appliqué, and fusible web. Use the following information to help determine which method is best for each appliqué project.

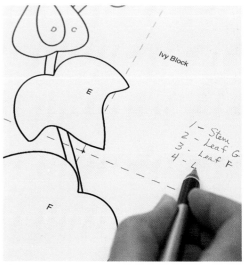

Photo 1F

Basting Method

With this method, a reusable template, marking tool, and thread are used to prepare appliqué pieces for hand or machine appliqué.

1. Place the templates on the right side of the fabric, positioning them at least ½" apart; trace (see Photo 1G, *right*).

2. Cut out the appliqué shapes, adding a ³⁄₁₆" seam allowance to all edges. Clip inside curves and points to within a thread of the marked lines, making clips closer together in the curved areas, as shown in Photo 1H, *far right*). Try to make the clips on the bias grain of the seam allowance, which means they will be often diagonal, rather than perpendicular, lines. This directional clipping prevents fabric from raveling while the edges are being worked. *Note: Some hand quilters who use the needle-turn appliqué method choose to stop their appliqué preparation with this step (for more information, see Needle-Turn Appliqué on page 181).*

3. Working from the right side of the appliqué piece and beginning at an inner point, use a contrasting color thread to baste the seam allowance under following the marked lines. For easier removal of the thread later, begin and end your basting thread on the right side of appliqué piece, as shown in Photo 1I, *right*).

4. For a sharp outer point, fold the fabric straight over the point (see Photo 1J, *above, far right*).

5. Then fold in an adjacent seam allowance, overlapping the folded point (see Photo 1K, *right*). Baste in place.

6. At the outer point, fold over the remaining adjacent seam allowance and continue basting around the shape (see Photo 1L, *far right*).

Photo 1G

Photo 1H

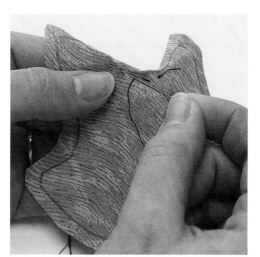
Photo 1I

Photo 1J

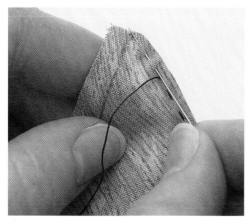
Photo 1K

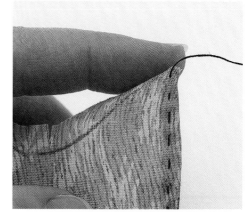
Photo 1L

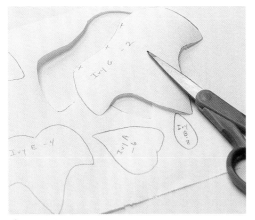

Photo 1M

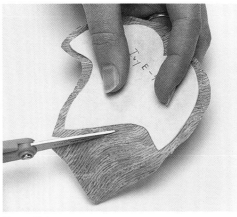

Photo 1N

Photo 1O

Photo 1P

Photo 1Q

Freezer-Paper Method 1

With this method, freezer-paper templates are used to hold the seam allowances of the appliqué pieces in place. This technique may be used to prepare pieces for hand or machine appliqué.

1. Trace the appliqué patterns on the dull side of the freezer paper. Cut out the shapes on the traced lines to make freezer-paper templates (see Photo 1M, *far left*).

2. Place the freezer-paper templates dull side up on the right side of the fabric. While holding the freezer paper in place, cut the shapes from fabric, adding a ³⁄₁₆" seam allowance to all edges, as shown in Photo 1N, *above left*.

3. Turn the freezer-paper templates shiny side up and place on the wrong side of the appliqué shape. Clip the inside curves or points on the appliqué shapes (see Photo 1O, *far left*). When clipping inside curves, clip halfway through the seam allowances, as shown in Photo 1P, *left*. Try to make the clips on the bias grain of the seam allowance, which means the clips often will be diagonal, rather than perpendicular, lines. This directional clipping prevents fabric from raveling while the edges are being worked.

4. Beginning at an inner point of the appliqué shape, use the tip of a hot, dry iron to push the seam allowance over the edge of the freezer paper. The seam allowance will adhere to the shiny side of the freezer paper (see Photo 1Q, *left*). ***Note:*** *Do not touch the iron soleplate to the freezer paper past the edge of the turned fabric.*

5. Continue working around the appliqué shape, turning one small area at a time and pressing the seam allowance up and over the freezer paper, as shown in Photo 1R, *right*. Make certain the appliqué fabric is pressed taut against the freezer-paper template. Small pleats in the fabric may appear around outer curves. If there is too much bulk in a seam allowance, make small V clips around outer curves to ease the fabric around the edge.

6. For a sharp outer point, fold the fabric straight over the point of the freezer-paper template; press to the freezer paper (see Photo 1S, *far right*).

7. With the tip of the iron, push an adjacent seam allowance over the edge of the freezer paper (see Photo 1T, *right*).

8. Repeat with the remaining adjacent seam allowance, pushing the seam allowance taut to ensure a sharp point (see Photo 1U, *far right*).

9. After all edges are pressed, let the appliqué shape cool, then either remove the freezer-paper template before proceeding with the desired hand- or machine-appliqué technique or leave in to stitch.

Removing a freezer-paper template after an appliqué shape has been stitched in place can be done in a couple of ways:
- Stitch the appliquéd shape to the foundation, leaving a small opening to pull out the template. Use the tip of the needle to loosen the freezer-paper template. Pull the template out through the opening and stitch the opening closed.
- Stitch the entire appliqué shape in place. From the wrong side, carefully snip through the appliqué foundation only. Remove the template through the opening, then stitch the opening closed.

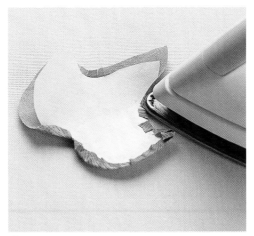
Photo 1R

Photo 1S

Photo 1T

Photo 1U

Creative Tip

Use leftover fabric and fusible scraps to make notecards, gift bags, t-shirt patches, and gift tags. Just fuse the fusible web to the wrong side of the fabric, cut out a motif or shape, and fuse to cardstock or clothing.

—BONNIE, SALES ASSOCIATE

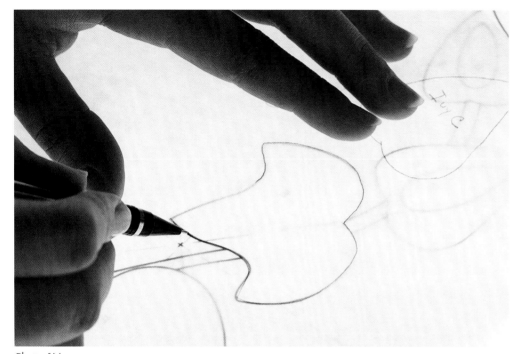

Photo 1V

Freezer-Paper Method 2

With this technique, entire freezer-paper templates are pressed to the appliqué foundation, shiny side down. The freezer paper is removed before the appliqué is sewn in place. This technique may be used to prepare pieces for hand or machine appliqué.

1. Trace a reverse image of the appliqué patterns on the dull side of the freezer paper (see Photo 1V, *left*). Cut out the shapes on the traced lines to make freezer-paper templates.
Note: To create a reverse image, tape the appliqué pattern facedown on a light box or sunny window.

2. Place the appliqué fabric wrong side up on a pressing surface (see Photo 1W, *below, far left*). With a dry iron on a cotton setting, press a freezer-paper shape, shiny side down, to the appliqué fabric. Leave the iron on the paper for a few seconds. Lift the iron to check that the template is completely adhered to the fabric. If the template is not completely adhered, press again.

3. Cut out the appliqué shape, adding a ³⁄₁₆" seam allowance to all edges. Clip inside curves or points on the appliqué shape, as shown in photos 1X and 1Y, *left* and *bottom, far left*. When clipping inside

Photo 1W

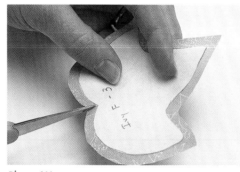

Photo 1X

Photo 1Y

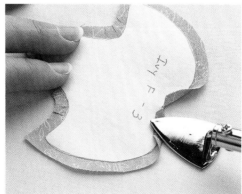

Photo 1Z

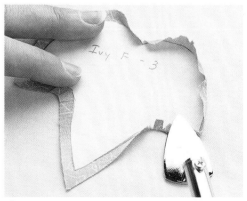

Photo 2A

Photo 2B

Photo 2C

curves, clip halfway through the seam allowance. Try to make the clips on the bias grain of the seam allowance, which means clips often will be on diagonal, rather than perpendicular, lines. This directional clipping prevents fabric from raveling while the edges are being worked.

4. Beginning at one inner point of an appliqué shape, use the tip of a dry, hot iron to push the seam allowance over the edge of the freezer paper to create a sharp edge (see Photo 1Z, *opposite*).
***Note:** The seam allowance will not adhere to the dull side of the freezer paper.*

5. Continue working around the appliqué shape, turning one small area at a time and pressing the seam allowance up and over the freezer paper, as shown in Photo 2A, *opposite*. Make certain the appliqué fabric is pressed taut against the edges of the freezer-paper template.

Small pleats in the fabric may appear around outer curves. If there is too much bulk in a seam allowance, make small V clips around outer curves to ease the fabric around the edge.

6. For a sharp outer point, fold the fabric straight over the point of the freezer-paper template; press.

7. With the tip of the iron, push an adjacent seam allowance over the edge of the freezer paper (see Photo 2B, *above left*). Repeat with the remaining adjacent seam allowance, pushing the seam allowance taut to ensure a sharp point.

8. After all edges are pressed, let the appliqué shape cool. Then remove the freezer-paper template, as shown in Photo 2C, *above*.

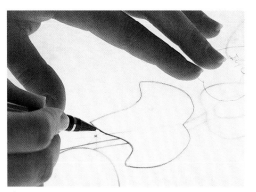
Photo 2D

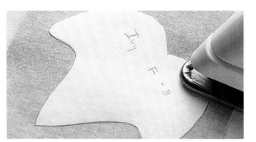
Photo 2E

Freezer-Paper Method 3

This method involves pressing entire freezer-paper templates, shiny side down, to the appliqué fabric. A water-soluble glue stick is used to hold the seam allowances in place. The freezer paper is not removed until after the appliqué is sewn in place. This technique may be used to prepare pieces for hand or machine appliqué.

1. Trace a reverse image of the appliqué patterns onto the dull side of the freezer paper, as shown in Photo 2D, *left*. Cut out the shapes on the traced lines to make freezer-paper templates.

2. Place the appliqué fabric wrong side up on a pressing surface. With a dry iron on a cotton setting, press a freezer-paper template, shiny side down, to the appliqué fabric (see Photo 2E, *left*). Leave the iron on

the paper for a few seconds. Lift the iron to check that the template is completely adhered to the fabric. If the template is not completely adhered, press again.

3. Cut out the appliqué shape, adding a ³⁄₁₆" seam allowance to all edges. Clip inside curves or points on the appliqué shape (see Photo 2F, *below, far left*). To make a sharp edge at a deep inside point, clip the seam allowance to within one thread of the freezer-paper template (see Photo 2G, *below left*). When clipping inside curves, clip halfway through the seam allowance. Try to make the clips on the bias grain of the seam allowance, which means the clips often will be diagonal, rather than perpendicular, lines. This directional clipping prevents fabric from raveling while the edges are being worked.

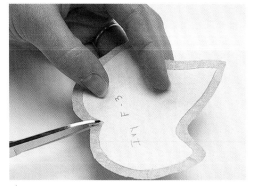
Photo 2F

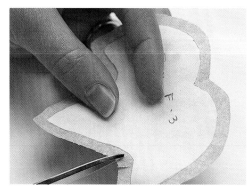
Photo 2G

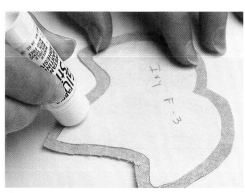
Photo 2H

Photo 2I

Photo 2J

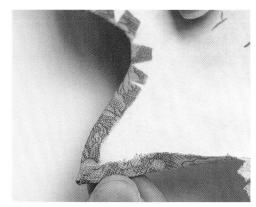
Photo 2K

4. Using a water-soluble glue stick, apply glue to the exposed seam allowance and to the outer edge of the freezer-paper template (see Photo 2H, *opposite*).

5. At a deep inside point, use the tip of your thumb to press the seam allowance on both sides of the clip down against the freezer-paper template, as shown in Photo 2I, *opposite*.
Note: *Small pleats in the fabric may appear around outer curves. If there is too much bulk in the seam allowance, make small V clips around outer curves to ease the fabric around the edge.*

6. Using the tip of your thumb and index finger, continue working the seam allowance over the edge by pinching the fabric (see Photo 2J, *opposite*). Work in small areas at a time.

7. To make a sharp outer point, fold and glue the fabric point straight over the point of the freezer-paper template. Push one adjacent edge of the seam allowance over the edge of the freezer paper; glue. Repeat with the remaining adjacent seam allowance as shown in Photo 2K, *opposite*.

8. The freezer-paper template is not removed until after the appliqué is stitched in place (see step 9 on *page 163* for information on removing templates after an appliqué has been sewn in place).

Freezer-Paper Method 4
This technique involves pressing the shiny side of the freezer-paper templates to the right side of the appliqué fabric. The seam allowances are not turned under. This technique may be used to prepare pieces for needle-turn appliqué (see *page 181*).

1. Trace finished-size appliqué patterns onto the dull side of the freezer paper (see Photo 2L, *right*). Cut out the shapes on the traced lines to make freezer-paper templates.

2. Place the appliqué fabric right side up on a pressing surface. With a dry iron on a cotton setting, press a freezer-paper template, shiny side down, to the appliqué fabric (see Photo 2M, *right*). Leave the iron on the paper for a few seconds. Lift the iron to check that the template is completely adhered to the fabric. If the template is not completely adhered, press again.

3. Cut out the appliqué shape, adding a ³⁄₁₆" seam allowance to all edges. Clip inside curves or points on the appliqué shape (see Photo 2N, *right*). When clipping inside curves, clip halfway through the seam allowance. Try to make the clips on the bias grain of the seam allowance, which means the clips often will be diagonal, rather than perpendicular, lines. This directional clipping prevents fabric from raveling while the edges are being worked.

4. Do not remove the template until the appliqué piece is stitched in place.

Photo 2L

Photo 2M

Photo 2N

Photo 2O

Double-Appliqué Method

This method eases the challenge of turning under seam allowances by facing the appliqué pieces with sheer, featherweight, nonfusible, nonwoven interfacing. This technique may be used to prepare pieces for hand or machine appliqué.

1. Place a rigid template wrong side up on the wrong side of the appliqué fabric; trace (see Photo 2O, *left*). The traced line is the stitching line.

2. With right sides together, layer the appliqué fabric with a like-size piece of sheer, featherweight, nonfusible, nonwoven interfacing (see Photo 2P, *below left*).

3. Sew the pieces together, stitching on the marked line. Cut out the appliqué shape, adding a ³⁄₁₆" seam allowance to all edges, as shown in Photo 2Q, *opposite*.

4. Trim the interfacing seam allowance slightly smaller than the appliqué fabric. This will enable the seam allowance to roll slightly to the back side of the appliqué once it is turned. Clip at the inner curves and points (see Photo 2R, *opposite*).

5. Clip a small slit in the center of the interfacing, being careful not to cut through the appliqué fabric (see Photo 2S, *opposite*).

6. Turn the appliqué right side out through the slit, as shown in Photo 2T, *opposite*.

7. Press the appliqué piece from the right side (see Photo 2U, *opposite*).

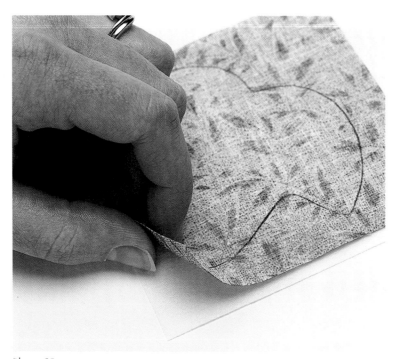

Photo 2P

Photo 2Q

Photo 2R

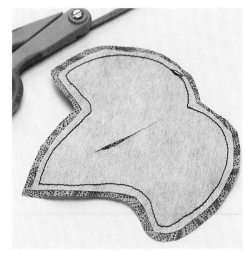

Photo 2S

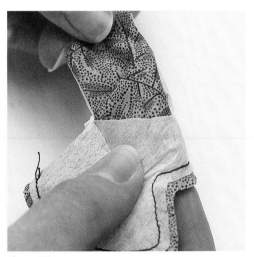

Photo 2T

Photo 2U

✃Creative Tip

To store fusible webbing and eliminate creasing, keep it rolled in an

aluminum foil box with the blade removed.

—CHRISTIE, SALES ASSOCIATE

Fusible Web Method

This method eliminates the need to turn under any seam allowances. Choose a lightweight, paper-backed fusible web that can be stitched through unless the appliqué edges will be left unfinished. If the appliqué edges will not be sewn in place, use a heavyweight, no-sew fusible web. (See Chapter 1—Tools and Materials for more information on fusible web.) This technique is commonly used for machine appliqué, but also can be used for hand appliqué.

1. Position the fusible web with the paper side up over the appliqué patterns; place on light box. Use a pencil to trace each pattern the specified number of times (see Photo 2V, *below left*). If you are tracing multiple pieces at one time, leave at least ½" between tracings.

Note: If the appliqué pattern is not designed especially for fusible web, create a mirror image of the pattern before tracing it. Otherwise the appliqués will be reversed when they are cut from fabric. To create a reverse image, tape the appliqué pattern facedown on a light box or sunny window and trace.

Cut out the traced appliqué patterns roughly ¼" outside the traced lines. Do not cut directly on the traced lines.

2. When working with multiple appliqué layers or to reduce the stiffness of the finished project, cut away the center of the fusible web shapes. To do this, cut ¼" inside the traced lines and discard the centers (see Photo 2W, *left*).

3. Place the fusible web shapes paper side up on the back of the designated appliqué fabrics. Press in place following the manufacturer's instructions (see Photo 2X, *below left*). Do not slide the iron, but pick it up to move it from one area to the next. Let the appliqué shapes cool.

4. Cut out the fabric shapes on the drawn lines, as shown in Photo 2Y, *below*. Peel off the paper backings.

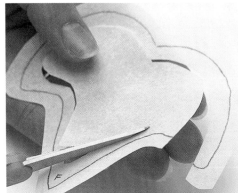

Photo 2V

Photo 2W

Photo 2X

Photo 2Y

Making and Applying Bias Stems and Vines

Fabric strips for curved appliqué stems and vines should be cut on the bias so they will be flexible enough to bend without wrinkles or puckers. (For information on cutting bias strips, see Chapter 4—Cutting Techniques.)

Quick Method 1

1. Cut a bias strip two times the desired finished width plus ½", as shown in photos 2Z and 3A, *right and far right*. For example, for a 1"-wide finished stem, cut a 2½"-wide bias strip.
Note: Handle strips carefully to avoid stretching.

2. Fold the bias strip in half lengthwise with the wrong side inside and press to make an appliqué stem (see Photo 3B, *below right*).

3. Trace the stem placement line on the appliqué foundation fabric as a seam guide (see Photo 3C, *far right*).

4. Pin the appliqué stem to the appliqué foundation with the raw edge next to the marked seam guide. Sew the stem in place by machine or hand using a ¼" seam allowance (see Photo 3D, *below*).

5. Fold the stem over the stitching line, covering the seam allowance and marked seam guide, as shown in Photo 3E, *below, bottom*. Trim the seam allowance if necessary. Press in place.

6. Secure the folded stem edge to the appliqué foundation using a machine blind hem stitch or slip-stitching by hand (see Photo 3F, *below, bottom*).

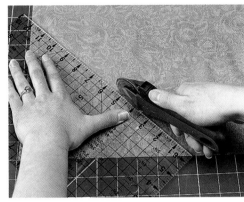
Photo 2Z

Photo 3A

Photo 3B

Photo 3C

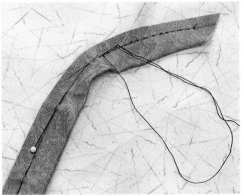
Photo 3D

Photo 3E

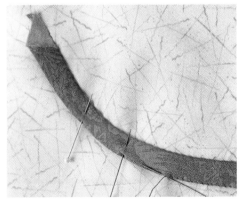
Photo 3F

Quick Method 2

1. Cut a bias strip three times the desired finished width (see Photo 3G, *below right*). For example, for a ¾"-wide finished stem, cut a 2¼"-wide bias strip.
Note: *Handle strips carefully to avoid stretching.*

2. Fold the bias strip in thirds lengthwise with wrong side inside. The first fold should be a thread short of meeting the second fold.

3. Trace the stem placement line on the appliqué foundation fabric as a seam guide.

4. Unfold the bias strip, and place it on the appliqué foundation with the raw edge next to the marked seam line; machine- or hand-sew on the first fold line (see Photo 3H, *below*).

5. Fold the bias strip over the stitching line, covering the seam allowance and marked seam guide. Trim the seam allowance if necessary. Press in place (see Photo 3I, *below right*).

6. Secure the second folded stem edge to the appliqué foundation using a machine blind hem stitch or slip-stitching by hand, as shown in Photo 3J, *below, far right*.

Photo 3G

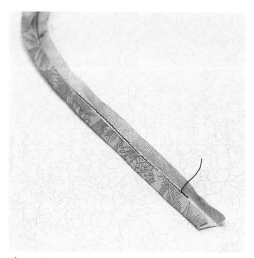

Photo 3H

Photo 3I

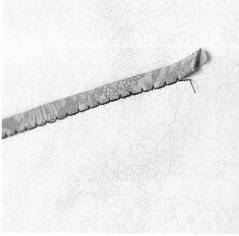

Photo 3J

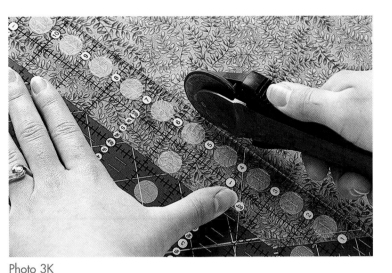
Photo 3K

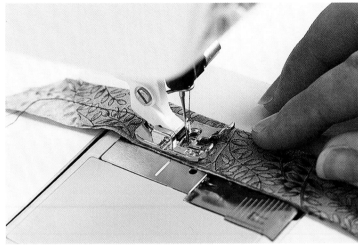
Photo 3L

Bias Bar Method

With this method, metal or heat-resistant plastic bias bars, purchased in a size to match the desired finished width of the bias stem, are used. (For more information on bias bars, see Chapter 1—Tools and Materials.) If instructions for strip width and seam allowance are provided with the bias bars, refer to them. If not, refer to the following.

1. Cut a bias strip twice the desired finished width plus ¾" (see Photo 3K, *above*). For example, for a ½"-wide finished bias stem, cut a 1¾"-wide bias strip. Handle the strip's edges carefully to prevent stretching. Fold the strip in half lengthwise with the wrong side together; lightly press.

2. Stitch the length of the strip with the folded edge on the machine seam guide (to the right of the presser foot), the raw edges to the left, and a seam allowance equivalent to the desired finished width (see Photo 3L, *top, far right*). For example, for a ½"-wide finished bias stem, stitch ½" away from the folded edge.

Photo 3M

3. Trim away the seam allowance, leaving only enough fabric to hold the seam intact (about ¹⁄₁₆"), (see Photo 3M, *above*.)

4. Slide the bias bar into the stem with the seam allowance centered on a flat side of the bar. Press the seam allowance to one side so that neither the seam nor the seam allowance is visible along the edges (see Photo 3N, *above right*).

5. Remove the bar from the stem, and press the stem again (see Photo 3O, *above right*).

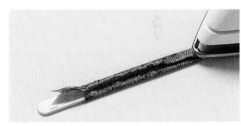
Photo 3N

Photo 3O

6. Trace the stem placement line on the appliqué foundation fabric as a seam guide.

7. Pin the bias stem to the appliqué foundation, covering the marked line, and secure the stem in place using a machine blind hem stitch or slip-stitching by hand.

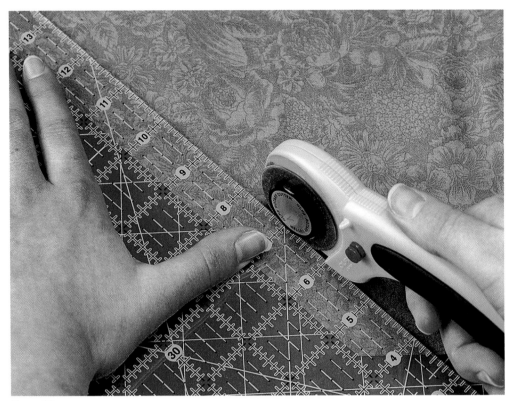

Photo 3P

Finger-Pressing Method

1. Cut a bias strip to the desired finished width plus ½" (see Photo 3P, *left*). For example, to make a ¼"-wide finished bias stem, cut a ¾"-wide bias strip. Handle the strip's edges carefully to prevent stretching.

2. Finger-press under ¼" along both long edges, as shown in Photo 3Q, *below*.

3. Pin the bias stem to the appliqué foundation and secure the stem in place using a machine blind hem stitch or slip-stitching by hand (see Photo 3R, *below bottom*).

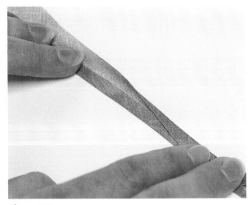

Photo 3Q

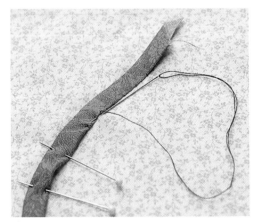

Photo 3R

✿Creative Tip

When machine or hand sewing, wet the eye of the needle, not the thread. It works like a magnet and makes threading much easier.

—LYNNE, SALES ASSOCIATE

Photo 3S

Photo 3T

Fusible Web Method

Using lightweight fusible web eliminates the need to turn under a strip's seam allowances. It is often the preferred method for making stems when the appliqués also are prepared with fusible web.

1. Cut a piece of lightweight fusible web the finished length of the desired stems by the width of a stem times the number of stems desired. For example, to make 13 stems that are each ¼" wide and 10" long, cut a piece of fusible web 3½×10". The extra ¼" allows for making the first cut on the edge of the fusible web.

Cut a bias edge on the appliqué fabric. Following the manufacturer's directions, press the fusible web piece to the wrong side of the appliqué fabric along the bias edge (see Photo 3S, *above*).

2. Trim the fabric to the edge of the fusible web. Then cut bias strips the desired finished widths and lengths of the appliqué stems (see Photo 3T, *above right*).

3. Trace the stem placement line on the appliqué foundation fabric as a guide.

4. Peel off the paper backings. Following the manufacturer's directions, press the stems in place on the appliqué foundation, covering the marked line (see Photo 3U, *right*). Sew the bias stems to the appliqué foundation using a machine blind hem stitch or slip-stitching by hand.

Photo 3U

Photo 3V

Photo 3W

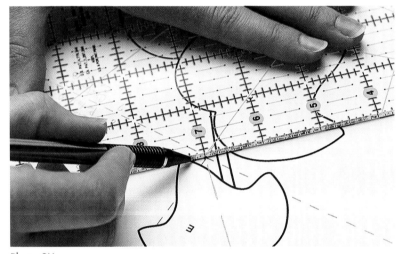

Photo 3X

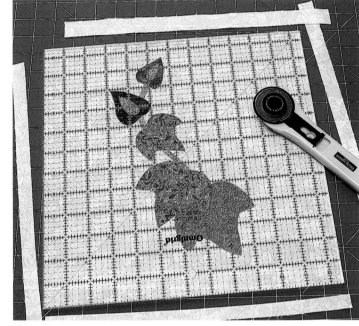

Photo 3Y

POSITIONING THE APPLIQUÉ PIECES

There are many ways to position pieces for appliqué. Some require more preparation than others. Experiment with different positioning methods to select the one that's best for you.

Folded Foundation Method

1. Cut the appliqué foundation fabric larger than the desired finished size to allow for any take-up in the fabric that might occur during the appliqué process. For example, for a 12" finished square, cut a 14"-square appliqué foundation. When the appliqué is complete, the foundation will be trimmed to 12½" square. (The extra ¼" on each side will be used for seam allowances when assembling the quilt top.)

2. Fold the square appliqué foundation in half vertically and horizontally to find the center. Lightly finger-press to create positioning guides for the appliqué pieces (see Photo 3V, *top, far left*).

3. Then fold the square appliqué foundation diagonally in both directions and lightly finger-press to make additional positioning guidelines (see Photo 3W, *top left*).

4. Draw corresponding vertical, horizontal, and diagonal positioning guidelines on the full-size appliqué pattern if they are not already marked (see Photo 3X, *above left*).

5. Prepare the appliqué pieces using the desired method. (See Preparing Appliqué Pieces beginning on *page 160*.) Referring to the appliqué pattern, pin and stitch the appliqué pieces to the foundation using the desired method; work from the bottom layer up.

6. After the appliqué is complete, trim the appliqué foundation to the desired finished size plus seam allowances (see Photo 3Y, *above*).

Marked Foundation Method

1. Cut the appliqué foundation fabric larger than the desired finished size to allow for any take-up in the fabric that might occur during the appliqué process. For example, for a 12" finished square, cut a 14"-square appliqué foundation. When the appliqué is complete, the foundation square will be trimmed to 12½" square. (The extra ¼" on each side will be used for seam allowances when assembling the quilt top.)

2. Using a faint pencil line and the full-size appliqué pattern, trace the design onto the appliqué foundation fabric (see Photo 3Z, *right*). To avoid having markings show after the appliqué is complete, lightly mark just inside the design lines and just at critical points (for example, where two lines intersect or at the tips of leaves).

3. Prepare the appliqué pieces using the desired method. (See Preparing Appliqué Pieces beginning on *page 160.*) Referring to the appliqué pattern, pin and stitch the appliqué pieces to the foundation using the desired method; work from the bottom layer up.

4. After the appliqué is complete, trim the appliqué foundation to the desired size plus seam allowances.

Light Box Method

1. Cut the appliqué foundation fabric larger than the desired finished size to allow for any take-up in the fabric that might occur during the appliqué process. For example, for a 12" finished square, cut a 14"-square appliqué foundation. When the appliqué is complete, the foundation square will be trimmed to 12½" square. (The extra ¼" on each side will be used for seam allowances when assembling the quilt top.)

Photo 3Z

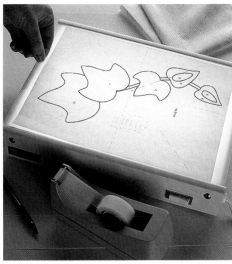

Photo 4A

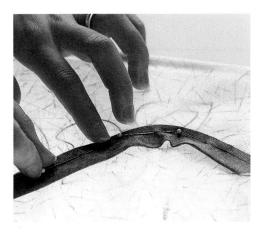

Photo 4B

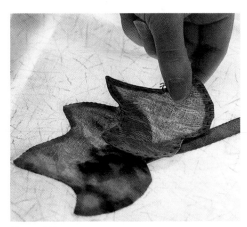

Photo 4C

2. Place the full-size appliqué pattern on a light box and secure it with tape. Center the appliqué foundation fabric atop the appliqué pattern (see Photo 4A, *top right*).

3. Prepare the appliqué pieces using the desired method. (See Preparing Appliqué Pieces beginning on *page 160.*) Return to the light box and pin the bottom layer of appliqué pieces in place on the appliqué foundation (see Photo 4B, *above*). Stitch the appliqué pieces to the foundation using the desired method.

4. After stitching the bottom layer of appliqué pieces, return the appliqué foundation to the light box. Match the next layer of appliqué pieces with the pattern, pin, and stitch (see Photo 4C, *above*). Continue in this manner until all appliqué pieces are stitched to the foundation.

5. Trim the appliqué foundation to the desired size plus seam allowances.

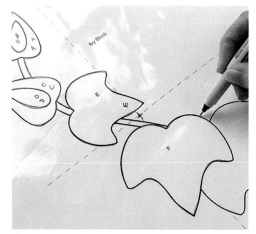

Photo 4D

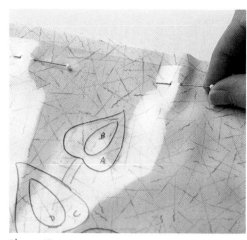

Photo 4E

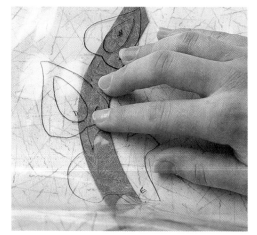

Photo 4F

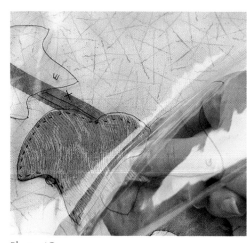

Photo 4G

Overlay Method

1. Cut the appliqué foundation fabric larger than the desired finished size to allow for any take-up in the fabric that might occur during the appliqué process. For example, for a 12" finished square, cut a 14"-square appliqué foundation. When the appliqué is complete, the foundation square will be trimmed to 12½" square. (The extra ¼" on each side will be used for seam allowances when assembling the quilt top.)

2. Position clear upholstery vinyl (or other clear flexible plastic) over the full-size appliqué pattern and precisely trace the design with a permanent marker (see Photo 4D, *far left*).

3. Center the vinyl overlay on the appliqué foundation fabric. Pin the top of the overlay to the foundation, as shown in Photo 4E, *above left*.

4. Prepare the appliqué pieces using the desired method. (See Preparing Appliqué Pieces beginning on *page 160*.) Once the appliqué pieces have been prepared, slide the bottom-most appliqué piece right side up between the appliqué foundation and the overlay (see Photo 4F, *far left*). When the piece is in place beneath its corresponding position on the vinyl overlay, remove the overlay and pin the appliqué piece to the foundation. Stitch the appliqué to the foundation using the desired method.

5. Pin the vinyl overlay on the foundation and position the next appliqué piece in the stitching sequence (see Photo 4G, *above left*). Pin and stitch it to the foundation as before. Continue adding appliqué pieces in this manner until all appliqués have been stitched in place.

6. Trim the appliqué foundation to the desired size plus seam allowances.

Holding Appliqué Pieces in Position

Once the appliqués and foundations have been prepared for stitching, the appliqué pieces can be held in place with pins, basting threads, spray adhesive, fusible web, or a fabric glue stick. The number of appliqué layers you are working with may influence your choice.

Pins

Use as many straight pins as needed to hold each appliqué piece in place on the appliqué foundation for both machine and hand appliqué (see Photo 4H, *right*). Pins are generally used to hold no more than two layers at a time and are pushed through from the top. Some hand appliquérs like to place pins on the back side of the work to prevent catching thread in pins as they work. Remove the pins as you stitch.

Basting

Sewing long stitches about ¼" from the turned-under edges is another way to secure prepared appliqué pieces to a foundation for both machine and hand appliqué. Begin and end the basting stitches on the right side of the appliqué for easier removal (see Photo 4I, *right*). Remove basting stitches when the entire appliqué work is complete or, if the basting threads impede stitching progress, remove them as you go.

Basting is the preferred method of quilters who wish to hold multiple appliqué layers in position at once before permanently stitching them in place.

Fabric Basting Spray

When lightly sprayed on the wrong side of appliqué pieces, this adhesive usually allows appliqué pieces to be positioned and repositioned (see Photo 4J, *right*). It can hold appliqués in place for both machine

and hand appliqué. Work in a well-ventilated area and cover the work surface with paper. Be careful to spray lightly, as overspraying can cause a gummy build-up that makes stitching difficult.

Fabric Glue or Glue Stick

Apply these adhesives lightly to the wrong side of the prepared appliqué pieces along the outer edges or in the center. Press the appliqué piece to the appliqué foundation fabric. Be sure to apply the glue sparingly to avoid a build-up that would be difficult to stitch through. This method can be used for both machine and hand appliqué.

Fusible Web

This adhesive is most often used to hold pieces in position for machine appliqué. For an appliqué project with multiple layers of pieces prepared with fusible web, hold the appliqué pieces in position before adhering them to the foundation (see Photo 4K, *below right*). To do so, place the full-size appliqué pattern beneath a clear, nonstick pressing sheet. Layer the prepared appliqué pieces in position right side up on the pressing sheet. Press lightly, just enough to fuse the pieces together, following the manufacturer's instructions. Do not slide the iron, but pick it up and move it from one area to the next. Let the pieces cool, then remove the fused appliqués from the pressing sheet and fuse them to the appliqué foundation.

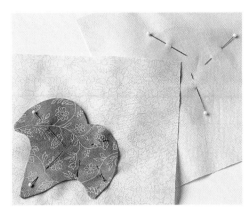

Photo 4H

Photo 4I

Photo 4J

Photo 4K

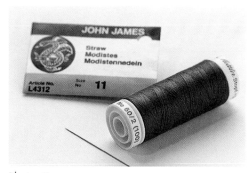

Photo 4L

Photo 4M

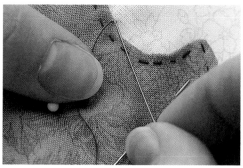

Photo 4N

Photo 4O

Photo 4P

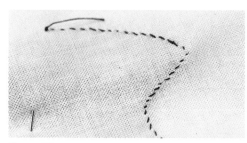

Photo 4Q

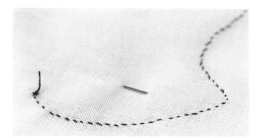

Photo 4R

HAND APPLIQUÉ

There are many ways to hand-stitch pieces in place on an appliqué foundation. Experiment with each method to determine which method is most comfortable for you.

For most hand appliqué, use a sharp, between, straw, or milliners needle and the finest thread you can find that matches the appliqué pieces (see Photo 4L, *top, far left*). The higher the number, the finer the thread, so look for silk or fine cotton machine-embroidery threads; they will make appliqué stitches nearly invisible (for more information on thread and needle choices, see Chapter 1—Tools and Materials).

Traditional Appliqué Stitch

This technique uses appliqué pieces that have had the seam allowances turned under. (For more information, see Preparing Appliqué Pieces, which begins on *page 160*.) For best results, use a sharp, between, straw, or milliners needle.

1. Prepare the appliqué pieces by turning the seam allowances under. Pin, baste, or glue an appliqué piece in place on the appliqué foundation.

2. Working with a length of thread no longer than 18", insert the needle into the wrong side of the appliqué foundation directly beneath the edge of the appliqué piece. Bring the needle up through the rolled edge of the appliqué piece (see Photo 4M, *above left, top*).

3. Hold the needle parallel to the edge of the appliqué with the point of the needle next to the spot where the thread just exited, as shown in Photo 4N, *above*.

4. Slide the point of the needle under the appliqué edge, into the appliqué foundation, and forward about 1/8" to 3/16", bringing the needle point out through the rolled edge of the appliqué (see Photo 4O, *above, far left*).

5. Give the thread a gentle tug to bury the stitch in the fabric and allow the appliqué shape to rise up off the foundation (see Photo 4P, *opposite*). Continue stitching in the same manner around the shape along the rolled edge.

6. On the wrong side of the appliqué foundation, the stitches will be slightly angled (see Photo 4Q, *opposite*).

7. End the thread by knotting it on the wrong side of the foundation, beneath the appliqué piece (see Photo 4R, *opposite*).

8. Once all pieces have been appliquéd, press the foundation from the wrong side and trim it to the desired size, including seam allowances.

Needle-turn Appliqué

This technique involves turning under the appliqué seam allowance as you stitch. For best results, use a straw or milliners needle. The extra length of these needles aids in tucking fabric under before taking stitches.

1. Prepare the appliqué pieces following Freezer-Paper Method 4 on *page 167,* or by completing steps 1 and 2 of the Basting Method on *page 161.* Pin, baste, or glue an appliqué piece in place on the appliqué foundation.

2. Working with a length of thread no longer than 18", insert the needle into the wrong side of the appliqué foundation directly beneath the edge of the appliqué piece. Bring the needle up between the appliqué and the foundation (see Photo 4S, *below*). Use the point of the needle to sweep the seam allowance under about 1" ahead of the stitching and secure the fabric with your thumb. The edge of the freezer-paper template or the drawn line serves as a guide for how much to turn under.

3. Hold the needle parallel to the edge of the appliqué with the needle's point at the spot where the thread just exited. Slide the point of the needle under a thread or two along the appliqué's rolled edge. Give the thread a gentle tug to bury the stitch in the fabric and allow the appliqué shape to rise up off the foundation (see Photo 4T, *below right*).

4. Then place the tip of the needle into the appliqué foundation and rock it forward, bringing the tip up into the rolled appliqué edge about ⅛" to ³⁄₁₆" away from the

previous stitch. Pull the needle through and gently tug the thread to bury the stitch as before.

5. Continue in the same manner around the entire appliqué, taking tinier stitches around inside corners and curves where the seam allowances are more scant. Use the needle point to manipulate the seam allowance to lie flat in outside curves.

6. End the thread by knotting it on the wrong side of the foundation, beneath the appliqué piece.

7. Once all pieces have been appliquéd, press the foundation from the wrong side and trim it to the desired size, including the seam allowances.

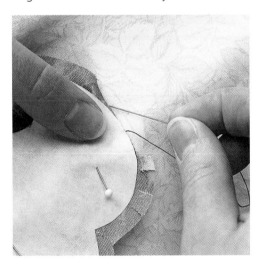

Photo 4S

Photo 4T

Photo 4U

Tack Stitch

This technique uses appliqué pieces that have had the seam allowances turned under. (For more information, see Preparing Appliqué Pieces, which begins on *page 160.*) For best results, use a sharp, between, straw, or milliners needle.

1. Prepare the appliqué pieces by turning the seam allowances under. Pin, baste, or glue an appliqué piece in place on the appliqué foundation.

2. Working with a length of thread no longer than 18", insert the needle into the wrong side of the appliqué foundation directly beneath the edge of the appliqué piece (see Photo 4U, *left*). Bring the needle up through the rolled edge of the appliqué piece.

3. Insert the needle down into the foundation right next to the appliqué edge where it came up (see Photo 4V, *far left*).

4. Bring the needle back up through the edge of the appliqué piece about 1/16" from the first stitch (see Photo 4W, *left*). Continue in the same manner to stitch the appliqué piece to the foundation.

5. Once all pieces have been appliquéd, press the foundation from the wrong side and trim it to the desired size, including the seam allowances.

Photo 4V

Photo 4W

Running Stitch

This method results in a more primitive or folk art look. It uses appliqué pieces that have had the seam allowances turned under. (For more information, see Preparing Appliqué Pieces, which begins on *page 160*.) For best results, use a sharp, between, straw, or milliners needle.

1. Prepare the appliqué pieces by turning the seam allowances under. Pin, baste, or glue an appliqué piece in place on the appliqué foundation.

2. Working with a length of thread no longer than 18", insert the needle into the wrong side of the appliqué foundation directly beneath the edge of the appliqué piece. Bring the needle up through the appliqué piece about 1/16" from the rolled edge.

3. Weave the needle in and out through both the edge of the appliqué piece and the foundation, staying about 1/16" from the outside edge of the appliqué (see Photo 4X, *below left*). Rock the needle in and out, taking small, evenly spaced stitches. Continue in this manner to secure the appliqué piece to the background.

4. Work with perle cotton and a larger needle to produce a larger running stitch, sometimes called a utility stitch or big stitch (see Photo 4Y, *below right*). The standard running stitch may also be done in matching thread (see Photo 4Y).

5. Once all pieces have been appliquéd, press the foundation from the wrong side and trim it to the desired size, including the seam allowances.

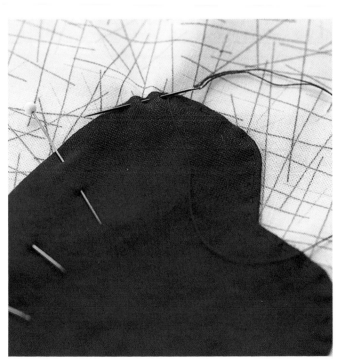

Photo 4X

Photo 4Y

Chapter 6 – Appliqué Techniques

183

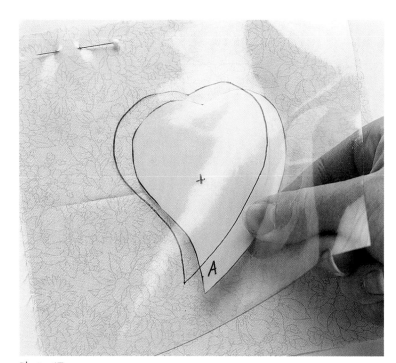

Photo 4Z

Photo 5A

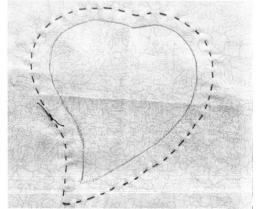

Photo 5B

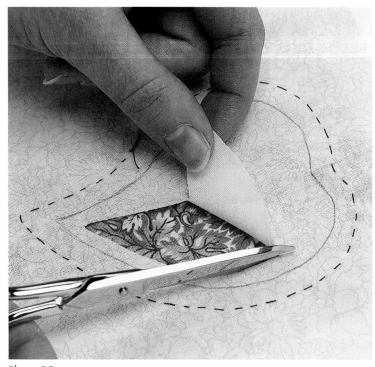

Photo 5C

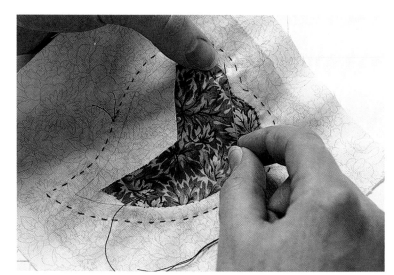

Photo 5D

Reverse Appliqué

With this method, the foundation fabric is sewn on top of the appliqué fabric. The foundation is then cut away to reveal the appliqué fabric underneath. For best results, use a straw or milliners needle.

1. Make a template for each appliqué piece. (See Making Appliqué Templates on *page 159*.) Make an overlay for the complete appliqué pattern. (See Overlay Method on *page 178*.)
Note: *Keep templates and overlays for letters and/or numbers on a straight baseline and mark the center point of each word or series of numbers.*

2. Mark the center of the foundation fabric. Position the overlay on the foundation fabric, aligning the marked centers. Pin the overlay in place. Slide a template under the overlay into position (see Photo 4Z, *opposite*).

3. Flip back the overlay and, using an erasable marking tool, carefully trace around the template on the foundation fabric (see Photo 5A, *opposite*).

4. Place the appliqué fabric right side up, directly beneath the traced motif on the foundation fabric. Baste around the outer edges of the motif, 5/16" away from the traced lines (see Photo 5B, *opposite*).

5. Starting in the middle of the motif, cut away a small portion of the foundation fabric, cutting 3/16" inside the traced line to create an edge for turning under (see Photo 5C, *opposite*).

6. Turn the raw edge under and slip-stitch the folded edge to the appliqué fabric beneath (see Photo 5D, *opposite*). Clip curves as necessary to make the edge lie flat.

7. Continue cutting away the foundation fabric a little at a time, turning under the raw edge and stitching the folded edge to the fabric below until the entire motif is revealed (see Photo 5E, *below left*).

8. Once the appliqué is complete, turn it over and trim the appliqué fabric to within 1/4" of the seam allowance (see Photo 5F, *below*).

9. Press the foundation from the wrong side and trim to the desired size, including the seam allowances.

❧Creative Tip

When hand sewing through thick fabric, use a small swatch of rubber lid grips to grasp the needle.

—Julie, Store Team Leader

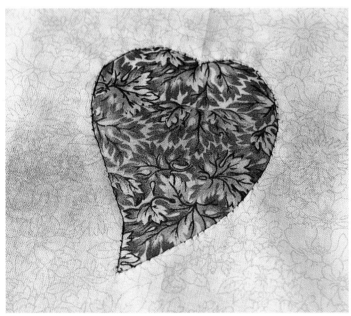

Photo 5E

Photo 5F

Chapter 6 – Appliqué Techniques

185

MACHINE APPLIQUÉ

Beginning and Ending Stitching

1. To begin stitching, bring the bobbin and needle threads to the top; this helps prevent thread tangles and snarls on the wrong side of your work. To begin this way, put the presser foot down and take one stitch. Stop and pull the bobbin thread to the top (see Photo 5G, *below, far left*).

2. Set the machine for a narrow zigzag or satin stitch. Holding the bobbin and needle threads to one side, take a few stitches on a curve or straight edge; do not start at an inner or outer point (see Photo 5H, *left*).
Note: If the machine has a variable stitch length, set the stitch length at 0 and take a few stitches, one on top of the next, to lock threads in place at the start.

3. Reset the machine to the desired stitch setting; stitch about 1" and trim off the thread tails (see Photo 5I, *below, far left*). Or, when the appliqué work is completed, use a needle to draw the thread tails to the wrong side of the work and bury them in the stitching.

4. To end, stitch one or two threads past the point where the stitching began and take one or two backstitches to secure the thread (see Photo 5J, *left*).
Note: If the machine has a variable stitch length, set the stitch length at 0 and take a few stitches, one on top of the next, to lock the threads in place.

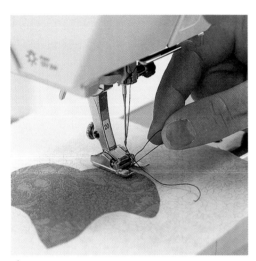

Photo 5G

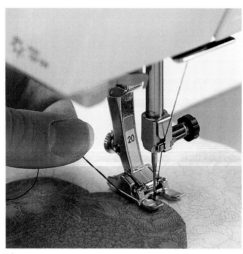

Photo 5H

Photo 5I

Photo 5J

Photo 5K

Photo 5L

Satin or Zigzag Stitch Appliqué

Variable-width satin or zigzag stitch makes a smooth, professional-looking finish on appliqué edges. Choose a thread color that matches or complements the appliqué fabric. Select a stitch width that corresponds to the size of the piece being appliquéd. Larger pieces can accommodate a wider, denser appliqué stitch than smaller appliqué shapes can.

With a machine satin stitch, it is not necessary to turn under the edges of the appliqué piece because the entire outer edge is held in place by the zigzag or satin stitch. The outer edge of the stitch just grazes the appliqué foundation. Depending upon the stability of the fabric, the appliqué design, and your personal preference, use fusible web, pins, or fabric glue to hold the appliqué pieces in place for machine stitching. Use a stabilizer behind the appliqué foundation (see About Stabilizers *below*).

1. Position the presser foot so that the left swing of the needle is on the appliqué and the right swing of the needle is just on the outer edge of the appliqué, grazing the appliqué foundation (see Photo 5K, *above left*).

2. Begin stitching on a curve or straight edge, not at an inner or outer point (see Photo 5L, *above*).

About Stabilizers

Stabilizers are used beneath appliqué foundations to add support and eliminate puckers and pulling on the fabric as you machine-appliqué. Some stabilizers are temporary and are removed once stitching is complete (as in the photo at *left*, where the stabilizer is removed by holding it firmly on one side of the stitching and gently pulling it away from the other side). Others are permanent and remain in the quilt or are only partially cut away after stitching. Many brands are available. Two of the most common types are tear-away and water-soluble stabilizers. Freezer paper also may be used as a stabilizer. Experiment with a variety of types to determine which works best for you.

Machine Appliqué Troubleshooting Tips

This machine-appliqué stitching is correctly placed. The outside edge of the stitch is just grazing the appliqué foundation.

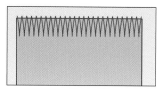

This stitching is too far inside the edge of the appliqué piece, so fabric threads from the appliqué will fray and poke out around the edges.

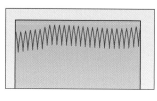

Here the stitches are too far outside the edge of the appliqué piece, so it may pull loose from the foundation.

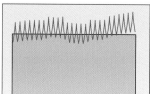

Gaps will occur in the stitching if the needle is down in the fabric on the wrong side of the needle swing when you pivot.

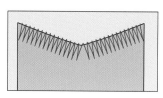

The stitches will slant if you try to pull or push the fabric through curves, rather than lifting the presser foot and pivoting the fabric.

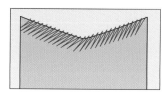

Pivoting too soon on an inside point will leave an incomplete line of stitches at the point.

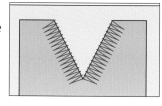

Pivoting at Corners, Curves, and Points

The position of the needle is critical when pivoting fabric to round a curve or turn a point or corner. The following illustrations show when to pivot. In each case, place the needle down in the fabric before pivoting. In each illustration the arrows indicate stitching direction, and the dots mark where the needle should be down for pivoting.

Turning Corners–Method 1

With this method the stitches cross over one another in the corners.

1. Stop with the needle down in the fabric on the right-hand swing of the needle, as shown in Illustration 1, *below, far left*.

2. Raise the presser foot and pivot the fabric. Lower the presser foot and stitch to the next edge (see Illustration 2, *below left*).

Turning Corners–Method 2

With this method the stitching lines abut, but they do not cross over one another.

1. Stop with the needle down in the fabric on the left-hand swing of the needle (see Illustration 3, *below*).

2. Raise the presser foot and pivot the fabric. Lower the presser foot and turn the handwheel until the right-hand swing of the needle is just about to go into the foundation fabric. Lift the presser foot and reposition the foundation fabric so the tip of the needle is above the point where the needle thread is coming out of the appliqué. Lower the presser foot and begin stitching to the next edge (see Illustration 4, *below*).

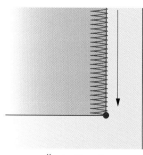

Illustration 1

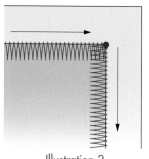

Illustration 2

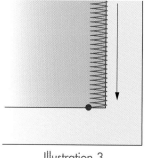

Illustration 3

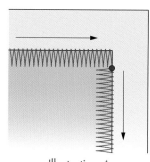

Illustration 4

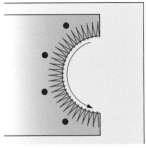

Illustration 5

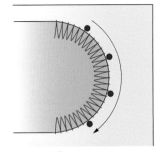

Illustration 6

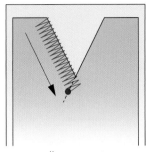

Illustration 7

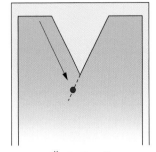

Illustration 8

Pivoting Inside Curves

Stop at the first pivot point with the needle down in the fabric on the left-hand swing of the needle. Raise the presser foot, pivot the fabric slightly, and begin stitching to the next pivot point (see Illustration 5, *above*). Repeat to round the entire inner curve.

Pivoting Outside Curves

Stop at the first pivot point with the needle down in the fabric on the right-hand swing of the needle. Raise the presser foot, pivot the fabric slightly, and begin stitching to the next pivot point (see Illustration 6, *above right*). Repeat to round the entire outer curve.

Pivoting Inside Points

1. With a marking tool, mark a line extending from the upcoming edge of the appliqué into the center. On the line, measure from the point a distance equal to the stitch width; mark the location with a dot (see Illustration 7, *above right, top*).

2. Stitch to the bottom of the inside point, stopping with the needle down in the fabric on the left-hand swing of the needle. The needle should be at the dot on the drawn marked line (see Illustration 8, *above, far right, top*).

3. Raise the presser foot and pivot the fabric. Lower the presser foot and turn the handwheel until the right-hand swing of the needle is just about to go into the

foundation fabric. Lift the presser foot and reposition the foundation fabric so the tip of the needle is above the point where the needle thread is coming out of the appliqué. Lower the presser foot and begin stitching to the next edge (see Illustration 9, *right*).

Pivoting Outside Points

Shapes with outside points are among the more difficult to appliqué. This method requires tapering the stitch width at the point. Practice on scraps to perfect your technique.

1. Stitch along the first edge of the appliqué, keeping the stitch width consistent until the left-hand swing of the needle begins to touch the opposite outside edge of the point (see Illustration 10, *above far right, middle*). Stop with the needle down in the fabric on the left-hand swing of the needle.

2. Gradually reduce your stitch width and continue sewing toward the point. Keep the right- and left-hand swings of the needle

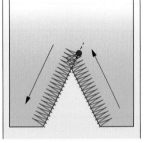

Illustration 9

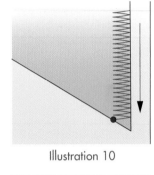

Illustration 10

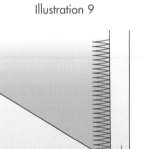

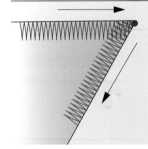

Illustration 11

Illustration 12

just grazing the outer edges and taper your stitch width until it's 0 at the point (see Illustration 11, *above left*). Stop with the needle down in the fabric.

3. Raise the presser foot and pivot the fabric. Lower the presser foot and begin stitching away from the point, increasing the stitch width at the same rate that you decreased it until you have returned to the original stitch width. Pivot the fabric slightly as needed to keep the right-hand swing of the needle grazing the foundation at the right-hand edge of the appliqué piece (see Illustration 12, *above*).

Photo 5M

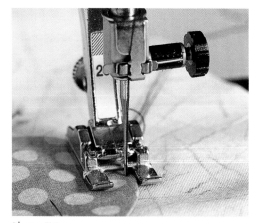

Photo 5N

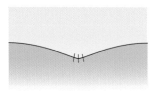

Illustration 13

Illustration 14

Mock Hand Appliqué
This method uses monofilament thread in the needle and the blind hem stitch to make virtually invisible stitches.
Note: Contrasting thread was used in these photos for illustration purposes only.

1. Prepare the appliqué pieces following Freezer-Paper Method 3 on *page 166*.

2. Position an appliqué piece so that the needle goes into the appliqué foundation right next to it (see Photo 5M, *left*). The needle should be so near the fold of the appliqué piece that it touches the fold but does not stitch through it.

Photo 5O

Photo 5P

When the needle jumps to the left, the stitch should be totally on the appliqué piece, as shown in Photo 5N, *below left*.

When the needle jumps to the right to complete a zigzag stitch, the needle should again be against the edge of the appliqué piece but go through the foundation only.

3. Secure inside and outside points with several stitches (see Illustrations 13 and 14, *bottom left*). Make certain the needle always touches the appliqué fold so no edges are missed (see Photo 5O, *below left*).

4. Continue stitching around the appliqué. Where the stitching began, stitch over the beginning stitches to secure the threads (see Photo 5P, *below left, bottom*). To lock the stitches, backstitch only two or three stitches.

5. When stitching is complete, check all edges of the appliqué to make sure no areas went unstitched. On the wrong side, carefully trim away the foundation fabric

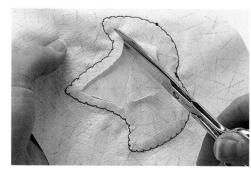

Photo 5Q

Photo 5R

from within each stitched shape, leaving a ¼" seam allowance (see Photo 5Q, *opposite*).

6. Use a spritzer bottle to wet the inside of the appliqué seam allowances (see Photo 5R, *opposite*). Make sure to spray the areas that were glued over the freezer paper.

7. Remove the paper. Once the water dissolves the glue, the freezer paper will slip right out (see Photo 5S, *below*).

8. Place a thick bath towel atop a pressing surface and lay the appliqué facedown on the towel. Cover the back of appliqué with a pressing cloth; press with a warm iron as shown in photos 5T, 5U, and 5V, *below*. The towel prevents edges of the appliqués from being flattened by the iron.
Note: Contrasting thread was used in the photographs for illustration purposes only. If monofilament thread had been used, no stitching line would be visible on the right side of the fabric.

Photo 5S

Photo 5T

Sewing Machine Setup for Mock Hand Appliqué

- Make certain the machine is clean and in good working order.

- Install a new size 60/8, 70/10, or 75/11 embroidery needle in the machine.

- Wind a bobbin with cotton 60-weight embroidery thread.

- Thread the needle with lightweight, invisible, nylon (monofilament) thread. Use clear thread for light-color fabrics; use smoke-color invisible thread for medium- and dark-color fabrics.

- Set the machine for a blind hem stitch with the stitch width and length both set at 1 mm. This stitch takes 2 to 5 straight stitches, then a zigzag, then 2 to 5 more straight stitches before zigzagging again.

Stitch a test sample using the same threads and fabrics as in the project. The distance between each zigzag should be ⅛" maximum, and the width of the zigzag should be the width of two threads. When the piece is finished, needle holes should be visible; the thread should not. If you gently pull on the edge of the appliqué, the stitching should be strong and without gaps.

Check the stitch tension on the test sample. There should be no bobbin thread showing on the top and no loops of nylon thread on the bottom. If the bobbin thread is showing on the top, loosen the top tension gradually until the bobbin thread no longer shows. Turn the sample over. If there are loops of nylon thread on the bottom, the top tension is too loose.

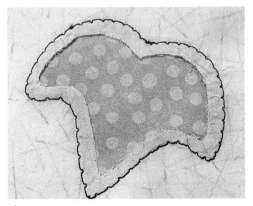

Photo 5U

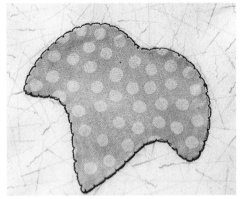

Photo 5V

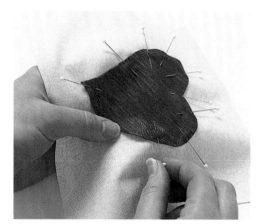
Photo 5W

Straight Stitch Appliqué

1. Prepare the appliqué pieces following the desired method. (For more information, see Preparing Appliqué Pieces, which begins on *page 160*.) Pin, baste, or glue the appliqués in place (see Photo 5W, *left*).

2. Set the stitch length at 0. Beginning on a straight edge or curve, take two or three stitches about ⅛" from the outer edge of the appliqué to anchor the thread. Hold the thread tails out of the way to prevent snarls on the underside (see Photo 5X, *below left*).

Note: Remove pins before the needle reaches them.

3. Adjust the stitch length to the desired number of stitches per inch (12 to 15) and continue sewing around the appliqué edge. Stay ⅛" from the outer edge (see Photo 5Y, *below left*).

4. To stitch inner and outer curves, stop with the needle down, lift the presser foot, pivot the appliqué foundation, lower the presser foot, and continue sewing (see Photo 5Z, *bottom, far left*).

5. To end the stitching, gradually reduce the stitch length to 0 as you meet the point where the stitching began. Make the last two or three stitches next to the stitches where you started. Do not backstitch or overlap stitches (see Photo 6A, *below left*). *Note: Contrasting thread was used in the photographs for illustration purposes only. In the right sample in Photo 6B, below, monofilament thread was used, so the stitching line does not appear as visible on the top side of the appliqué.*

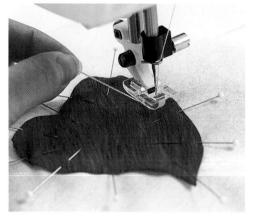
Photo 5X

Photo 5Y

Photo 5Z

Photo 6A

Photo 6B

Decorative Stitch Appliqué

This technique is often done on a sewing machine using the blanket or buttonhole stitch. Other decorative stitches also may be used, such as the featherstitch. (For information on decorative stitches done by hand, see Chapter 10—Specialty Techniques.)

1. Prepare the appliqué pieces following the desired method. (For more information, see Preparing Appliqué Pieces, which begins on *page 160*.) Pin, baste, or glue the appliqués in place.

2. Use a tear-away stabilizer beneath the appliqué foundation. (See About Stabilizers on *page 187*.)

3. Beginning on a straight edge or a curve, take a few stitches; hold the thread tails out of the way to prevent thread snarls on the wrong side of the project. The right swing of the needle should graze the appliqué foundation. The left swing of the needle should be completely on the appliqué piece.

4. For inside curves, stop with the needle down in the fabric on the left needle swing, lift the presser foot, pivot the appliqué foundation, lower the presser foot, and continue sewing (see Photo 6C, *above right*).

5. For outside curves, stop with the needle down in the fabric on the right needle swing, lift the presser foot, pivot the appliqué foundation, and continue sewing (see Photo 6D, *above, far right*).

6. Adjust the stitch length as necessary at corners and where the stitching meets at the end (see Photo 6E, *above right*).

Photo 6C

Photo 6D

Photo 6E

Fusible Web Appliqué

To finish the edges of appliqué pieces that have been fused to the appliqué foundation, follow the instructions for Satin or Zigzag Stitch Appliqué, which begin on *page 187*, Decorative Stitch Appliqué at *left*, or Hand Embroidery Stitches in Chapter 10—Specialty Techniques. Be sure to prepare appliqués with a sew-through fusible web. (See Preparing Appliqué Pieces—Fusible Web Method, which begins on *page 170*.)

Wool Appliqué

Felted wool—wool that has been napped and shrunk—is easy to work with because the edges will not ravel, so there is no need to turn them under. Use templates to cut felted wool into appliqué pieces. Do not include seam allowances. (See Making Appliqué Templates, which begins on *page 159*.)

Use a basic running stitch or decorative hand- or machine-embroidery stitches to attach wool appliqués to an appliqué foundation. Or, for added dimension, tack wool appliqué pieces at their centers only.

To felt wool for use in appliqué, machine-wash it in a hot-water/cool-rinse cycle with a small amount of detergent, machine-dry on hot, and steam-press. It is the disparity in temperatures, along with the agitation, that causes the wool to felt. To use wool from a piece of clothing, cut it apart and remove the seams so it can shrink freely.

Chapter 7

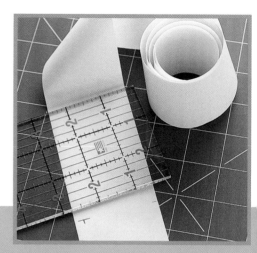

ASSEMBLING
THE QUILT TOP
AND BACKING

Your creative expression has only just begun as you

combine blocks, borders, and sashing into a beautiful

quilt, front and back.

TRIP AROUND THE WORLD

Lovely pastel quilts with carefully shaded prints could be made easily in the 1930s by purchasing kits of die-cut pieces. Kit manufacturers delivered on their promise of accurately cut pieces, harmonious colors, and relief from having to cut individual pieces with scissors. They stacked solid colors and coordinated prints in sets in the kits, carefully separating them with cardboard dividers. And because all the sewing was done in straight lines, almost anyone could be a successful quiltmaker. For this quilt, "Trip Around the World," bands of rainbow-colored squares were sewn together according to the package directions. Simple quilting around each square was an easy way to finish the top.

Assembling *the Quilt Top*

Once you've planned your quilt and have cut and pieced or appliquéd the blocks, it's time to sew them together and perhaps add a border or two. Knowing the fundamentals of setting blocks together and adding borders will help you assemble a quilt top accurately.

SQUARING UP THE BLOCKS

Often the quilt you are assembling is one you've worked on from start to finish. Sometimes, you may have set the blocks aside for a while before you begin the quilt top assembly. Still other times, you may receive a set of finished quilt blocks from another source, and your first experience working with them is when you're ready to sew them together. However you've acquired the blocks, it is essential that all blocks be squared up before they're assembled into a quilt top. If you piece together a quilt top with some blocks that are too large and ease in the excess fabric, you'll end up with a quilt that has waves. If you piece a quilt with some blocks that are too small and try stretching the fabric to fit, you'll have a quilt that isn't square at the corners and pulls in, creating drag lines across the surface.

Measure each block to be certain they are all the same size. Check to be sure they have ¼" seam allowances on all edges and that the corners are square. Use a large, acrylic square ruler atop the block to check your work.

If the pieces were cut accurately and ¼" seams were used throughout the piecing process, the blocks will be the correct size (see Photo 1A, *below, far left*).

If you are squaring up a block to a dimension that is not easily visible on the ruler, use pieces of narrow masking tape on the underside of the ruler to create a guide (see Photo 1B, *below left*). Place the inside edge of the tape on the measurement line, so you can see at a glance if a block is too small.

SETTING THE QUILT BLOCKS

The word *set* refers to how the blocks are arranged in the quilt top. Blocks can be put together in a variety of ways, including block to block (see illustration *below*), or with sashing and/or setting squares. (See Chapter 3—Planning Your Quilt for information on choosing a setting for your quilt blocks.) As a review, several assembly options for straight and diagonal (on point) block settings appear on *page 198*.

Photo 1A

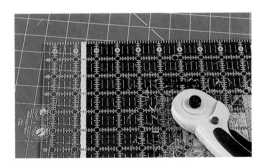

Photo 1B

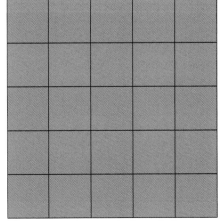

Straight Set, Block-to-Block

Straight Set with Alternate Squares

Straight Set with Sashing Strips and Squares (Cornerstones)

Diagonal Set with Continuous Sashing

Straight Set with Alternate Blocks

Diagonal Set

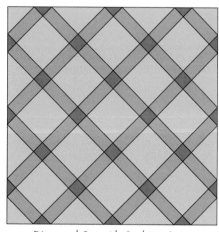

Diagonal Set with Sashing Strips and Squares

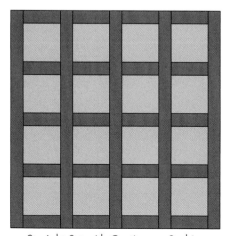

Straight Set with Continuous Sashing

Diagonal Set with Floating Blocks

Vertical or Zigzag Set

ASSEMBLING STRAIGHT-SET BLOCKS AND ROWS

(See Chapter 3—Planning Your Quilt for information on choosing a straight setting for quilt blocks.)

1. After selecting the desired straight-set block arrangement, lay out the blocks in horizontal rows (see Photo 1C, *below left, top*). If you are including sashing between blocks, lay out the sashing pieces now, too. *Note: Fabric squares were substituted for pieced blocks in the photographs that follow.*

2. With right sides together and raw edges aligned, join the blocks in each row (see Photo 1D, *below center, top*).

3. Press the seam allowances to one side, pressing each row in alternate directions (see Photo 1E, *below right, top*). For example, press the seam allowances in row 1 and all odd-numbered rows to the right, and press the seam allowances in row 2 and all even-numbered rows to the left. Then, when the rows are assembled, the alternated seam allowances will lock together, ensuring matching seams.

4. Pin together rows 1 and 2, taking care to match the seam intersections (see Photo 1F, *below left, bottom*). It may be necessary to ease the blocks slightly to ensure that the raw edges align. If one row is significantly shorter or longer, check the

seam allowances to see if one is too narrow or too deep. If so, remove the seam and restitch it before joining the rows. Sew the rows together, backstitching at the beginning and end to secure the seam line and stabilize the quilt edge. Trim any threads and/or dog-ears.

5. Continue joining rows in pairs (for example, join row 3 to row 4, row 5 to row 6, and so forth; see Photo 1G, *below center, bottom*).

6. Then sew together the joined rows to complete the quilt center (see Photo 1H, *below right, bottom*). Press all seam allowances in the same direction.

Photo 1C

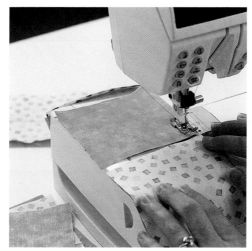

Photo 1D

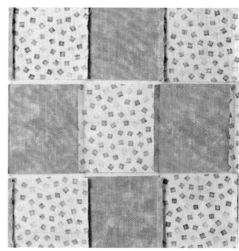

Photo 1E

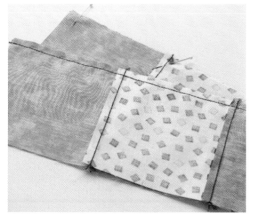

Photo 1F

Photo 1G

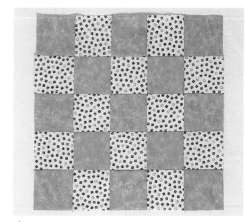

Photo 1H

Chapter 7 – Assembling the Quilt Top and Backing

199

ASSEMBLING DIAGONALLY SET BLOCKS AND ROWS

(See Chapter 3—Planning Your Quilt for information on choosing a diagonal setting for quilt blocks.)

Quilt tops with blocks set diagonally, or on point, can be a bit more challenging to piece than straight-set blocks. Because you are sewing in diagonal rows, you may have a greater tendency to stretch or distort the quilt blocks as you piece them together.

It is essential to cut side setting triangles and corner setting triangles so the straight grain edge will be along the outer edges of the quilt. This will help prevent the quilt from becoming distorted or sagging. (See Chapter 4—Cutting Techniques for complete information on cutting setting triangles and setting squares.)
Note: Some quilters prefer to cut their side and corner setting triangles 1/2" to 1" larger than required and trim away the excess fabric after piecing the top. The measurements given in the Setting Triangles and Setting Squares charts in Chapter 4 are mathematically correct and do not allow for any excess fabric.

1. After selecting the desired diagonally set block arrangement, lay out blocks and setting squares in diagonal rows (see Photo 1I, *above right*). If sashing will be included between blocks, lay out the sashing pieces now, too.

2. Add the side setting triangles and corner setting triangles to the layout (see Photo 1J, *above, far right*).

3. With right sides together and raw edges aligned, join the blocks (or blocks and sashing) in each row (see Photo 1K, *right*). Sew the setting triangles to the ends of each row. Do not add the corner triangles.

Photo 1I

Photo 1J

Photo 1K

Photo 1L

Photo 1M

Photo 1N

Photo 1O

4. Press the seam allowances to one side, pressing each row in alternate directions (see Photo 1L, *far left*). For example, press the seam allowances in row 1 and all odd-numbered rows to the right, and press the seam allowances in row 2 and all even-numbered rows to the left. Then when the rows are assembled, the alternated seam allowances will lock together, ensuring matching seams.

5. Pin together rows 1 and 2, taking care to match seam intersections (see Photo 1M, *left*). It may be necessary to ease the blocks a slight bit to ensure that the raw edges align. If one row is significantly shorter or longer, check the seam allowances to see if one is too narrow or too deep. If so, remove the seam and restitch it before joining the rows. Sew the rows together, backstitching at the beginning and end to secure the seam line and stabilize the quilt edge. Trim any threads and/or dog-ears.

6. Continue joining rows in pairs (for example, join row 3 to row 4, row 5 to row 6, and so forth). Then sew together the joined rows.

7. Sew the setting corner triangles to the pieced rows to complete the quilt center, as shown in see Photo 1N, *far left*. (The ¼" seam allowances of the corner triangles will extend beyond the edge of the quilt center.) Press all seam allowances in the same direction. Trim any threads and dog-ears (see Photo 1O, *left*).
Note: *If side and corner triangles were cut larger than specified, trim them now, leaving a ¼" seam allowance outside the corners of the pieced blocks.*

Chapter 7 – Assembling the Quilt Top and Backing

ꝯCreative Tip

To keep from losing your scissors while machine-piecing,

tie a small pair to your sewing machine with a long

ribbon. Use the scissors to trim threads while sewing.

—*ANN, STORE ASSOCIATE*

Illustration 1

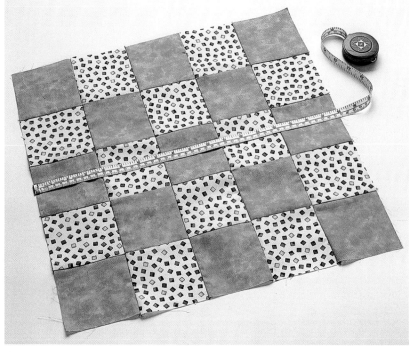

Photo 1P

BORDERS

Just as a mat and frame enhance a picture, borders can make a big difference in the finished appearance of a quilt. There are myriad possibilities for adding single or multiple rows of borders to a quilt (see Chapter 3—Planning Your Quilt for information on choosing a border design for a quilt).

Adding Straight Borders

Referring to the chart *opposite*, determine the border strip width to cut, then add ½" for seam allowances to the desired finished border strip width. Then follow these instructions to add straight borders to a quilt top (see Illustration 1, *above left*).

1. Place the assembled quilt center on a flat surface.

2. To determine the length of the border strips for the side edges, measure through the center of the quilt center from top to bottom.

3. To determine the length of the top and bottom borders, measure through the

center of the assembled quilt center from side to side (see Photo 1P, *above*). Add twice the width of the side border strip (including seam allowances), then subtract 1" (for the seam allowances). For example, if the quilt center measures 18" from side to side and the side border strips are 2½" wide, add 18" + 5" - 1" = 22". In this case, cut the top and bottom border strips 2½×22" long.

4. Cut the border strips on the lengthwise grain of fabric for less stretch and more stability. Cut on the crosswise grain only if the quantity of yardage on hand is limited. Rotary-cut straight borders whenever possible (see Chapter 4—Cutting Techniques for more information on cutting border strips).

Determining Yardage for Straight Borders

The border strip width will be cut the desired finished width plus ½" for seam allowances.

Side Border Strips:
Measure vertically (top to bottom) through the center of the quilt center (including seam allowances). For side edges, you will need 2 strips, each = _____" long (A).

For example, if the measurement is 40", including seam allowances, (A) = 40".

Top and Bottom Border Strips:
Measure horizontally (side to side) through the center of the quilt center (including seam allowances). _____".

Multiply width of side border strips (including seam allowances) by 2.

Add to first measurement + _____".

Subtract 1" for seam allowances, -1".

For top and bottom edges, you will need 2 strips, each = _____" long (B).

For example, if the measurement is 30", including seam allowances, and the width of the side border strips is 3", including seam allowances, then 30" + (3" × 2) - 1" = 35" (B).

Yardage Required to Cut Border Strips Lengthwise:
For border width up to 10½":
Divide larger of (A) or (B) by 36" = _____ yards.

For example, if (A) measures 40" and (B) is 35", (A) is larger than (B), so 40" (A) divided by 36" = 1.11 yards, which rounded up would be 1⅛ yards.
***Note:** With a border up to 10½"-wide, you can cut at least four border strips the length (parallel to selvage) of the 42"-wide fabric. In some cases, if border strips are narrower, you may be able to cut more strips from the length.*

For border width 10¾" to 20":
Divide (A + B) by 36" = _____ yards.

For example, if A is 60" and B is 40" and you want to add a 15"-wide border, 60"(A) + 40"(B) = 100" of border length needed divided by 36" = 2.77 yards, which rounded up would be 2⅞ yards.
***Note:** With a border up to 20"-wide, you can cut at least two border strips the length (parallel to the selvage) of the 42"-wide fabric. In some cases, if the border strips are narrower, you may be able to cut three strips from the length.*

Yardage Required to Cut Border Strips Crosswise:
Take measurements for (A) and (B) as described at left.
(A + B) × 2 = _____ (C), or total inches of border needed.

Divide (C) by 42" (round up to next whole number) = _____ (D) or number of strips that will need to be cut.

Add 1 strip to allow for diagonal seaming of border strips + 1 = _____ (E).

Multiply (E) × width of border, then divide by 36" = _____ yards.

For example, 40" (A) + 35" (B) × 2 = 150" (C) of border needed. 150" (C) divided by 42" = 3.57, rounded up would be 4 (D) strips to cut. 4 (D) + 1 = 5 (E) strips. 5 (E) strips × 3"-wide border, divided by 36" = .42 or ½ yard.
Note: *For information on piecing crosswise border strips, see page 206.*

5. Fold each side border strip in half crosswise and press lightly to mark the center (see Photo 1Q, *right*).

6. Fold the pieced quilt center in half and press lightly to mark the center of the side edges (see Photo 1R, *opposite*).

7. With right sides together and raw edges aligned, pin and sew the border strips to the side edges of the pieced quilt center with ¼" seam allowances, matching the center fold lines (see Photo 1S, *opposite*). To ease in a slight amount of fullness, sew with the longer fabric piece next to the feed dogs.

8. Press the seam allowances toward the border (see Photo 1T, *opposite*).

9. Repeat steps 5 and 6 to mark the centers of the top and bottom border strips and the pieced quilt center.

10. Pin and sew the top and bottom border strips to the top and bottom edges of the quilt center as before (see Photo 1U, *opposite*).

11. Press the seam allowances toward the border.

12. Repeat the steps as necessary to add additional borders.

Photo 1Q

Photo 1R

Photo 1S

Photo 1T

Photo 1U

Piecing Crosswise Border Strips

Cutting borders lengthwise is preferable to cutting them crosswise. But if only a limited amount of the "perfect" fabric is available for a quilt project, cutting crosswise strips may be the only option. Follow these steps to join crosswise border strips with diagonal seams.

1. Cut crosswise fabric strips the desired width of the border plus ½" for seam allowances. Cut enough strips to equal the total length needed for each side of the quilt, plus one extra strip. The extra strip will provide you with enough additional length to allow for the fabric that is lost as a result of diagonal seams.

2. Position the strips perpendicular to one another with raw edges aligned and right sides together.

3. Mark, then join the strips with diagonal seams to make a border strip (see Photo 1V, *below left*). ***Note:*** *In most cases, diagonal seams are preferable to straight seams because they are visually less distracting in the finished quilt (see Photo 1W, below left, bottom).*

4. Press the seam allowance open (see Photo 1X, *below*).

5. Trim the seam allowance to ¼". Trim the border strip to the desired length, including seam allowances (see Photo 1Y, *below, bottom*).

Photo 1V

Photo 1W

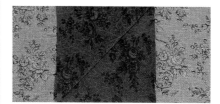

Photo 1X

Photo 1Y

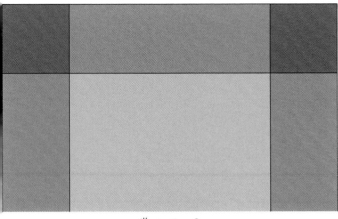

Illustration 2

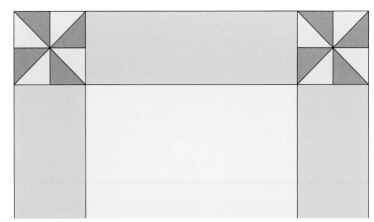

Illustration 3

Adding Straight Borders with Corner Squares or Blocks

Referring to the chart on *page 208*, determine the border strip width to cut, then add ½" for seam allowances to the desired finished border strip width. Then follow these instructions to add straight borders with corner squares or blocks to a quilt top (see illustrations 2 and 3, *above and above right*).

1. Lay the quilt top on a flat surface.

2. To determine the length of side border strips, measure through the center of the assembled quilt center from top to bottom (including the seam allowances).

3. To determine the length of the top and bottom border strips, measure through the center of the quilt center from side to side (including the seam allowances).

4. To determine the dimensions of corner squares or blocks, measure the width of the side border strip including seam allowances.

5. Cut the border strips on the lengthwise grain of the fabric, if possible. It has less stretch and more stability than the crosswise grain.

6. Fold each side border strip in half crosswise and press lightly to mark the center.

7. Fold the quilt center in half and press lightly to mark the center of the side edges.

8. With right sides together and raw edges aligned, pin and sew the side border strips to the side edges of the quilt center with ¼" seams, matching the center fold lines. Press the seam allowances toward the border.

9. Sew a corner square or block to each end of the top and bottom border strips (see Photo 1Z, *above right*). Press the seam allowances toward the border strips.

10. Pin and sew the borders to the top and bottom edges of the quilt center, matching the center fold lines, ends, and seams (see Photo 2A, *right*). Press the seam allowances toward the border.

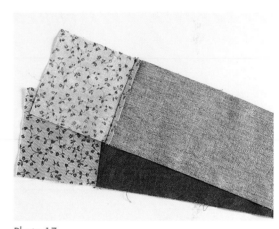

Photo 1Z

Photo 2A

Determining Yardage for Straight Borders with Corner Squares or Blocks

The border strip width will be cut the desired finished width plus ½" for seam allowances.

Side Border Strips:
Measure vertically (top to bottom) through the center of the quilt center (including seam allowances). For side edges, you'll need 2 strips, each = _____ " long (A).

For example, if the measurement is 40", including seam allowances, (A) = 40".

Top and Bottom Border Strips:
Measure horizontally (side to side) through the center of the quilt center (including seam allowances). For top and bottom edges, you'll need 2 strips, each = _____ " long (B).

For example, if the measurement is 35", including seam allowances, (B) = 35".

**Corner Squares
(Pieced Blocks May Be Substituted):**
Measure the width of the side border (including seam allowances). _____ "
Multiply sum by 4 = _____ ".
For corner squares or blocks, you'll need 4 squares from a _____ "-long strip (C).

For example, if finished width of the side border is 3", (3" + ½") × 4 = 3½ × 14" long strip needed. You will subcut the strip into four 3½" squares.

Yardage Required to Cut Border Strips Lengthwise:

For border width up to 10½":
Divide larger of (A) or (B) by 36" = _____ yards.

For example, if (A) measures 40" and (B) is 35", (A) is larger than (B), so 40" (A) divided by 36" = 1.11 yards, which rounded up would be 1⅛ yards.
***Note:** With a border up to 10½" wide, you can cut at least four border strips the length (parallel to the selvage) of the 42"-wide fabric. In some cases, if your border strips are narrower, you may be able to cut more strips from the length.*

For border width 10¾" to 20":
Divide (A + B) by 36" = _____ yards.

For example, if the quilt center measures 60×40" and you want to add a 15"-wide border, 60" (A) + 40" (B) = 100" of border length needed divided by 36" = 2.77 yards, which rounded up would be 2⅞ yards.
***Note:** With a border up to 20" wide, you can cut at least two border strips the length (parallel to the selvage) of the 42"-wide fabric. In some cases, if the border strips are narrower, you may be able to cut three strips from the length.*

Yardage Required to Cut Border Strips Crosswise:
Take measurements for (A) and (B) as described at left.

(A + B) × 2 = _____ (D), or total inches of border needed.

Divide (D) by 42" (round up to next whole number) = _____ (E), the number of strips that will need to be cut.

Add 1 strip to allow for diagonal seaming of border strips + 1 = _____ (F).

Multiply (F) × width of border, then divide by 36" = _____ yards.

For example, 40" (A) + 35" (B) × 2 = 150" (D) of border needed. 150" (D) divided by 42" = 3.57, rounded up would be 4 (E) strips to cut. 4 (E) + 1 = 5 (F) strips. 5 (F) strips × 3"-wide border, divided by 36" = .42 or ½ yard.
***Note:** For information on piecing crosswise border strips, see page 206.*

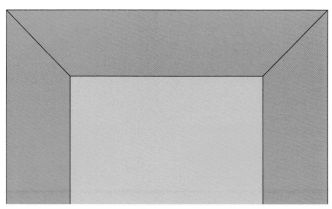

Illustration 4

Adding Mitered Borders

Referring to the chart on *page 211*, determine the border strip width to cut, then add ½" for seam allowances to the desired finished border strip width. Then follow these instructions to add mitered borders to a quilt top (see Illustration 4, *left*).

1. Lay the assembled quilt center on a flat surface.

2. To determine the length of the side border strips, measure through the center of the quilt center from top to bottom, then add twice the finished width of the border to allow for mitering, plus 1" for seam allowances.

3. To determine the length of the top and bottom border strips, measure through the center of the quilt center from side to side, then add twice the finished width of the border to allow for mitering, plus 1" for seam allowances.

4. Cut the border strips on the lengthwise grain of the fabric, if possible. It has less stretch and more stability than the crosswise grain.

5. Fold each border strip in half crosswise and press lightly to mark the center. Fold the assembled quilt center in half and press lightly to mark the center of the side edges.

6. To ensure accuracy when pinning border strips to the quilt top, measure and mark the length of the quilt center on each side. Divide the quilt center's length by 2, and measure this amount in both directions from the center crease on the border strip (see Photo 2B, *above, far left*). Make a mark at each measured point, which should correspond to the quilt center corner.

Photo 2B

Photo 2C

Photo 2D

Photo 2E

7. With right sides together and centers and corner marks aligned, pin a side border strip to one side edge of the quilt center, allowing the excess border strip to extend beyond the corner edges. Sew together, beginning and ending 1/4" from the quilt center's corners (see Photo 2C on *page 209*). Repeat with the opposite side border strip.

8. Repeat steps 6 and 7 with top and bottom border strips. Press the seam allowances toward the border strips.

9. With the wrong side up, overlap the border strips at one corner.

10. Align the edge of a 90° right triangle with the raw edge of a top border strip so the long edge of the triangle intersects the seam in the corner (see Photo 2D on *page 209*). With a pencil, draw along the edge of the triangle between the border seam and the raw edge.

11. Place the bottom border strip on top and repeat the marking process (see Photo 2E on *page 209*).

12. With the right sides of adjacent border strips together, match the marked seam lines and pin (see Photo 2F, *above right*).

13. Beginning with a backstitch at the inside corner, stitch exactly on the marked lines to the outside edges of the border strips. Check the right side of the corner to see that it lies flat (see Photo 2G, *above, far right*).

14. Trim the excess fabric, leaving a 1/4" seam allowance (see Photo 2H, *above right*).

Photo 2F

Photo 2G

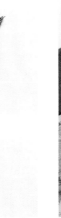

Photo 2H

Photo 2I

15. Press the seam open (see Photo 2I, *above right*).

16. Repeat steps 9 through 15 to mark and sew the remaining border corners in the same manner.

Determining Yardage for Mitered Borders

The border strip width will be cut the desired finished width plus ½" for seam allowances.

Side Border Strips:
Measure vertically (top to bottom) through the center of the quilt center (including seam allowances). _____"
Determine finished width of border _____".
Add twice the finished width of the border to allow for mitering + _____".
Add 1" for seam allowances + _____".
For side borders you will need 2 strips, each = _____" long (A).

For example, if the side edge measurement is 40", including seam allowances, and the finished width of a border strip is 3", then 40"+ 6" + 1" = 47" (A).

Top and Bottom Border Strips:
Measure horizontally (side to side) through the center of the quilt center (including seam allowances). _____"
Determine finished width of border _____".
Add twice the finished width of the border to allow for mitering + _____".
Add 1" for seam allowances + _____".
For top and bottom borders you will need 2 strips, each = _____" long (B).

For example, if the measurement is 35", including seam allowances, and the finished width of the border is 3", then 35" + 6" + 1" = 42" (B).

Yardage Required to Cut Border Strips Lengthwise:
For border width up to 10½":
Larger of (A) or (B) divided by 36" = _____ yards.

Using the example above, (A) is larger than (B), so 47" (A) divided by 36" = 1.30 yards, which rounded up would be 1⅓ yards.
***Note:** With a border up to 10¼" wide, you can cut at least four border strips the length (parallel to the selvage) of the 42"-wide fabric. In some cases, if your border strips are narrower, you may be able to cut more strips from the length.*

For border width 10¾" to 20":
Divide (A + B) by 36" = _____ yards.

For example, if the quilt center measures 60×40" and you want to add an 11"-wide border, 60" + 22" + 1"= 83"(A) and 40" + 22" + 1"= 63"(B). 83" + 63" divided by 36" = 4.05 yards, which rounded up would be 4⅛ yards.
***Note:** With a border up to 20" wide, you can cut at least two border strips the length (parallel to the selvage) of the 42"-wide fabric. In some cases, if your border strips are narrower, you may be able to cut three strips from the length.*

Yardage Required to Cut Border Strips Crosswise:
Take measurements for (A) and (B) as described above.
(A + B) × 2 = _____ (C), or total inches of border needed.
Divide (C) by 42" (round up to next whole number) = _____ (D) or the number of strips that will need to be cut.
Add 1 strip to allow for diagonal seaming of border strips + 1 = _____ (E).
Multiply (E) × width of border, then divide by 36" = _____ yards.

For example, 47" (A) + 42" (B) × 2 = 178" (C) of border needed. 178" (C) divided by 42" = 4.24, which rounded up would be 5 (D) strips. 5 (D) + 1 = 6 (E) strips. 6 (E) strips × 3"-wide border, divided by 36" = .5 or ½ yard.
***Note:** For information on piecing crosswise border strips, see page 206.*

Multiple Borders with Mitered Corners

If you are making more than one mitered border (see Illustration 5, *below*), join strips for each edge together lengthwise (matching the center lines) and sew the joined border strips to the assembled quilt center edges as a unit. Press the seam allowances in alternate directions on adjoining border edges and the seam allowances will match more easily at the miter line.

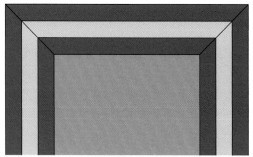

Illustration 5

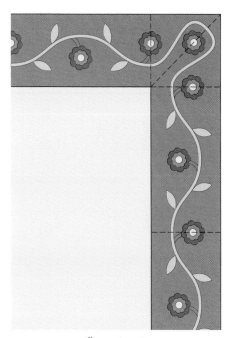

Illustration 6

Appliqué Borders

Appliquéing borders (see Illustration 6, *below left*) may be done before or after joining the border strips to the quilt center, depending on your personal preference.

Appliquéing Border Strips Before Joining Them to the Quilt Center

To appliqué border strips before joining them to the quilt center, follow these steps.

1. Some patterns that call for the appliqué to be done before the borders are added will have the border strips cut larger than necessary to assure that fabric "taken up" in appliqué stitching will not affect the overall desired size of the finished border. You may wish to cut the border strips longer and wider than specified if the pattern does not allow for this.

2. Appliqué the pieces using your desired method (see Chapter 6—Appliqué Techniques for more information on appliqué methods). If excess width and length are added, do not place appliqué pieces too near the outside edge, as they could be cut off in trimming the outer edge,

Photo 2J

or covered by the binding. Do not add any appliqués at the border strip ends that will cover or come within 1" of a straight or mitered seam.

3. After appliquéing is completed, trim the border strips to the specified size if excess allowance was added. Join the border strips to the assembled quilt center following the instructions for your desired method (see Adding Straight Borders on *page 202* or Adding Mitered Borders on *page 209*).

4. Complete the unfinished appliqué where it crosses or comes near the seams.

Appliquéing Border Strips After Joining Them to the Quilt Center

To appliqué border strips after joining them to the quilt center, follow these steps.

1. Some patterns call for the outer edge of the border strips to be trimmed after the appliqué is added to allow for the fabric that might be "taken up" in appliqué stitching. You may wish to cut the border strips larger than specified if the pattern does not allow for this.

2. Join the border strips to the assembled quilt center following the instructions for the desired method (see Adding Straight Borders on *page 202* or Adding Mitered Borders on *page 209*).

3. Appliqué the pieces using your desired method (see Chapter 6—Appliqué Techniques). If excess width and length are added to the strips, do not appliqué pieces too near the outside edge, as they could be cut off in trimming, or covered by the binding.

4. After appliquéing is completed, trim the border strips to the specified size if excess allowance was added (see Photo 2J, *left*).

Pieced Borders

Borders made up of blocks or pieced units (see Illustration 7, *right*) are sewn to quilt edges in the same way as straight borders. Follow the instructions for Adding Straight Borders on *page 202* or Adding Straight Borders with Corner Squares or Blocks on *page 207* to create the desired length border strips from blocks or pieced units. (See Chapter 3—Planning Your Quilt for information on how to design a pieced border.) Pay attention to the layout of the pieced blocks and, if the units are directional, how they turn the corners. It is best to match all four corners of a quilt top.

If this isn't possible, use corner blocks rather than pieced units to avoid taking the focus off the center of the quilt (see Illustration 8, *far right*).

Make sure that the finished size of the border block divides evenly into the finished size of the assembled quilt center. This will prevent you from having to use partial blocks in the border.

Pieced Borders with Diagonally Set Blocks

Borders that contain blocks or units set diagonally, or on point (see Illustration 9, *right*), are easiest to use on a plain quilt center or a quilt center with blocks set on point. Refer to the Diagonal Measurements of Squares chart in Chapter 4—Cutting Techniques for mathematical help in planning a diagonally set border. Make sure that the finished size of the border block divides evenly into the finished size of the pieced quilt center. This will prevent you from having to use partial blocks in the border. (For information on designing a diagonally set border, see Chapter 3—Planning Your Quilt.)

Illustration 7

Illustration 8

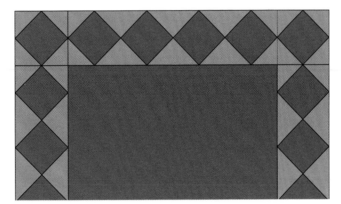

Illustration 9

Scalloped Borders

Scallops on borders (see Illustration 10, *below*) are marked after the border strips are sewn to the assembled quilt center. They are cut after the hand or machine quilting is complete. To plan a scalloped border, follow these steps.

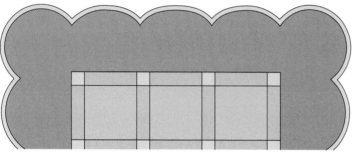

Illustration 10

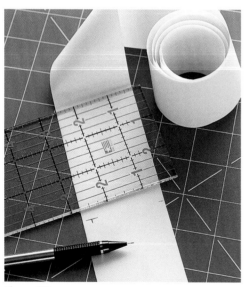

Photo 2K

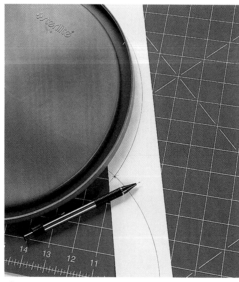

Photo 2L

1. Once the border strips have been added, measure the width and length of the assembled quilt top.

2. Decide on the approximate width of each scallop. In choosing a width, select a number that is divisible into both the width and length of the quilt top. Use the approximate width to determine how many scallops per edge. For example, if the quilt top measures 50×70" and you'd like each scallop to be 10" wide, the top and bottom borders would have five scallops each and the side borders would have seven scallops each.

3. Draw the desired scallop on a strip of paper as long as a border (see Photo 2K, *below, far left*). Rolls of adding machine paper work well for marking shallow scallops. In this example, place two dots 10" apart on the top edge of the paper to mark the top of the scallop. Draw a line between these dots. Make another set of dots between 1 and 2" directly below the first marks. The depth between the first and second marks will determine how deep the indentations or Vs are in the scallops (the sharper the V, the more difficult it is to bind).

4. Using a compass, jar lid, plate, or other rounded edge as a guide, join the second set of marks with a gentle curve that just touches the line drawn between the first set of marks (see Photo 2L, *left*).

5. Once you've created a scallop you like, draw it along the complete length of the paper strip to make a template. Repeat to make as many different-size templates as needed.

6. Position the paper templates on the quilt top and check the corners. Blend the curves of the scallops to round the corners. Once you've blended the edges of one corner, make a paper template of it and trace three more identical paper templates for the remaining corners. Use these paper templates to mark the pattern on the quilt top (see Chapter 4—Cutting Techniques for information on marking a quilt top). Cut through all three layers on the marked lines. Refer to *page 260* for instructions on binding a scalloped edge.

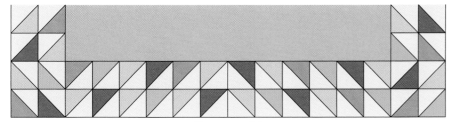

Illustration 11

Directional Borders

Directional borders (see Illustration 11, *above*) are those which have designs running in a particular sequence or order. For instance, sawtooth borders are made up of a series of triangle-squares. Since borders need to appear the same on all four sides, careful planning is required to turn corners smoothly and keep the design moving in the right direction. Sketch the border on paper before proceeding with assembly. Occasionally, directional borders require a special corner unit or block to make the transition from side to side. See Chapter 3—Planning Your Quilt for more information.

Spacer Borders

Spacer borders are plain borders that are sewn between the quilt center and outer pieced borders. Think of a spacer border as an inside mat or one part of a double mat on a framed picture. Spacer borders are a good solution when the dimensions of the pieced border and the pieced quilt center are not compatible, or whenever you'd like to have some visual breathing room between the quilt center and the outer border.

Spacer borders can be the same width on all sides of a quilt, or they can be one width on the sides and another on the top and bottom (see Illustration 12, *top, far right*).

When the same fabric used for the assembled quilt center is used for a spacer border, it can make the center blocks appear to float within the confines of the spacer border (see Illustration 13, *below*).

A spacer border of contrasting fabric calls attention to the separation between the quilt center and the outer border (see Illustration 14, *below right*).

Illustration 12

Illustration 13

Illustration 14

Photo 2M

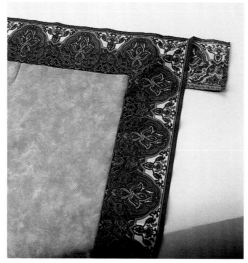

Photo 2N

Photo 2O

Using Border Prints For Mitered Borders

Mitered borders made of a print or striped fabric add complexity to the look of a quilt with little extra work. It may be necessary to purchase extra fabric so all the corners will match.

Mitered Border-Print Borders on a Square Quilt

To make a square quilt with a print border, place like motifs at the center of each side edge so the mitered corners and edges will match.

1. Determine the yardage and measurements for the border strips following the Determining Yardage for Mitered Borders chart on *page 211*. The yardage needed depends on the pattern repeat of the border print across the width of the fabric. For example, if you're making a 4"-wide finished border and the motif is repeated every 6" across the width of the fabric, all borders can be cut from one length of fabric. If you are making a 4"-wide finished border and the motif is printed only once across the width of the

fabric, only one border can be cut from one length of fabric. A total of four lengths will be needed to make the border.

2. Cut the four border strips from the same lengthwise repeat of the border print.

3. Join the border strips to the assembled quilt center following the instructions for Adding Mitered Borders on *page 209*, beginning with Step 5.

Mitered Border-Print Borders on a Rectangular Quilt

1. Determine the yardage and measurements for the border strips following the Determining Yardage for Mitered Borders chart on *page 211*. The yardage needed depends on the pattern repeat of the border print across the width of the fabric, the pattern repeat of the border print along the length of the fabric, and where the border strips will join. Cut the two side border strips first from the same lengthwise repeat of the border print, selecting a motif to be at their centers.

2. Join each side border strip to the side edges of the quilt center, following directions given in Adding Mitered Borders on *page 209*, steps 5 through 7.

3. Fold the border strip corners back at 45° angles as if to miter (see Photo 2M, *above, far left*).

4. Cut the top and bottom border strips from the same lengthwise repeat of the border print, selecting the same motif used at the center of the side border strips for the centers of the top and bottom border strips.

5. Lay the quilt center with its attached side border strips right side up on a work surface (see Photo 2N, *above left*). Align the centers of the top border strip and the upper edge of the quilt center, allowing the excess top border strip to extend under the side border strips.

6. Make a pleat at the center of the top border strip and pull the border strip fabric into the pleat until the desired motif appears at a corner (see Photo 2O, *above*). Pleat an equal amount of fabric from each side of the center on the top border strip.

Photo 2P

Photo 2Q

Photo 2R

7. Fold the pleat to the wrong side of the top border strip and pin (see Photo 2P, *above*). The pleat should align with the marked midpoint on the top edge of the quilt center.

8. Pin the border strips with right sides together at the corners (see Photo 2Q, *above right*).

9. Sew the pleat along the fold lines. Trim the seam allowance to ¼" and press open. Then sew the border strip to the quilt center, joining the corners following Adding Mitered Borders on *page 210*, beginning with Step 9 (see photos 2R and 2S, *above, far right* and *right*).

10. Repeat steps 5 through 9 to add the bottom border strip.

Photo 2S

Assembling *the Quilt Backing*

Most quilters use a single fabric for the quilt back, thus keeping the focus on the quilt top. Some, however, enjoy adding a design to the quilt back, almost making the quilt reversible. Whichever you choose, the backing gives you another opportunity to be creative with fabric choices and colors.

BACKING DESIGN IDEAS

There are many options for using multiple fabrics in your backing. Piece leftover fabrics from the quilt top or from an entirely different quilt project (see Illustrations 15 and 16, *below and below right*).

If there are unused blocks from the quilt top, join them to create a pieced quilt back (see Illustration 17, *below, bottom*).

Another option is to enlarge a block used on the quilt top and use it as a focal point on the quilt back (see Illustration 18, *below, bottom*). This is a good way to include a novelty print or a piece of treasured fabric that is "too good" to cut into pieces.

A quilt back is also a wonderful place to showcase an embroidered verse, a photo-transfer collage, or a sampling of

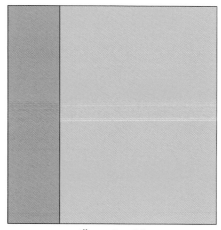

Illustration 15

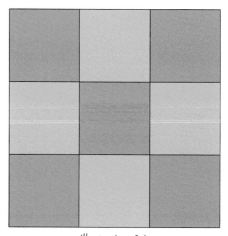

Illustration 16

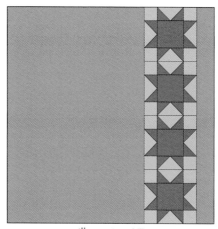

Illustration 17

Illustration 18

coordinating test blocks remaining from previous projects.

If you're concerned about the quality of the hand or machine quilting, choose a backing fabric that will camouflage the stitches, such as a particularly busy one or one that matches the thread color used on the quilt top.

Although muslin is an inexpensive option for a quilt back, keep in mind that it shows every quilting detail and does little to enhance the beauty of the finished quilt.

Consider that a pieced back with many seams can make hand quilting difficult, since the needle must pierce several layers of fabric. A pieced back is of less concern when a project is to be machine-quilted.

Backing fabrics should have the same care requirements as the quilt top and should be preshrunk if the quilt top fabrics were.

PREPARE THE BACKING FABRIC

Like batting, the quilt back needs to be larger than the quilt top to allow for fabric that is taken up during quilting and for stabilization when using a quilting frame. Always add 6" to both the length and width measurements so there is an extra 3" of fabric all around.

Trim off the selvage of all backing fabrics. The selvage edge is tighter than the rest of the yardage and can cause puckering or inward curving in the finished quilt if it is used as a part of the backing.

PLANNING THE QUILT BACK

If the quilt top is wider or longer than the backing fabric width, the backing must be pieced. If seams are necessary, decide whether the seams on the back should be horizontal or vertical.

If the quilt is 40 to 60" wide, horizontal seams save on yardage (see Illustration 19, *right*).

If the quilt is wider than 60", use one or two vertical seams (see Illustration 20, *right*).

A quilt 81 to 120" wide requires a backing that is pieced with two vertical seams (see Illustration 21, *below right*).

The quilt top's measurement determines how many pieces are in the backing. For example, if one dimension of the quilt top is less than 36", use a single piece of 45"-wide fabric for the backing. This width will cover the 36" dimension plus the additional 6". In this case, add 6" to the remaining quilt top dimension and divide by 36" to determine the yardage necessary. ***Note:*** *The calculations assume 42" of usable fabric can be cut from a 44/45"-wide fabric.*

Manufacturers offer fabrics in widths of 60", 90", and 108", but they are available in a limited color and design assortment.

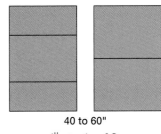

40 to 60"

Illustration 19

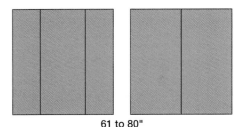

61 to 80"

Illustration 20

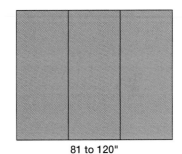

81 to 120"

Illustration 21

Chapter 7 – Assembling the Quilt Top and Backing

219

Backing Yardage Guide

Quilt Top Width	Seam Orientation	Yardage to Purchase
40–60"	Horizontal	2 × width +12" ÷ 36"=
61–80"	Vertical	2 × length +12" ÷ 36"=
81–120"	Vertical	3 × length +18" ÷ 36"=

Examples					
Width × Length	Seam Orientation	Figures	Add 6" per piece	Divide by 36"	Purchase
47×74"	Horizontal	47"× 2 widths	94"+12"=	106"÷36"=	3 yds.
70×84"	Vertical	84"× 2 lengths	168"+12"=	180"÷36"=	5 yds.
95×110"	Vertical	110"× 3 lengths	330"+18"=	348"÷36"=	9⅔ yds.

Backing for a Quilt Top 40–60" Wide

Horizontal seams are most economical for quilts that are 40 to 60" wide. Determine the width of the quilt top. Multiply this measurement by 2. Add 12", then divide by 36" to find the yardage you need to purchase for backing.

For example, if the finished quilt top is 50" square, the backing piece must measure 56" square. To figure backing yardage, multiply 50" × 2 = 100"; 100" + 12" = 112"; 112" divided by 36" = 3.11 yards. In this case you should purchase a minimum of 3⅛ yards of 44/45"-wide backing fabric.
Note: The calculations and diagrams assume 42" of usable fabric can be cut from a 44/45"-wide fabric.

Piecing Method 1

To piece a quilt back with two horizontal seams (see Illustration 22, *right*), first cut off a length of 56" (42×56"). Then cut two 8×56" pieces from the remaining 56" length. For added stability, use ½" seam allowances when piecing the quilt backing. Sew an 8"-wide piece to each long side of the first piece to make a pieced back that measures 56" square. Press the seam allowances open.

Piecing Method 2

To piece a quilt back with a single seam (see Illustration 23, *right*), first cut off a length of 56" (42×56"). Then cut a 15×56" piece from the remaining fabric. For added stability, use ½" seam allowances when piecing the quilt backing. Sew together the two pieces along a pair of long edges to make a pieced back that measures 56" square. Press the seam allowance open.

Piecing Method 3

To piece a quilt back and have the horizontal seam centered (see Illustration 24, *right*), cut the fabric length in half. For added stability, use ½" seam allowances when piecing the quilt backing. Sew together the two pieces along a pair of long

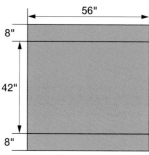

Illustration 22

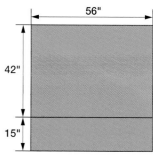

Illustration 23

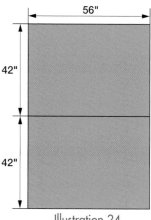

Illustration 24

edges to make a pieced back that measures 56×83". Press the seam allowance open. When layering the backing, batting, and quilt top, position the batting and quilt top so that the backing seam is centered. Then trim off the excess backing fabric.

Backing for a Quilt Top 61–80" Wide

Vertical seams are most economical for quilts that are 61 to 80" wide.

Determine the length of the quilt top. Multiply this measurement by 2. Add 12", then divide by 36" to find the yardage necessary for backing.

For example, if your quilt top is 65×80", you'll need a backing piece that measures 71×86". To figure backing yardage, multiply 80" × 2 = 160"; 160" + 12" = 172"; 172" divided by 36" = 4.77 yards. In this case you should purchase a minimum of 4⅞ yards of 44/45"-wide backing fabric.
Note: *The calculations and diagrams assume 42" of usable fabric can be cut from a 44/45"-wide fabric.*

Piecing Method 1

To piece a quilt back with one vertical seam (see Illustration 25, *below left*), cut the fabric length in half crosswise. For added stability, use ½" seam allowances when piecing the quilt backing. Sew the two pieces together along a pair of long edges to make a pieced back that measures 83×86". Press the seam allowance open.

Piecing Method 2

To piece your quilt back with two vertical seams (see Illustration 26, *below*), cut the yardage in half crosswise (42×86"). Cut one of the pieces in half lengthwise to get two 21×86" pieces. For added stability, use ½" seam allowances when piecing the quilt backing. Sew one narrow piece on either side of the first piece to make a pieced back that measures 82×86". Press the seam allowances open.

Backing for a Quilt Top 81–120" Wide

Vertical seams are most economical for quilts that are 81 to 120" wide.

Determine the length of the quilt top. Multiply this measurement by 3. Add 18", then divide by 36" to find the yardage necessary for backing.

For example, if your quilt top is 85×100", you'll need a backing piece that measures 91×106". To figure backing yardage, multiply 100" × 3 = 300"; 300" + 18" = 318"; 318" divided by 36" = 8.83 yards. In this case a minimum of 8⅞ yards of backing fabric is necessary.

Piecing Method

The only efficient way to piece a backing this large is with two vertical seams (see Illustration 27, *below*). Cut the total yardage into three equal lengths of 106". For added stability, use ½" seam allowances when piecing the quilt backing. Sew together the three lengths along long edges to make a pieced back that measures 124×106". Press the seam allowances open.

When layering the backing, batting, and quilt top, you'll have excess fabric on the side edges. Either evenly space the seams or have them offset. Once the backing is positioned, trim off the excess backing fabric, leaving an extra 3" of fabric on all edges.

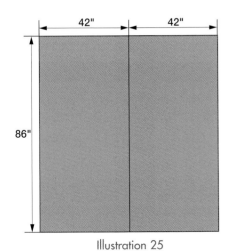

Illustration 25

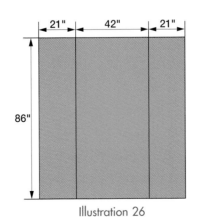

Illustration 26

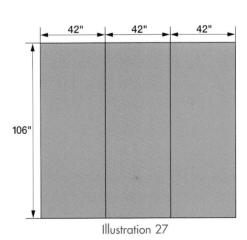

Illustration 27

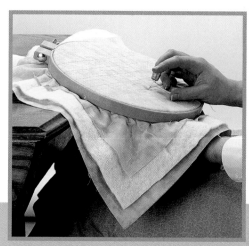

QUILTING
IDEAS

Choosing the right batting and quilting

designs can enhance the intricacy or

simplicity of your quilt.

NINE-PATCH CHECKERBOARD STAR

Amish and Mennonite quiltmakers in Pennsylvania are famous for their quilts with simple but visually distinctive surface designs and dense, decorative quilting. This Nine-Patch Checkerboard Star from Berks County, Pennsylvania, is made in colors that were popular among Mennonite quilters and others in the second half of the 19th century: green, double pink, and gold. Green and pink also were used to make the attractive inner sawtooth border. The brown print setting fabric nearly hides the wonderful feather quilting in the sashing strips and the cables quilted in the outer border.

Quilting *Ideas*

A beautiful quilt top and backing deserve a batting that will enhance the finished project and be suited to its use. Once the batting is in place, the process of quilting can begin. Whether you choose to quilt by hand or machine, the quilting designs you select for your project can add to its overall appearance and durability.

SELECTING A QUILT DESIGN

Instructions for making a quilt generally come with detailed steps, numerous patterns, and helpful diagrams. How the project should be quilted often goes unsaid. Many quiltmakers simply quilt in the ditch or in an allover meandering pattern because they don't know what else to do.

If "quilt as desired" is the instruction, those three words needn't leave you wondering how to proceed. Instead, look at them as an invitation to begin the next phase of completing a fabulous quilt project.

Questions to Ask

Take some time and ask yourself the following questions. They'll help you make decisions on how to quilt a project.

Is this a quilt I hope will remain in my family for several generations?
When creating an heirloom quilt, consider quilting the project with elaborate designs and intricate details. For other projects, simple quilting designs that are easy to complete may be more appropriate.

Is this quilt going to be laundered often?
Select machine quilting for quilts that will receive lots of use.

How much time do I have to complete this quilt?
Save hand quilting for projects where you can afford to invest the time. If time is limited but you want to hand-quilt a project, select easy-to-do designs and motifs.

What's my preferred quilting method, by hand or by machine?
Just as when selecting a project, if you're excited about the process you've chosen, you'll be more likely to finish it successfully. Whether you want to hand- or machine-quilt may also affect your choice of a quilting design, as some lend themselves better to one technique than the other. For example, if you're going to machine-quilt, a continuous line design is often the best option since there will be less starting and stopping.

Do I want my quilting stitches to be visible in the quilt top?
Whether quilting by hand or machine, save intricate, close quilting for projects that will showcase the stitching and more basic designs for those with busier fabrics and more pieces where it's likely the quilting stitches won't show.

Does this quilt have a traditional, folk art, or contemporary mood?
Sometimes the feel of a quilt will drive the quilting design. For example, a traditional quilt may call for a feathered wreath design, but a folk art quilt may look best with big stitches quilted in perle cotton.

Finding Inspiration

Ideas for quilting motifs and designs don't have to be limited to the precut stencils, templates, and books of quilting designs available at your local quilt shop. Look around you for inspiration.

One way to generate designs is to think about the theme of a project. For example, for a holiday quilt, consider holiday-related items, such as ornaments, strings of lights, trees, holly, garland, mittens, snowflakes, reindeer, and stockings, as potential quilting motifs. Evaluate the possibilities based on difficulty and where they might work best on the quilt.

A round ornament could be stitched as a simple circle, for instance, while a reindeer would probably require a stencil. A wavy line with occasional loops could represent garland on a narrow inner border.

Another place to find a quilting design is within the fabric of the quilt. Are there motifs in one of the prints, such as oak leaves or flowers, that could work as a quilting design?

The architecture of buildings can provide numerous concepts. The exteriors of old brick buildings often provide interesting grid arrangements that can be translated into quilting patterns, for instance. Wrought-iron fences and gates might suggest beautiful scrollwork, perfect for border designs. Door arches, moldings, or pressed-tin ceilings may offer ideas for your next medallion-style quilt.

Even household items, such as picture frames, jewelry, and kitchen tiles, can produce quilting design ideas. The bubbles in an aquarium, for example, may suggest the perfect pattern for a goldfish quilt.

Examine both new and old quilts that you like. Ask yourself: Why do I like this quilt? What about it appeals to me? Is it the pieced or appliquéd pattern? Is it the colors? Or is it the quilting design that brings it all together?

QUILTING TERMINOLOGY

Understanding these general quilting terms will help you gain confidence.

Allover designs, particularly geometrics, can be stitched over an entire quilt without regard to shapes or fabrics. Allover designs can be quilted from either the top side or the backing.

Backgrounds and fillers fill in open interior spaces, such as setting squares, circles, or hearts, with stitching. Stitch squares, diamonds, clamshells, or other small regular shapes in open areas as well as in the background outside an appliqué or quilted motif. The closely spaced lines of a filler tend to flatten the area, creating a low-relief, textured appearance.

Big, or utility, stitches require a heavier thread, such as perle cotton, and a large hand stitch. They result in a folk art appearance.

Echo quilting involves stitching multiple lines that follow the outline of an appliqué or other design element, repeating its shape. The evenly spaced quilting lines should be ¼ to ½" apart. Echo quilting can completely fill a background.

In the ditch means stitching just inside a seam line. The stitches disappear into the seam, which makes a patch, block, or motif stand out from its background. It's an easy method to do by machine.

Outline quilting is done ¼" from a seam line or edge of an appliqué shape, just past the extra thickness of the pressed seam allowance. To quilt as close as possible to a seam line, choose the side opposite the pressed seam allowance.

Stippling, also called allover meandering or puzzle quilting, can be stitched by hand or machine. It involves random curves, straight rows of regularly placed stitches (lined up or staggered), or random zigzags. For the best effect, stippling should be closely spaced.

BORDER DESIGNS AND BALANCE

Borders and quilt centers are usually quilted separately. One option is to leave the border unquilted, but that tends to make the final project look unbalanced. That's also the result if the border quilting doesn't fit the rest of the project. Don't skimp on quilting in the borders; try to keep the amount of quilting equal to the rest of the quilt.

To balance the quilting designs, include the borders when you begin thinking about quilting designs for the blocks. Think about what will coordinate with or complement the quilting designs selected for the rest of the quilt top.

If you've selected a particular motif or design for the quilt center, is there a way to continue that same motif or a variation of

the motif in the border? For example, if the blocks are quilted with a simple flower, can it be repeated in the border, maybe adding a connecting vine-and-leaf pattern? If you are crosshatching the blocks, can you crosshatch through the border as well?

As you select quilting designs, evaluate the fabric used in the border. Is it a solid or a subtle print that will really show off a quilting design? Or is the fabric so busy it will hide any type of quilting?

If there is a solid inner border and a print outer border, quilt a recognizable pattern in the solid border; it will show up better. Crosshatch or stipple the busier fabric.

Auditioning Designs

Once you have an idea for a border quilting design, it's best to create a paper template or tracing paper overlay to see how the design will fit in the length of the borders and how it will turn the corners. Use a temporary quilting pencil or marker to draw it on the quilt top. Always test the pencil or marker on scraps of the fabrics used in the quilt top before marking on the actual top. (See Marking the Quilt Top, which begins on *page 228*, for more information.)

Adjusting Border Designs to Fit

There is no single formula for success in adjusting border designs to fit a quilt. Because of the variety of factors involved—border width and length, quilting design width and repeat—the ways to adjust a border design are numerous.

An important consideration in adjusting the design is that it is best for all sides and corners to match. The most challenging method is to adjust the length of a continuous design. However, there are options other than adjusting a border design's width and length.

Extending the Quilt Center Design

If an overall design, such as crosshatching or stippling was used on the quilt center, consider extending it onto the borders as well, as shown in Illustration 1, *right*.

Meandering Vine Design

Meander a vine design along each border, as shown in Illustration 2, *right*. At the corners, be sure to turn the design in an identical manner, creating mirror images in opposite corners of the quilt.

Repeated Block Design

Repeat a block design used in the quilt center in the border (or choose a different design), evenly spacing the design along the length. Pay particular attention to the direction of the motifs. You may wish to point them all in one direction if the motif has a definite top and bottom, as shown in Illustration 3, *right*. Or point all the designs toward or away from the quilt center.

Combining Elements

If you choose a rhythmic or wavy design, such as swags or feathers, but the motifs don't fit the border length, combine them with a block design at the midpoint of each border, as shown in Illustration 4, *right*.

Adjusting the Length of the Design

Adjusting a continuous line design takes the most time and effort of any adjustment, but when completed results in a design which appears to seamlessly circle the entire quilt. The instructions that follow are for modifying a stencil design. Drawing the design first on paper (shelf liner or freezer paper) will help prevent incorrect markings on the quilt top.

Though the steps of adjusting border designs are generally the same, how extra length is taken out so that the design fits is unique to each project.

As a rule, it's best not to modify a design at the corners. Instead, adjust the design somewhere near, but not at, the midpoint.

1. Cut two lengths of paper, one equal in width and length to the quilt's finished side borders and one equal in width and length to the top/bottom borders. Do not include the seam allowances. (If the quilt is square, one strip will do.) Label the strips and mark the center of each.

2. Trace the stencil's corner design on the ends of each strip. Use the registration marks on the stencil to make sure the design is properly aligned on the paper border.

3. Align the center registration mark on the stencil with the midpoint marked on the border. Beginning from this point, slide the stencil between the midpoint and corner to figure how many repetitions of the design will fit. The alterations will likely be different for the side and top/bottom borders.

If the amount of design adjustment is small, it may be possible to adjust a bit of length in one motif without noticeably altering the design.
Note: *If the amount to be added or reduced is too great, the design will be distorted, calling attention to the motif that was squeezed or stretched to fit.*

If the amount is significant, it will be necessary to add or delete a part of several motifs to make the adjustment. When doing so, keep in mind the overall shape of the design and use the stencil as much as possible to trace the design on the paper.

4. Once you're pleased with the paper patterns, transfer the modified design to the quilt top. (See Marking the Quilt Top on *page 228*.)

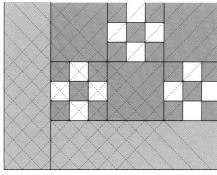

Illustration 1

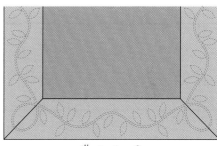

Illustration 2

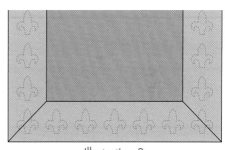

Illustration 3

Illustration 4

Photo 1A

Photo 1B

Photo 1C

Marking the Quilt Top

Quilting designs generally are marked on a quilt top before it's layered with batting and a backing. First select a marking method; several options follow. Then select the appropriate marking tool, keeping in mind that some marking tools are more permanent than others (see Chapter 1—Tools and Materials for more information).

Secure the quilt top to a large, flat work surface with tape or clips to prevent shifting. Position the quilting design in the center of the quilt top to begin. Reposition the design and quilt top as needed to mark the entire quilt center or quilt top. Before marking the borders, see Adjusting Border Designs to Fit on *page 226* for more information.

Using a Tracing Method

There are several tracing methods to transfer a quilting design to a quilt top. Because these methods involve placing a light source behind the layered quilting design and quilt top, tracing works best on small- to medium-size projects.

Light Bulb and Glass-Top Table

1. Place a bright light beneath a glass-top table. Or, pull apart a table that accommodates leaves and place a piece of glass or clear acrylic over the opening.

2. Tape the quilting design to the top of the glass. Secure the quilt top over the design and trace the design onto the fabric (see Photo 1A, *above left*).

Light Box

1. Tape the quilting design to a light box. Turn on the light source.

2. Secure the quilt top over the design, and trace the design onto the fabric (see Photo 1B, *above*).

Sunny Window

1. Tape the quilting design to a clean, dry window on a sunny day.

2. Tape the quilt top over the design and trace the design onto the fabric (see Photo 1C, *above right*).

Using Stencils and Templates

1. To transfer a quilting design using a stencil or template, place the pattern on the quilt top and secure it in place with tape or weights.

2. Mark the pattern on the fabric.

Using Tear-Away Patterns

1. Mark the quilting design on tracing paper, tissue paper, or tear-away stabilizer (see Photo 1D, *opposite*). Make one pattern for each time the design will be used on the quilt top.

2. Baste or pin the pattern to the quilt top. Quilt along the design lines through both the paper and the quilt (see Photo 1E, *opposite*).

3. Gently tear the paper patterns away from the quilt top, as shown in Photo 1F, *opposite*.

Photo 1D

Photo 1E

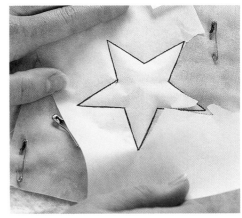

Photo 1F

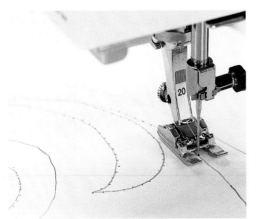

Photo 1G

Photo 1H

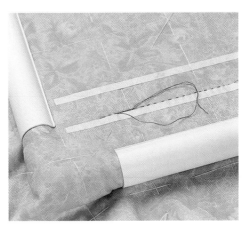

Photo 1I

Using Perforated Patterns

1. Mark the quilting design on sturdy paper. Sew over the paper's design lines with a sewing machine and an unthreaded needle, as shown in Photo 1G, *above*. Or, trace the lines with a needle-pointed tracing wheel.

2. Secure the quilt top to a firm surface, then secure the perforated pattern to the quilt top. Go over the perforations with chalk, pounce, or stamping powder (see Photo 1H, *above right*).

Using Tape

Use quilter's tape, painter's tape, or masking tape to mark straight-line quilting designs, as shown in Photo 1I, *above right*. (See Chapter 1—Tools and Materials for more information on tapes.) The tape can be put in place before or after the quilt layers are sandwiched together. Reposition the tape as needed until the quilting is complete, then remove it.

Note: *To avoid a sticky residue on fabric, do not leave tape in place for extended periods of time.*

BATTING

Batting is the soft layer between the quilt top and backing that gives a quilt dimension and definition and offers warmth.

Because it comes in various thicknesses and fibers, batting can make a quilt flat or puffy, stiff or drapable. It is available by the yard or packaged to fit standard bed sizes.

Batting should complement the nature and use of the finished quilt. Check package labels, talk to other quilters, and test samples to find the batting with the qualities that are important for the project.

Manufacturing Process

All battings start out as individual fibers that are carded and processed into a sheet or web. Without further treatment, these battings would be difficult to use as the unbonded fibers would come apart or clump together inside a quilt. An untreated batting also would be susceptible to bearding or fiber migration (when batting fibers come through the quilt top).

To make a sheet or web of batting more stable, and hence more useable, it's either bonded or needle-punched, treatment processes that result in battings with different characteristics.

Bonding

Manufacturers chemically bond batting fibers by adding a resin or using heat. Resin bonding helps wool or polyester battings resist bearding.

Bonded batts usually have a higher loft and airier appearance than needle-punched batts. A bonded batting holds up well with use and does not require extensive quilting. If a batting is not bonded, it can be difficult to work with and have an uneven appearance.

Needle-Punched

This treatment process involves running a barbed needle through the batting fibers to "tangle" them and provide some stability to the web. For additional stability, a scrim—a loosely woven piece of fabric that resembles a net—can be added to a batting sheet or web before it's needle-punched.

The loft of needle-punched batting varies according to the number of layers used in the manufacturing process. The fewer the layers, the lower the loft; the lower the loft, the better fine-quilting details can be seen.

Bleaching

Natural batting fibers are ecru in color. They can be bleached to create bright white battings for use with white or very light-color fabrics.

BATTING QUALITIES

Carefully read the manufacturer's label to learn the specific qualities of a particular batting.

Bearding

Some battings beard, or have fibers migrate through the quilt top, more than others, but any bearding is a problem when light battings are used with dark fabrics, or the reverse. Test battings with the quilt's fabrics to see if bearding will be a problem. (See Testing on *page 233* for more information about selecting the best batting for a specific project.) Don't use an untreated batting. Though bearding can be attributed to a problem with the batting choice, it also could be caused by a very loosely woven fabric. Knowing what qualities to watch for can make a significant difference in your satisfaction with the finished quilt.

Drapability

The density or sparseness of the quilting and the loft of the batting will affect the drape, or relative stiffness or softness, of the finished quilt. In general, a thinner batting and more dense quilting will result in a quilt with a softer drape. A thicker batting in a quilt that has been tied, rather than heavily quilted, will have less drape.

Grain Line

Battings can have a grain line just as fabric does. The lengthwise grain is stable and doesn't have much give, while the crosswise grain will be stretchy. In order to prevent unwanted distortion, match the batting's lengthwise grain with the backing fabric's lengthwise grain. Quilt the lengthwise grain first to limit distortion.

Loft

The thickness of a batting is referred to as its loft. Differing loft levels result in differing appearances in a finished quilt. Refer to the chart on *page 232* to choose a loft compatible with your finishing method.

Keep in mind that the higher the loft, the less drapability in the finished quilt.

Resilience

Resilience refers to the batting's ability to regain its original shape. A resilient batting, such as one made from polyester, will spring back when unfolded and resist creasing. This is a desirable feature for a finished quilt with a puffy appearance. Cotton battings are less resilient and more prone to creasing, but some of their other qualities may compensate and make their use desirable. A cotton/polyester blend batting is somewhere in between in terms of resilience.

Warmth

Cotton battings have the ability to absorb moisture, thus offering cooling comfort in the summer and a natural warmth in the winter. Wool battings provide warmth with

little weight. Synthetic fibers, such as polyester, lack the breathability of natural fibers.

Washability and Shrinkage

Although polyester and wool battings resist shrinkage, cotton battings can shrink from 3 to 5 percent. Check the package label, then decide whether or not to preshrink a batting. Some quilters prefer the puckered, antique look that comes from a batting that shrinks after it's been quilted.

SELECT YOUR BATTING

Choose a batting for your project based on the finished quilt's intended use and desired appearance.

Quilting Distance

The distance between quilting stitches is largely determined by batting qualities. The manufacturer's label will specify the maximum distance between stitching rows. If the recommended maximum distance is exceeded, the batting will shift and bunch up later.

If a finished quilt project will be tied, it is essential to select a quilt batting that allows a wide distance between stitches. A heavily quilted design will require a different choice of batting. Always refer to the package label to see if the batting you're considering is compatible with the amount of quilting planned for a project.

Intended Use

Consider the intended use of a quilt. Is it a baby quilt that will be washed and dried extensively? Will it be placed on a child's bed and get pulled and tugged? Are you making a wall hanging that needs to maintain sharp, crisp corners? Or a quilt that will drape loosely over a bed and tuck beneath the pillows? Is it an heirloom project that will be used sparingly and only

General Batting Characteristics

BATTING TYPE	ADVANTAGES	DISADVANTAGES	CHARACTERISTICS
100% Cotton	Natural fiber so batting breathes. Resists fiber migration. Readily available.	May have seeds and plant residue that can release oils and stain the quilt. Often cannot be prewashed. Shrinks 3 to 5% when washed. May be too dense for beginning hand quilters to needle.	Can give a puckered appearance if washed after quilting. Soft, drapable. Good for experienced quilters' fine, hand-quilting stitches or machine quilting.
Cotton/Polyester Blends: 80/20, 50/50	Some natural fibers so batting breathes. Resists fiber migration. Easy for beginning hand quilters to needle. Readily available.	Some shrinkage, which can be avoided in many cases, if desired, by prewashing.	Low to medium loft. Drapable. Good for hand quilting and machine quilting.
Wool and Wool Blends	Natural insulator. Preshrunk. Available in black.	May have inconsistent loft. May need to be encased in cheesecloth or scrim if not bonded.	Blend of fibers from different animal breeds. Resiliency enhances quilting stitches. Soft, drapable. Good for hand and machine quilting.
Silk	Good choice for quilted garments. Does not shrink. Can be washed.	Expensive. Not widely available. Damaged by exposure to direct sunlight.	Has excellent body and drape. Lightweight. Good for hand quilting and machine quilting.
Flannel	Lightweight alternative to traditional batting. Readily available.	Extreme low loft limits quilting pattern development.	100% cotton. Lightweight, thin. Good for machine quilting.
Polyester	Resilient, lightweight. Cannot be harmed by moths or mildew. Readily available. Available in black.	Synthetic fibers lack breathability.	Available in many lofts. Suitable for hand quilting and machine quilting. High loft is good for tied quilts, comforters.
Fusible	No need to prewash. Eliminates need for basting. Good choice for small projects.	Limited batting options and sizes. Adds adhesive to quilt. Difficult for hand quilters to needle.	Good for machine quilting. Eliminates need for basting.

laundered once every few years? Or is it a decorative item that will never be washed? Is it a table runner that needs to lie extremely flat? Questions such as these will help evaluate which batting is best for a particular project.

Desired Appearance

Consider the fabrics in the quilt top and the backing. Are they light or dark colors? Will a dark batting show through the fabric? Would a white batting beard through the top?

Did you wash and dry your fabrics before making your quilt top, or do you want the layers to shrink as one after you've finished the project to result in an antique appearance?

What loft do you want your quilt to have? Do you want it to be big and puffy or flat and drapable?

Quilting Method

Will a project be quilted by hand or machine, or will it be tied? Do you want to use perle cotton and a utility stitch to create a folk art look?

The batting type dictates the spacing between rows of quilting, so decide on dense or sparse stitching before selecting a batting. The manufacturer's label will specify the maximum distance. If this distance is exceeded when quilting, the batting will shift and bunch up, causing the finished project to look uneven. To tie a project, select a batting that specifies a wide distance between stitches.

Fibers

Consider whether you want natural, synthetic, or a blend of fibers. Each has different qualities. (For more information, see the General Batting Characteristics chart, *opposite*.)

Size

The quilt batting needs to be larger than the quilt top to allow for take-up during quilting and for stabilization when using a quilting frame. Add 6" to both the length and width measurements to allow an extra 3" of batting around the entire quilt.

Testing

To be sure that the batting will be satisfactory, test it with similar fabrics, thread, quilting technique, and washing

process (if desired) used in the quilt top. Record the results for future reference. Because same-type battings from different manufacturers can vary in qualities and results, keeping records of the battings you use and your personal preferences will help you make future selections.

In addition, when looking at other quilters' finished projects, ask the makers what battings they used. The answers can help you determine the finished appearance you prefer.

PREPARE THE BATTING

Once the quilt top is marked, it's time to prepare the batting.

1. Remove the batting from its packaging and spread it out on a large flat surface to allow the folds to relax overnight. Or fluff the batting in a clothes dryer for a few minutes on an air-dry setting to remove wrinkles.

2. Trim the batting so that it's at least 3" larger on all sides than the quilt top.

Creative Tip

When I baste a quilt sandwich, I use number-two safety pins and just love them.

My favorite tool is the safety pin closer. It really saves my fingers.

—CINDY, NATIONAL EDUCATION TRAINER

Photo 1J

Photo 1K

Photo 1L

ASSEMBLE THE LAYERS

Take ample time layering the quilt top, batting, and backing. Being careful at this point will save frustration when quilting. It is best to assemble the layers on a large, flat surface where the entire quilt top can be spread out.

1. If the quilt backing is pieced, press all the seam allowances open. This will prevent added bulk when you are quilting.

2. Place the quilt backing wrong side up on a large, flat surface. Tape, clip, or otherwise secure the quilt backing to the work surface (see Photo 1J, *above*).

3. Center and smooth the batting in place atop the quilt backing (see Photo 1K, *above right*). If desired, baste the batting and backing together with a single large cross-stitch in the center to prevent the layers from shifting. (This is especially important when working on a surface that is smaller than the quilt top.)

4. Center the quilt top right side up on top of the batting. To be sure that it is centered, fold it in half with right side inside (see Photo 1L, *above right*). Align the center fold of the quilt with the center of the batting, then unfold the quilt top and smooth out any wrinkles.

5. Square up the quilt top (for more information, see Chapter 7—Assembling the Quilt Top and Backing). To check that the quilt top has not been stretched or pulled out of alignment during the layering process, place a large, square ruler in one corner (see Photo 1M, *opposite*). The edges of the ruler should be flush with the quilt top's edges.

If the quilt is squared up, pin the border in that corner to hold it in place. Repeat in the remaining three corners. If the quilt top is not square, repeat Step 4, taking care not to stretch the quilt top out of shape.

6. Pin or baste all the layers together, beginning at the center. Be careful not to

shift the layers, and work toward the edges, smoothing fabrics as you go. (Refer to the basting instructions that follow for additional information.)

Thread Basting

This method is most common for hand quilters because it works better in a hoop than pins.

1. With stitches about 2" long, baste the three layers together by stitching a horizontal line and a vertical line through the center of the quilt sandwich to form quadrants on the quilt top. Then baste diagonally in both directions (see Photo 1N, *opposite*).

2. Add basting stitches 3 to 4" apart over the entire surface of the quilt top (or follow the batting manufacturer's directions for spacing).
Note: *If you'll be quilting in a hoop, use 1 to 2" long basting stitches spaced 1 to 2" apart. Because the hoop will be repeatedly moved and repositioned, the shorter stitch length and closer stitches will help prevent shifting.*

Pin Basting

Machine quilters generally pin baste because it is easier to remove pins than basting threads from underneath stitching.

1. Pin the three layers together with rust-proof safety pins, making a horizontal line and a vertical line through the center of the quilt sandwich to form quadrants on the quilt top.
Note: Be sure to use rust-proof pins, as they won't stain fabrics if left in place for an extended period of time.

2. Add pins over the surface of the quilt top at 3 to 4" intervals (see Photo 1O, *below right*).

Spray Basting

Basting sprays are best for small quilt projects, such as wall hangings. Follow the manufacturer's directions to adhere the layers to one another. Take care not to overspray, which can lead to a gummy buildup on your quilting needle. (See Chapter 1—Tools and Materials for more information on basting sprays.)

Photo 1M

Photo 1N

Photo 1O

Photo 1P

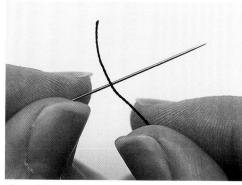

Photo 1Q

HAND QUILTING

Hand quilting results in broken lines of stitches and a quilt with a soft look. Methods of hand quilting vary as much as quilters do. Adapt the techniques that follow to suit your style.

Practice pays when it comes to hand quilting. If you're new to the process, start with straight lines, then try to echo patterns. As you gain proficiency, you'll be motivated to do more, which will lead to even better results.

Small, evenly spaced stitches are the hallmark of hand quilting. A beginner should aim for evenly spaced, uniform-size stitches. Your quilting stitches will generally decrease in size as you gain experience.

Hand-Quilting Setup
(See Chapter 1—Tools and Materials for more information on hand-quilting tools, supplies, and work space setup.)

Some hand quilters like to hold their quilts loosely in their laps as they stitch, a method referred to as "lap quilting."

Wooden hoops or frames are often used to hold quilt layers together for quilting, keeping them smooth and evenly taut. The layers of a quilt should be basted together before inserting them into a hoop or frame.

Some quilters prefer hoops to frames because they are smaller and lighter, take up less storage space, are portable, and can be retightened as needed.

The size and style you choose—whether it's a hoop you can hold in your lap, a hoop attached to a floor stand, or a large quilting frame—depends upon your personal preference and the mobility you desire. You might try several types before deciding which works best for you. (See Chapter 1— Tools and Materials for more information.)

Hand quilters generally use a size 10 or 12 between needle and 100% cotton hand-quilting thread. (Hand-quilting thread differs from machine-quilting thread in that it is heavier and is usually coated to help it glide more easily through the fabric.)

Be sure that you're comfortably seated, with the hoop or frame at an angle you can easily see and reach without straining your shoulders, arms, and hands. The quilt layers should be securely basted so they won't shift (see Photo 1P, *above left*).

Starting and Stopping Hand-Quilting Stitches
Stitch with an 18" length of hand-quilting thread in your needle. Begin and end stitching by burying the thread tail between the layers of the quilt; this prevents knots from showing on the front or back of the quilt.

Securing Thread to Begin
1. With your needle threaded, hold the thread tail over the needle, extending it about ½" above (see Photo 1Q, *above*).

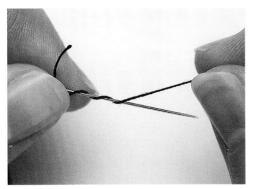

Photo 1R

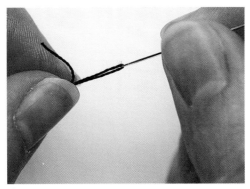

Photo 1S

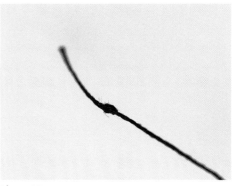

Photo 1T

2. Holding the thread tail against the needle with one hand, use the other hand to wrap the thread around the needle clockwise two or three times (see Photo 1R, *above*).

3. Pinching the thread tail and wraps with your thumb and forefinger, grasp the needle near the point and gently pull it through the thread wraps (see Photo 1S, *above right*).

4. Continue pinching the thread wraps until the thread is pulled completely through and forms a small, firm knot near the end of the thread tail (see Photo 1T, *above, far right*). This is called a quilter's knot.

5. Insert the needle into the quilt through the quilt top and batting, but not into the backing, a few inches from where you want to quilt, as shown in Photo 1U, *center right*.

Bring the needle back to the surface in position to make the first stitch.

6. Tug gently on the thread to pop the knot through the quilt top and embed it in the batting, as shown in photos 1V and 1W, *center, far right* and *right*.

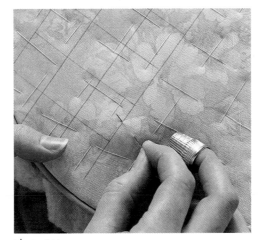

Photo 1U

Photo 1V

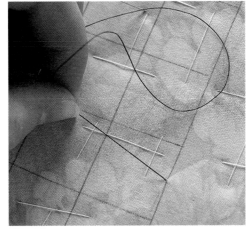

Photo 1W

❧Creative Tip

To keep a thimble from falling off your finger, try cutting a 1½" circle of Skid Pad, positioning it over your finger, and gently sliding the thimble over it. Trim the excess so your thread doesn't get caught on it.

—COLLEEN, SALES ASSOCIATE

Chapter 8 – Quilting Ideas

Securing Thread to End

1. Wind the thread twice around the needle close to the quilt top, as if making a French knot (see Photo 1X, *below*).

2. Holding the thread wraps next to the quilt top, run the needle tip through the quilt top and batting layers only.

3. Rock the needle tip back up, bringing the needle out ½ to 1" away from the stitching, as shown in Photo 1Y, *below*.

4. Tug gently on the thread to pop the knot through the quilt top and embed it in the batting (see Photo 1Z, *below left, bottom*).

5. Holding the thread tail taut, clip the thread close to the quilt top, releasing the end to snap below the surface of the quilt top, as shown in Photo 2A, *below bottom*.

Hand-Quilting Running Stitch

For this classic hand-quilting stitch, wear a thimble on the middle finger of your stitching hand.

1. Hold the needle between your thumb and index finger. Place your other hand under the quilt, with the tip of your index finger on the spot where the needle will come through the quilt back. With the needle angled slightly away from you, push the needle through layers until you feel the tip of the needle beneath the quilt (see Photo 2B, *opposite*).

2. When you feel the needle tip, slide your finger underneath the quilt toward you, pushing up against the side of the needle to help return it to the top (see Photo 2C, *opposite*). At the same time, with your top hand roll the needle away from you. Gently push the needle forward and up through the quilt layers until the amount of the needle showing is the length you want the next stitch to be.

3. Lift the eye of the needle with your thimble finger, positioning your thumb just ahead of the stitching. Rock the eye of the needle upward until the needle is almost perpendicular to the quilt top and the tip is in the fabric. Push down on the needle until you feel the tip beneath the quilt again (see Photo 2D, *opposite*).

4. As in Step 2, push the needle tip with your underneath finger and roll the eye of the needle down and forward with your thimble finger to return the needle tip to the top (see Photo 2E, *opposite*).

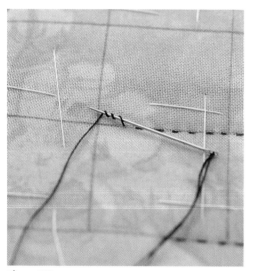

Photo 1X

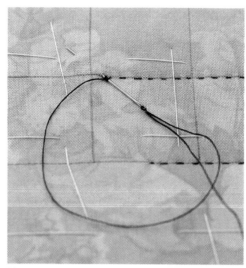

Photo 1Y

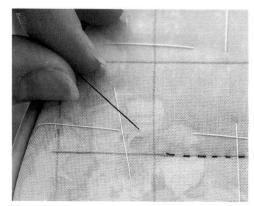

Photo 1Z

Photo 2A

5. Repeat this rock-and-roll motion until the needle is full, as shown in Photo 2F, *below, far right*.

6. Pull the needle away from the quilt top until the stitches are snug (see Photo 2G, *below bottom*).

Remember that uniformity in stitch length is more important than the length of each stitch (see Photo 2H, *bottom right*).

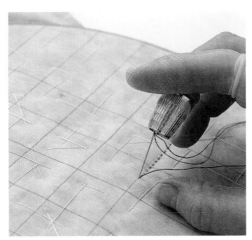

Photo 2B

Photo 2C

Photo 2D

Photo 2E

Photo 2F

Photo 2G

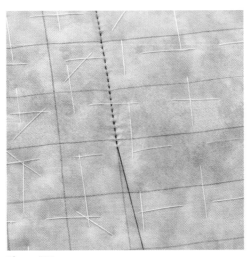

Photo 2H

Hand-Quilting Stab Stitch

Although it's less commonly used than the running stitch, some hand quilters prefer the stab stitch. Wear a thimble on the middle finger of both hands.

1. Hold the needle between your thumb and index finger. Place your other hand under the quilt. Put the needle tip in the fabric with the needle straight up and down. Push the needle through layers and pull it completely through with your underneath hand (see Photo 2I, *below*).

2. With the underneath hand, push the needle back through all the quilt layers a stitch distance from where it went down;

pull the needle and thread completely through all the layers with the upper hand to complete a quilting stitch (see Photo 2J, *below*).

3. Repeat this stab-and-pull-through motion, making one quilting stitch at a time. Remember that uniformity in stitch length is more important than the actual length of individual stitches.

Traveling with the Needle

If you finish a line of hand-quilting with plenty of thread still in the needle, you may want to move to another area without knotting the thread and starting again. The technique for doing so is referred to as

"traveling," which is often used for continuous quilting designs such as feathers. If the distance you need to travel is more than 1 to 2", however, it is best to knot the thread and begin again.

1. When you finish a line of stitching, run the needle point through the quilt top and batting only, moving it towards the next quilting area. If you are using a contrasting thread that is darker than the quilt top, be sure to slide the needle deep into the batting. Bring the needle tip out about half a needle length away (see Photo 2K, *below left*). Do not pull the needle all the way through unless you have reached the point where the next stitching line is to begin.

2. If you have not reached the starting point of the next stitching line, grasp the tip of the needle only. Leaving the eye of the needle between the quilt layers, pivot the needle eye toward the point where the next stitching line will begin (see Photo 2L, *below*).

Photo 2I

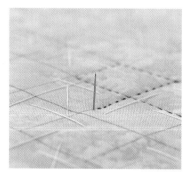

Photo 2J

Photo 2K

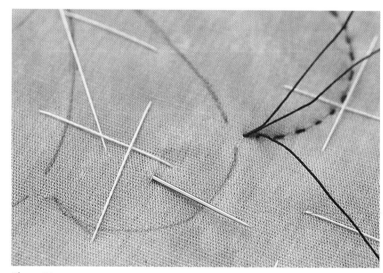

Photo 2L

3. With a thimble on your middle finger, push the tip of the needle, eye first, toward the next starting point. Bring the eye of the needle out at the starting point (see Photo 2M, *below*). Pull out the entire needle, eye first. Begin stitching where desired.

Hand-Quilting Designs

The designs that can be created with hand quilting are almost limitless. You can create straight lines of quilting stitches or intricate curves.

MACHINE QUILTING

Though some believe machine quilting to be a modern method, there are examples from the early days of sewing machines. With the versatility of today's sewing machines, as well as the expanded availability of long-arm quilting machines outside the commercial market, machine quilting continues to grow in popularity. With practice and perseverance you can create keepsake-quality quilts with a sewing machine.

Machine-quilting stitches are continuous and even, giving a quilt a precise look. Just as in hand-quilting, practice pays when it comes to machine quilting. If you're new to the process, start with straight lines that are stitched from edge to edge to avoid lots of stopping and starting. Then try grid patterns and more intricate designs. As you gain proficiency and become more comfortable working with the sewing machine in this way, you'll be motivated to do more, which will lead to even better results.

Machine-Quilting Setup

(See Chapter 1—Tools and Materials for more information on machine-quilting tools, supplies, and work space setup.)

Make sure the machine is clean and in good working order. Arrange a large, flat working surface that's even with the bed (throat plate) of the machine. It is important that the work surface support the weight of the quilt to prevent pulling and shifting of layers. Make certain the quilt layers are securely basted.

Be sure that you're comfortably seated, with the machine in a position that allows you to see and reach without straining your shoulders, arms, and hands.

For straight-line machine quilting, set up the machine with a walking (even-feed) foot and a straight-stitch throat plate. (Free-motion machine quilting requires a different presser foot. See Free-Motion Quilting on *page 245* for information on this technique.) Set the stitch length for 8 to 12 stitches per inch.

The style of needle most often used is a sharp 80/12. Experiment with smaller needles (75/11 or 70/10) if the holes left in the fabric by the needle are too large.

The most common thread choice is 50-weight, three-ply, 100% cotton machine-quilting thread. If you want the finished stitches to be invisible, use very fine, transparent, nylon, monofilament thread (.004 mm) in the needle and lightweight cotton or bobbin-fill thread in the bobbin.

Photo 2M

Creative Tip

To minimize the raveling and tangling that can

occur when prewashing small cuts of fabric,

place the pieces in a lingerie bag.

—SHARON, STORE ASSOCIATE

Photo 2N

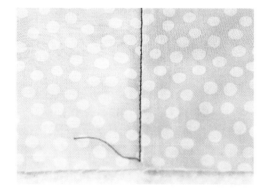

Photo 2O

Photo 2P

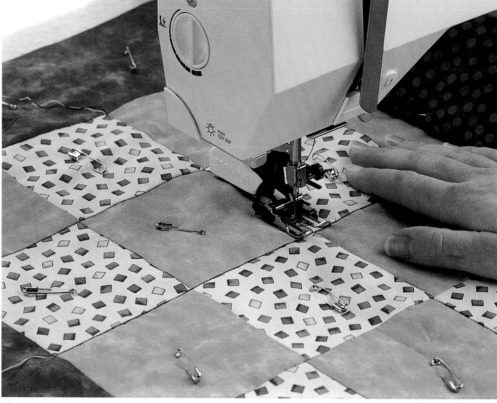

Photo 2Q

Starting and Stopping Machine-Quilting Stitches

1. At the beginning of a line of stitching, pull the bobbin thread to the quilt top. Lock the stitches by setting the machine's stitch length to the shortest setting and sewing forward about ¼".

2. Stop sewing, reset the stitch length to the preferred setting, and continue sewing.

3. To finish a line of stitching, return the machine's stitch length to the shortest setting, and sew forward about ¼".

4. Raise the presser foot, remove the quilt, and clip the threads.

Photo 2R

Photo 2S

In-the-Ditch Machine Quilting

Quilting "in the ditch" means stitching just inside a seam line, as shown in Photo 2N, *opposite*.

The stitches disappear into the seam, which makes a patch, block, or motif stand out from its background (see Photo 2O, *opposite*). This is one of the easiest methods to do by machine.

1. Attach a walking (even-feed) foot. Find the lengthwise center seam line of the basted quilt sandwich. With the needle just to one side of that seam line, sew along it from border to border (see Photo 2P, *opposite*).

2. Turn the quilt crosswise; adjust all the layers so they are smooth. Stitch the crosswise center seam in the same manner (see Photo 2Q, *opposite*).

3. Return the quilt sandwich to the lengthwise direction and stitch in the ditch along the seam lines in a quadrant to the right of the center seam, working from the center outward toward the border (see Photo 2R, *above left*).

4. Turn the quilt and stitch in the ditch on the seam lines in a quadrant on the opposite side of the center line (see Photo 2S, *above right*). Work from the center outward toward the border.

5. Repeat in the remaining two quadrants of the quilt.

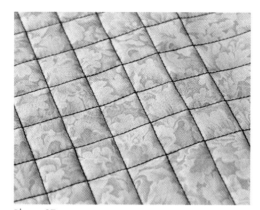

Photo 2T

Channel or Grid Machine Quilting

For straight lines that do not necessarily follow the seam lines, do channel or grid quilting.

Channel Quilting

Channel quilting consists of parallel rows of straight lines going in one direction across a quilt top. Some sewing machines come with a quilting bar that attaches to the machine to serve as a guide for evenly spaced rows. Use the bar when the quilting rows are farther apart than a presser foot width or when the guides on the machine bed are covered. The bar is particularly useful when you're quilting straight rows across a large project.

When channel quilting, mark at least the center line on the quilt top before stitching. Follow the steps described in In-the-Ditch Machine Quilting on *page 243*, anchoring the center line first, then stitching each half of the quilt. Work from the center outward toward the border until an area is completely quilted.

Grid Quilting

Grid quilting involves stitching parallel rows of straight lines in two directions across a quilt top (see Photo 2T, *above left*). When quilting in a grid, mark at least the horizontal and vertical center lines on the quilt top before stitching. The same quilting bar used for channel quilting can help keep rows straight for grid quilting. Follow the steps described in In-the-Ditch Machine Quilting on *page 243*, anchoring the center lines first, then stitching quadrant by quadrant until finished.

Free-Motion Quilting

Free-motion machine quilting is used to stitch curved lines and designs. Sew with the sewing machine's feed dogs in the down position in order to control the stitch length and direction.

It takes practice to achieve the steadiness and speed control necessary for creating small, uniform-size stitches. Start with a small project and simple quilting designs and work up to a larger quilt with more complicated designs.

1. Attach a darning foot to the sewing machine and drop or cover the feed dogs (see Photo 2U, *right*).

2. Position the basted quilt sandwich beneath the darning foot. Bring the bobbin thread to the surface of the quilt top.

3. Lower the presser foot.
Note: Even though the darning foot does not touch the quilt top when the presser foot is lowered, lowering it before stitching will help prevent the quilt from "jumping" up and down as the needle goes in and out; it also engages the tension discs which will make the stitches more even and taut.

Hold both the needle and the bobbin threads in one hand. Take three to six stitches in the same area to lock the stitches. Move the quilt sandwich in the direction you wish to go. (With the feed dogs down, the fabric layers will not move unless you move them.)

4. Clip the tails of the needle and bobbin threads.

Photo 2U

Photo 2V

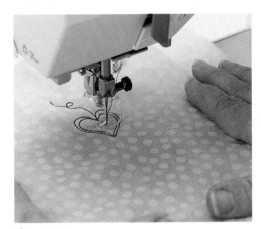
Photo 2W

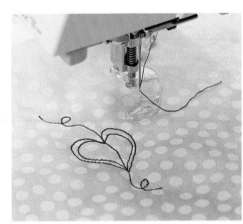
Photo 2X

5. Move the quilt sandwich slowly with the machine stitching at a medium-fast, constant speed (see Photo 2V, *top right*). Guide the fabric layers in the direction they need to go. Do not turn the quilt (see Photo 2W, *above*). Because the feed dogs are lowered, you will be able to move the quilt sandwich freely from side to side and front to back. Use as little hand pressure as possible to move and control the quilt.

6. End the stitching by taking three to six stitches in the same area to lock the stitches (see Photo 2X, *above*). Remove the quilt top from the machine and clip the thread ends.

Photo 2Y

Photo 2Z

Folding A Large Project for Machine Quilting

When you're working on a large quilt, it can be difficult to control the bulk of many fabric layers, especially between the needle and the inside of the machine arm. Many machine quilters find it is easier to roll the project and work on small areas at a time.

1. Evenly roll or fold up opposite sides of the quilt sandwich. Secure the sides as desired (see Photo 2Y, *left*).
Note: *It may be wise to invest in clips specially designed for this purpose.*

2. Evenly roll or fold up a remaining quilt side, again securing as desired (see Photo 2Z, *below left*).

3. Place the project beneath the needle and presser foot and begin quilting, as shown in Photo 3A, *below.*

4. Reroll or refold the layered quilt sandwich to stitch new areas.

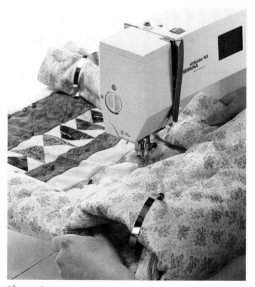

Photo 3A

Photo 3B

Photo 3C

Photo 3D

Machine-Quilting Designs

Machine quilting can produce almost a limitless number of designs. Besides the straight lines and intricate curves described on previous pages, there are quilting designs created specifically for sewing machines. The advantage of these designs is that they involve minimal starting and stopping. Arrows on the stitching patterns indicate the direction to sew. For inspiration, see Selecting a Quilt Design, beginning on *page 225*.

TYING A QUILT

Tying, or tufting, is a quick alternative to hand or machine quilting. A tie is a stitch taken through all three layers of the quilt and knotted on the quilt top surface or, occasionally, on the back of the quilt. Tied quilts have a puffier look than those that are quilted. For extra puffiness, use a thicker than customary batting or multiple layers of batting. Make certain the batting is appropriate for tying, because there will be large unquilted areas between ties. (See *page 231* for more information on selecting batting.)

1. Use perle cotton, sport-weight yarn, or narrow ribbon for the ties and a darner or chenille needle (see Chapter 1—Tools and Materials for more information on needles). Make a single running stitch through all quilt layers, beginning and ending on the quilt top and leaving a 3" tail (see Photo 3B, *above left*).

2. Make a single backstitch through the same holes and all three layers, ending on the quilt top, as shown in Photo 3C, *above*.

3. Clip the thread, yarn, or ribbon, leaving a second 3" tail (see Photo 3D, *above right*).

4. Tie the tails in a square knot (right over left, then left over right) close to the surface of the quilt (see Photo 3E, *right*). Avoid pulling too tight and puckering the fabric.

5. Clip the thread tails as desired.

Photo 3E

Chapter 9

FINISHING
TECHNIQUES

Complete your quilt by binding it, adding an
identification label, and stitching on a sleeve to hang
it for all to admire.

AMISH MAPLE LEAF CRIB QUILT

Amish mothers often made a crib quilt for each new baby in the family. Their style was to choose bright, cheerful patterns and compose them in the same solid-color cotton fabrics they used to make clothing for their families. This quilt was made by a member of a central Indiana Amish community in 1938. When the quilt is held to the light, a striped cotton blanket can be seen inside. This kind of filler would stay smooth as the quilt was used and washed over and over.

Finishing *Techniques*

Binding your quilt, adding a label, and perhaps stitching on a hanging sleeve bring you the satisfaction of fully completing a project. Again, creativity is enhanced when you're able to make informed decisions about techniques. And when you're adding these finishing touches, it's the perfect time to begin thinking about your next quilt.

PREPARING THE QUILT FOR BINDING

Taking the time to properly prepare a quilt for binding will result in a better finished appearance.
Note: To use the backing fabric as binding, see Self-Binding, which begins on page 261.

1. Lay the quilted project faceup on a rotary-cutting mat on a flat surface.

2. Position a large acrylic square ruler in one corner of the quilt, aligning adjacent edges of the ruler with adjacent edges of the quilt top. Place a long acrylic ruler above the square ruler, aligning the long edge with the quilt top edge. Using a rotary cutter, cut away the batting and backing that extend beyond the quilt top edge (see Photo 1A, *below*).

Reposition the rulers and cutting mat as needed to trim around the entire quilt.
Note: Align the square ruler on two edges before positioning the second ruler to square up the quilt corner; this will help keep the quilt straight. A slight bit of the quilt top edge is sometimes trimmed away. If one corner is significantly off when the ruler is aligned, refer to Chapter 7—Assembling the Quilt Top and Backing for information on squaring up quilt blocks.

Or, rather than rotary-cutting the excess batting and backing, mark the cutting line along the ruler edge, then use scissors to trim on the line.

Photo 1A

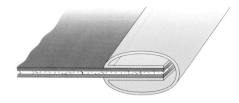

Illustration 1

Illustration 2

Photo 1B

Binding Length

Determine how much binding it will take to go around all sides of the quilt. Many patterns list the number of binding strips or the total length needed to complete a project.

To determine the binding length yourself, lay the quilt flat and measure through the center of each border strip as shown in Photo 1B, *above* (do not measure along the outer edge of the quilt); add the lengths of each side together. Add approximately 15" to allow for diagonally seaming strips and finishing the ends of continuous binding (binding in one long strip with no breaks except where it begins and ends).

DETERMINING BINDING TYPE AND WIDTH

Before cutting binding strips, decide whether to use single-fold or double-fold (French-fold) binding. Also determine whether to cut the binding on the straight grain or bias grain. On a project that has curved or scalloped edges, cut the strips on the bias grain.

Single-Fold Binding

Single-fold binding, as its name implies, is a single thickness of fabric (see Illustration 1, *right*). It requires less fabric than double-fold binding, but also provides less protection for a quilt's edges. Because of this, single-fold binding is generally used in quilts that will not be handled frequently, such as wall hangings, miniature quilts, and quilts with curved or scalloped edges where less bulk in the binding is desired.

Single-fold binding is cut twice the desired finished binding width plus ½" for seam allowances. For example, for ¼"-wide finished single-fold binding, cut 1"-wide binding strips. The binding strips for single-fold binding can be cut on the straight or bias grain. To bind a quilt with curved edges, cut the strips on the bias grain.

Double-Fold Binding

Double-fold, or French-fold, binding is the most common binding type. It provides the most durable finish on a quilt's edges (see Illustration 2, *above right*). It is cut wider than single-fold binding because it is pressed in half (doubled) before it is attached to the quilt top. Double-fold binding is cut four times the desired finished binding width plus ½" for seam allowances. For example, for ½"-wide finished double-fold binding, cut 2½"-wide binding strips. The binding strips for double-fold binding can be cut on the straight or bias grain. To bind a quilt with curved edges, cut the strips on the bias grain.

Self-Binding

This method of binding uses the quilt backing, rather than separate strips, as binding. (See Self-Binding, which begins on *page 261*, for more information.)

Bias Strip Width Chart

Use this chart to determine how wide to cut fabric strips to make single- or double-fold binding.

Desired Finished Width	Single-fold Width To Cut Strip	Double-fold (French-fold) Width To Cut Strip
¼"	1"	1½"
⅜"	1¼"	2"
½"	1½"	2½"
⅝"	1¾"	3"
¾"	2"	3½"
⅞"	2¼"	4"
1"	2½"	4½"

STRAIGHT-GRAIN BINDING

For most quilts, binding strips may be cut on the straight grain. Use a fabric's crosswise straight grain rather than its lengthwise grain for more give and elasticity. If the quilt has curved edges, cut the strips on the bias.

1. Cut crosswise strips the desired width (see Determining Binding Type and Width, *opposite*). Cut enough strips to equal the total length needed (see Photo 1C, *below*).

2. Position and pin the strips perpendicular to one another with the raw edges aligned and right sides together. Mark,

then join the strips with diagonal seams to make one continuous binding strip (see Photo 1D, *below*).

3. Trim the excess fabric, leaving ¼" seam allowances. Press the seam allowances open. Trim the dog-ears (see Photo 1E, *below right*).

BIAS BINDING

When binding a quilt that has curved edges, cut the strips on the bias grain to help the binding lie flat.

Cutting Bias Strips
1. Begin with a fabric square or rectangle. Use a large acrylic ruler to square up the

edge of the fabric and find the 45° angle (see Photo 1F, *bottom, far left*).

2. Cut enough strips to total the length needed, handling the edges carefully to avoid stretching and distorting the strips (see Photo 1G, *below left, bottom*).

3. Position and pin the strips perpendicular to one another with the raw edges aligned and right sides together. Mark, then join the strips with diagonal seams to make one continuous binding strip.

4. Trim the excess fabric, leaving ¼" seam allowances. Press the seam allowances open. Trim the dog-ears (see Photo 1H, *below, bottom*).

Chapter 9 – Finishing Techniques

Photo 1C

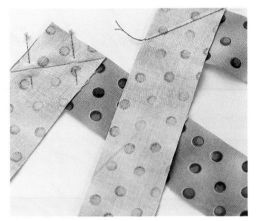

Photo 1D

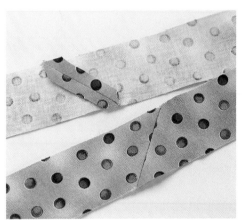

Photo 1E

Photo 1F

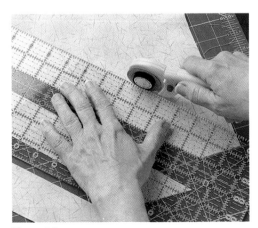

Photo 1G

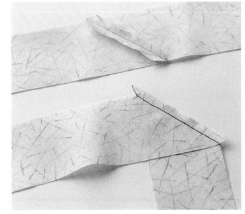

Photo 1H

Photo 1I

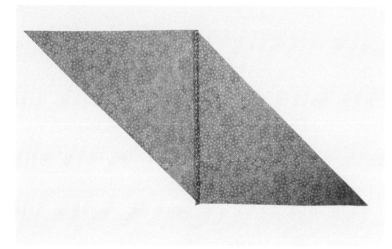

Photo 1J

Making Continuous Bias from a Square

Rather than cutting individual bias strips, cut and seam a square to make a continuous bias strip.

1. Cut a square from the binding fabric on the straight grain. Use the chart on *below* to determine the size of square you need.

2. Cut the square in half diagonally to form two triangles (see Photo 1I, *above left*).

3. With right sides together, align two short triangle edges. Sew the triangles together with a ¼" seam allowance to make a parallelogram (see Illustration 3, *opposite*). Press the seam allowances open (see Photo 1J, *above right*).

4. Use a quilt marker or pencil and a ruler to draw lines parallel to the long bias edges, spacing the lines the desired width of the binding strip (see Illustration 4, *opposite*). For example, space the lines 1½" apart for a 1½"-wide binding strip (see Photo 1K, *opposite*).

5. With right sides together, bring the straight-grain edges together and align the raw edges. Shift one straight-grain edge so the top corner is offset by the width of one drawn line (see Photo 1L, *opposite*).

6. Sew the offset edges together using a ¼" seam allowance. Press the seam allowances open (see Photo 1M, *opposite*).

7. At the extended edge, begin cutting on the drawn lines to make one continuous bias strip (see Photo 1N, *opposite*).

8. Trim the strip's ends so they are square.

Amount of Continuous Bias That Can Be Cut from a Square

To calculate the length of a continuous bias strip that can be cut from a square, find the square's area (multiply the square's measurement by itself) and divide by the desired width of the bias strip. For example, to figure the total inches of 2½"-wide bias a 12" square yields, multiply 12×12 and divide by 2.5 = 57".

BIAS WIDTH	1"	1¼"	1½"	1¾"	2"	2¼"	2½"
12" square	144"	115"	96"	82"	72"	64"	57"
18" square	324"	259"	216"	185"	162"	144"	129"
27" square	729"	583"	486"	416"	364"	324"	291"
36" square	1,296"	1,036"	864"	740"	648"	576"	518"

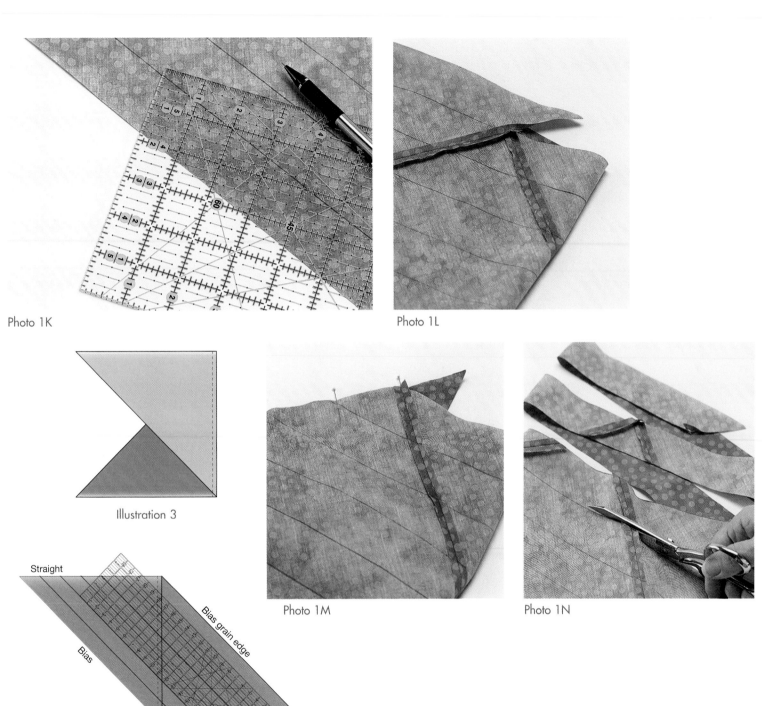

Photo 1K

Photo 1L

Illustration 3

Photo 1M

Photo 1N

Straight

Bias

Bias grain edge

Straight grain edge

Illustration 4

255

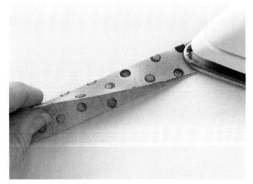

Photo 1O

Photo 1P

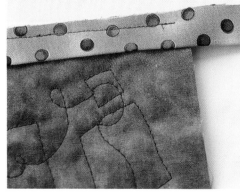

Photo 1Q

Photo 1R

PREPARING BINDING

Single-Fold Binding

Single-fold binding requires little preparation before being sewn to the quilt.

1. With the wrong side inside, fold under 1" at one end of the binding strip; press.

2. For a creased binding edge, turn under and press a ¼" seam allowance on one long edge of the strip before joining the other long edge to the quilt. This pressed edge will be hand-stitched to the back of the quilt after the binding strip is sewn to the quilt top.

Double-Fold (French-Fold) Binding

1. With the wrong side inside, fold under 1" at one end of the binding strip; press (see Photo 1O, *above left*).

2. With wrong sides inside, fold the strip in half lengthwise; press (see Photo 1P, *left*).

SEWING ON BINDING

The instructions that follow can be used to attach single-fold or double-fold binding. Binding is generally attached to a quilt with a ¼" seam allowance. This leaves ¼" of binding showing on the quilt front and the balance of the binding turned to the quilt back.

To have a narrower or wider binding show on the quilt front, adjust the width of the seam allowance to equal the binding width that you want to show on the quilt front. (To determine how wide to cut the binding, see Determining Binding Type and Width on *page 252.*)

Cut and sew a sample binding strip on a layered quilt sandwich to be sure the strips are wide enough to cover the stitching line on the quilt back.

Continuous Binding with Mitered Corners

The photographs *below* and *opposite* show double-fold binding. On single-fold binding, the raw binding edge (the edge not turned under) is the one to align with the edge of the quilt. (See Single-Fold Binding.)

1. Beginning in the center of the bottom edge, place the binding strip against the right side of the quilt top, starting with the folded end and aligning the binding strip's raw edges with the quilt top's raw edge (see Photo 1Q, *far left*).

2. Starting 2" from the folded end, sew through all the layers (see Photo 1R, *left*). End the stitching line before the corner at a distance equal to the width of the seam allowance. For example, with a ¼" seam allowance, stop sewing ¼" from the corner. Backstitch, then clip the threads. Remove the quilt from beneath the sewing-machine presser foot.

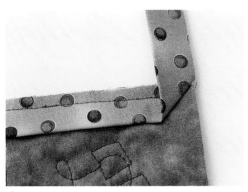
Photo 1S

Photo 1T

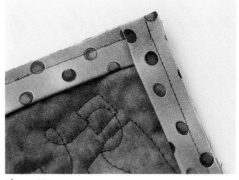
Photo 1U

3. Fold the binding strip upward, creating a diagonal fold, and finger-press (see Photo 1S, *above*).

4. Holding the diagonal fold in place with your index finger, bring the binding strip down in line with the next edge, making a horizontal fold that aligns with the first raw edge of the quilt (see Photo 1T, *above right*).

5. Begin sewing again at the top of the horizontal fold, stitching through all layers (see Photo 1U, *above, far right*).

6. Sew around the quilt, turning each corner in the same manner. At the starting point, lap the raw end of the binding strip inside the folded end (see Photo 1V, *above right, middle*).

7. Finish sewing to the starting point. Backstitch to secure (see Photo 1W, *above, far right*).

8. Turn the binding over the edge of the quilt to the back. Hand-stitch the binding to the backing fabric, making sure to cover the binding stitching line. Hand-stitch the folded edge of the binding down where the binding strips meet (see Photo 1X, *right*).

9. Fold a miter in each corner as you reach it. Take a stitch or two in each fold to secure it (see Photo 1Y, *far right*).

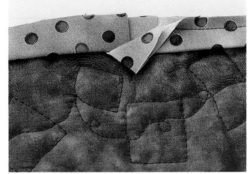
Photo 1V

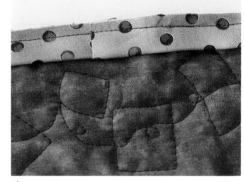
Photo 1W

Photo 1X

Photo 1Y

Joining Binding Ends With No Overlap

Some quilters prefer to seam the ends of a binding strip together, rather than overlapping them as described in Continuous Binding with Mitered Corners, steps 6 and 7, on *page 257*. Seaming the ends means less bulk.

1. Prepare the binding strips as for double-fold (French-fold) binding, but do not fold under an end. (See Preparing Binding—Double-Fold Binding on *page 256*.)

2. Beginning in the center of the bottom edge, place the binding strip against the right side of the quilt top; align the binding strip's raw edges with the quilt top's raw edge and leave a 6 to 10" tail (the larger the project, the longer the tail).

3. Starting 6 to 10" from the end (depending on the length of the binding strip tail), sew the binding to the quilt following steps 2 through 5 under Continuous Binding with Mitered Corners, which begins on *page 256*. Stop sewing within 10 to 20" from where you began stitching (see Photo 1Z, *left*).

4. Remove the quilt from under the presser foot and place it on a flat surface.

5. Lay the first binding tail in place on the quilt top, aligning the raw edges. Repeat with the second binding tail. Crease the second binding tail where it meets the first tail's straight cut end (see Photo 2A, *far left*). From the crease, measure the distance of the binding strip's cut width.

Photo 1Z

Photo 2A

Photo 2B

Photo 2C

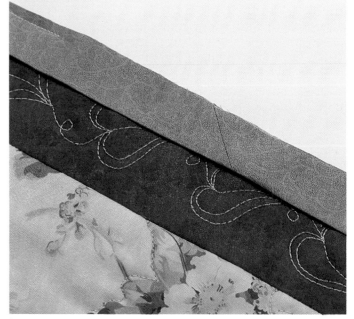

Photo 2D

For example, these binding strips were cut 2" wide, so we measured 2" from the crease and cut the second tail straight across at that mark (see Photo 2B, *opposite*).

6. Open the tails; with right sides together, place one on top of the other at a right angle (see Photo 2C, *opposite*).

7. Join the strips with a diagonal seam. Before stitching, check to be sure the strips are not twisted. Trim the seam allowance to ¼" and finger-press open.

8. Fold the binding strip in half lengthwise as it was previously. It should lie perfectly flat (see Photo 2D, *opposite*).

9. Continue sewing the binding strip to the starting point. Backstitch to secure.

10. Turn the binding over the edge of the quilt to the back. Hand-stitch the binding to the backing fabric, making sure to cover the binding stitching line.

Binding Inside Corners

Sometimes a project may require binding around an inside corner. Knowing where to stop stitching and pivot the quilt is the key to turning an inside corner smoothly. This technique may be used with single-fold or double-fold binding.

1. Sew a binding strip to the quilt with a ¼" seam allowance. At an inside corner, sew ¼" past the corner so that when you pivot, the needle will be ¼" from the next edge (see Illustration 5, *above right, top*). Backstitch once, then return to the original stopping point. With the needle down, pivot the layers to stitch the next portion in place.

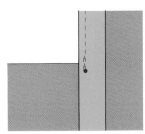

Illustration 5

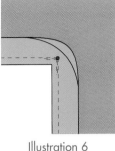

Illustration 6

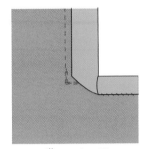

Illustration 7

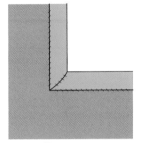

Illustration 8

2. Use the point of a seam ripper to make the binding lie flat as necessary. Continue sewing along the edges, repeating steps 1 and 2 at each inside corner, until the binding strip is sewn to the quilt (see Illustration 6, *top, far right*).

3. Turn the binding over the edge of the quilt to the back (see Illustration 7, *above*). Work the binding's inside corners to create a small pleat on each side.

4. Hand-stitch the pleats in place, then hand-stitch the binding to the backing fabric, making sure to cover the binding stitching line (see Illustration 8, *above right*).

Binding Curved or Scalloped Edges

Use strips cut on the bias to bind a quilt that has curved edges or scallops because it has enough give to bend smoothly around the curves.

1. Prepare the bias strips as desired for single-fold or double-fold binding. (See Preparing Binding on *page 256*.)

2. Beginning in the center of the bottom edge, place the binding strip against the right side of the quilt top, starting with the folded end and aligning the binding strip's raw edges with the quilt top's raw edge. *Note: Do not begin at an inside point.*

3. Starting 2" from the folded end, sew through all the layers, easing the binding around the curves (see Photo 2E, *left*). *Note: Do not stretch the binding around the curves or the quilt edges will cup once the binding is turned to the quilt back.*

4. When you return to the starting point, lap the raw end of the binding strip inside the folded end.

5. Finish sewing to the starting point. Backstitch to secure.

6. Clip the seam allowance at each inner point (see Photo 2F, *below left*).

7. Turn the binding over the edge of the quilt to the back. Hand-stitch the binding to the backing fabric, folding a small mitered tuck at each inner point. Make sure to cover the binding stitching line (see Photo 2G, *below*).

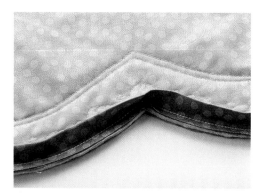

Photo 2E

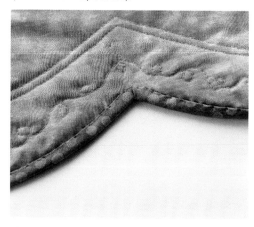

Photo 2G

Photo 2F

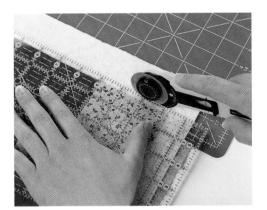

Photo 2H

Photo 2I

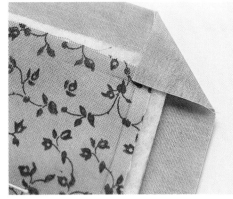

Photo 2J

Photo 2K

Photo 2L

SELF-BINDING

Self-binding methods use the backing fabric to bind the quilt. This type of binding tends to be less durable than traditional binding, but can be practical when you have limited fabric on hand and want the binding to match the backing fabric.

Self-Binding with Backing Fabric, Mitered Corners

1. Mark the ¼" seam line on the quilt top. Trim the batting so it extends beyond the marked seam line the desired finished binding width (see Photo 2H, *above*). For example, to have ¼" of binding showing on the quilt front, trim the batting ½" beyond the marked seam line.

To keep from inadvertently cutting into the backing fabric, slip the edge of the rotary-cutting mat between the backing and the batting.

2. Trim the backing to leave twice the desired finished binding width plus ¼" for a seam allowance (see Photo 2I, *above right, top*). For example, for a ½" finished binding, cut the backing so it extends 1¼" beyond the seam line.

3. Press one corner of the backing over the quilt top so the tip meets the corner of the marked seam line (see Photo 2J, *above right, top*).

4. Trim the tip of the corner on the pressed line (see Photo 2K, *above*).

5. Turn up a ¼" seam allowance on the backing; press (see Photo 2L, *above right*).

6. Fold one pressed edge of the backing over the quilt top, covering the seam line. Pin in place (see Photo 2M, *right*).

7. Fold over the adjacent edge, making a mitered corner. Hand-stitch the binding to the quilt top, making sure to cover the marked seam line (see Photo 2N, *right*).

Photo 2M

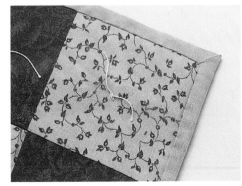

Photo 2N

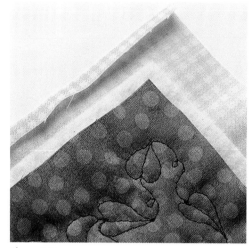

Photo 2O

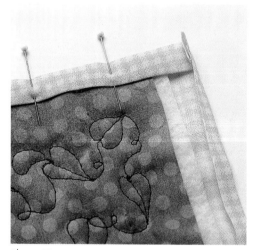

Photo 2P

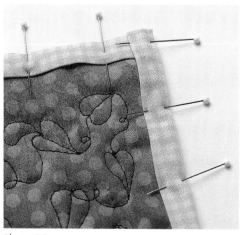

Photo 2Q

Self-Binding with Backing Fabric, Butted Corners

1. If desired, mark a seam line on the quilt top ¼" from its raw edges. Trim the batting so it extends beyond the seam line to the desired finished binding width. For example, to have ¼" of binding showing on the quilt front, trim the batting ½" beyond the seam line.

To keep from inadvertently cutting into the backing fabric, slip the edge of the rotary-cutting mat between the backing and the batting.

2. Trim the backing to leave twice the desired finished binding width plus ¼" for a seam allowance. For example, for a ½" finished binding, cut the backing so it extends 1¼" beyond the seam line.

3. Turn up a ¼" seam allowance on opposite edges of the backing; press (see Photo 2O, *above left*).

4. Fold the backing to the front again, covering the seam line; pin. In the same manner, fold, press, and pin the remaining backing edges (see photos 2P and 2Q, *left and below left*).

5. Hand-stitch the binding to the quilt top, making sure to cover the seam line.

Knife-Edge Self-Binding

With knife-edge self-binding, both the quilt top and backing are turned under to meet evenly at the edges of the quilt, leaving the edges with an unbound appearance. To use this technique, quilt no closer than ½" from the quilt's edges.

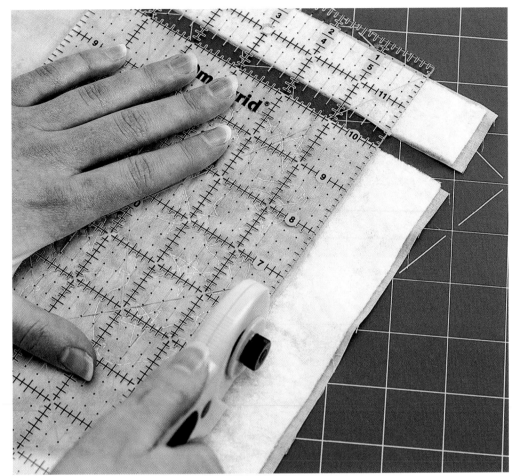

Photo 2R

Photo 2S

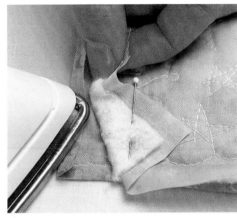

Photo 2T

Photo 2U

1. If desired, mark a seam line on the quilt top ¼" from its raw edges. Trim the quilt top, batting, and backing to ¼" beyond the seam line, even with the edge of the quilt top (see Photo 2R, *above*).

2. Fold the quilt top and backing out of the way, then trim the batting only to just beyond the seam line (see Photo 2S, *above right, top*).

To keep from inadvertently cutting into the backing fabric, slip the edge of the rotary-cutting mat between the backing and the batting.

3. Turn opposite quilt top edges under ¼"; press (see Photo 2T, *above right*). Turn corresponding backing edges under ¼"; press. Repeat with the remaining quilt top and backing edges.

4. Align the folded edges, enclosing the batting, and pin together (see Photo 2U, *right*). Baste, if desired. Hand-stitch the folded edges together.
Note: *You may wish to finish and stabilize this area by quilting ¼ to ½" away from the folded outer edges.*

SPECIALTY BINDINGS

These techniques for adding a special binding or finish to a quilt may take a bit more time than traditional bindings. However, they generally add an extra element that distinguishes the quilt.

Prairie Points

Prairie points, fabric triangles made of folded squares, add a dimensional accent to a quilt edge. To bind a quilt with prairie points, quilt no closer to the edges than ½".

1. Trim the quilt batting and backing even with the quilt top edges (see Photo 2V, *below left*). If desired, mark a seam line on the quilt top ¼" from its raw edges. Then trim an additional ¼" of batting.

To keep from inadvertently cutting into the backing fabric, slip the edge of your rotary-cutting mat between the backing and the batting.

To make it easier to join the prairie points to the quilt top, baste the backing out of the way.

2. Assess the project and determine a size for the prairie points. The size of the prairie points depends on the size of the quilt project. A large quilt may be able to handle large prairie points, while a small quilt could easily be overwhelmed by a border of wide prairie points.

The finished height of the prairie point will be half the size of the square minus ¼" for a seam allowance. For example, a 3" square folded into a prairie point will add 1¼" to the quilt's width on each side after being sewn to the quilt.

To figure how many prairie points are needed, first determine how much to make each prairie point overlap. A 3" square yields a prairie point with a 3" base, but quilters generally overlap the prairie points by ½ to 1", so each one will take up less than 3" of the quilt's edge. Experiment with different amounts of overlap before cutting

squares to make the final prairie points. Once a size for the squares is determined, make a few prairie points and experiment to determine the desired spacing.

3. Cut the number of squares in the desired size. Fold a square in half diagonally with the wrong side inside to form a triangle; press. Fold the triangle in half and press, making a prairie point (see Illustration 9 and Photo 2W, *below*). Repeat to make the desired number of prairie points.

4. Pin prairie points to a side edge of the quilt top with raw edges aligned and the prairie points pointing toward the quilt center. Space them evenly and make sure all the double-folded edges face the same direction. Overlap adjacent edges or slip the single-folded edges between the double-folded edges (see Photo 2X, *opposite*).

5. When the prairie points are placed satisfactorily, join them to the quilt top, stitching on the seam line and keeping the backing free from the stitching.

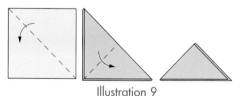

Illustration 9

Photo 2V

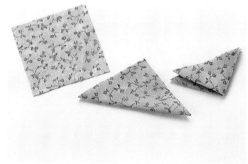

Photo 2W

6. Repeat steps 4 and 5 along the remaining edges.

7. Turn under a ¼" seam allowance on all edges of the quilt backing; press.

8. Open up the prairie points so the points face away from the quilt center and the seam allowances turn to the inside. Pin together the backing and prairie points, enclosing the batting and seam allowances (see Photo 2Y, *below*). Baste, if desired.

9. Hand-stitch the folded backing edge to the base of the prairie points, covering the machine stitching (see Photo 2Z, *below right*).

10. If desired, finish and stabilize the border by quilting ¼ to ½" away from the outer edges.

Photo 2X

Photo 2Y

Photo 2Z

Covered Cording/Piping

Covered cording, also called piping, is sometimes used to finish a quilt edge. To add covered cording, quilt no closer to the quilt top edges than ½".

1. Trim the quilt batting and backing even with the quilt top edges. If desired, mark a seam line on the quilt top ¼" from its raw edges. Then trim an additional ¼" of batting.

To keep from inadvertently cutting into the backing fabric, slip the edge of the rotary-cutting mat between the backing and the batting.

To make it easier to join the covered cording to the quilt top, baste the backing out of the way.

2. Encase a length of cording in a continuous bias strip (see Cutting Bias Strips on *page 253* and Making Continuous Bias From a Square, which begins on *page 254*). The width of the bias strip depends on the diameter of the cording. The larger the cording, the wider the bias strip will need to be. The strip needs to be wide enough to cover the cording, plus ½" for seam allowances. Regardless of the width of the bias strip, the method used to cover the cording is the same.

With the wrong side inside, fold under 1½" at one end of the bias strip, then fold the strip in half lengthwise. Insert the cording next to the folded edge, with a cording end 1" from the folded end. Using a cording or zipper foot, machine-sew through both fabric layers right next to the cording (see Photo 3A, *left*).

3. Beginning at the center of one edge, pin the covered cording around the quilt top with the covered cording's stitching line on the seam line (see Photo 3B, *far left*).

4. Begin stitching 1½" from the folded end, stitching on the seam line and keeping the backing free from the stitching. Round the corners slightly, pivoting with the needle in the fabric at each corner and making sure the corner curves match. As you stitch each corner, gently ease the covered cording into place. Clip the seam allowance of the covered cording just next to the quilt top seam line (see Photo 3C, *left*).

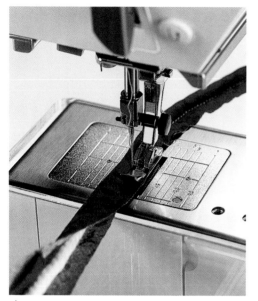
Photo 3A

Photo 3B

Photo 3C

Photo 3D

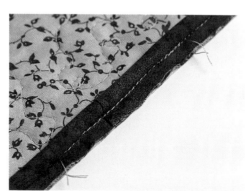
Photo 3E

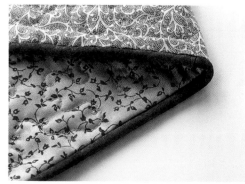
Photo 3F

5. Within 2 to 3" of the starting point, end the stitching. Remove 1" of stitching at each end of the cording cover and pull back the bias strip ends. Trim the cording so the ends abut and whipstitch them together (see Photo 3D, *opposite*).

6. Refold the bias strip so it covers the cording, lapping the folded end over the raw end. Finish stitching the covered cording to the quilt top (see Photo 3E, *opposite*).

7. Turn under a ¼" seam allowance on the quilt backing; press.

8. Open up the covered cording so that it sits on the quilt edge and turn the seam allowance to the inside. Pin the backing to the covered cording's seam line, enclosing the batting and seam allowances. Baste, if desired.

9. Hand-stitch the folded backing edge to the back of the covered cording, covering the machine stitching (see Photo 3F, *opposite*).

Pieced Bias Binding

Create a scrappy border by joining straight-grain strips into sets, then cutting the sets into bias strips. Once sewn to the quilt, the pieced binding gives the appearance of diagonal stripes along the quilt's edge.

1. Cut 42"-long strips on the crosswise straight grain in the desired width or widths. (The strips may be cut in uniform or varying widths.)

2. Join the strips with ¼" seam allowances to make a striped binding set (see Photo 3G, *above right*). For example, join five 1½×42" strips to make a 5½×42" binding

Photo 3G

set. Press the seam allowances open. Repeat to make the desired number of binding sets.

3. Cut bias strips from the binding sets in the desired width, as shown in Photo 3H, *right* (see Determining Binding Type and Width on *page 252* and Bias Binding, which begins on *page 253*).

4. Join the strips to make a continuous bias strip (see Photo 3I, *right*).

5. Prepare the continuous bias strip as for double-fold (French-fold) binding. (See Preparing Binding—Double-Fold Binding on *page 256*.)

6. With raw edges aligned, join the pieced binding to the quilt. (See Sewing on Binding, which begins on *page 256*.)

7. Turn the binding over the edge of the quilt to the back. Hand-stitch the binding to the backing fabric, making sure to cover the binding stitching line (see Photo 3J, *right*).

Photo 3H

Photo 3I

Photo 3J

Chapter 9 – Finishing Techniques

267

Photo 3K

HANGING QUILTS FOR DISPLAY

To hang a quilt for display, you'll need to add tabs or a hanging sleeve. Quilts smaller than 23" square may be hung with purchased hanging clips or sewn-on tabs. Larger quilts require a hanging sleeve attached to the back, which allows the quilt to hang straight with little distortion. The sleeve may be added before or after the binding.

Adding a Hanging Sleeve Before Binding

1. Assemble the quilt up to the point of attaching the binding.

2. Measure the quilt's top edge. Cut a 6 to 10"-wide strip that is 2" longer than the quilt's top edge.

3. Fold under 1½" on both short edges. Sew 1¼" from each folded edge.

4. Fold the hemmed strip in half lengthwise with the wrong side inside; pin. Join the long edges using a ¼" seam allowance to make a hanging sleeve. Do not press the seam allowance open.

5. Aligning raw edges, pin or baste the sleeve to the quilt backing. Sew the hanging sleeve and binding to the quilt at the same time, using a scant ¼" seam allowance along the edge where the sleeve is attached to accommodate the added bulk of the hanging sleeve. (See Sewing on Binding, which begins on *page 256* for more information on attaching binding to a quilt.)

6. Hand-stitch the binding to the hanging sleeve, covering the sleeve's stitching line. Then hand-stitch the long folded edge of the hanging sleeve to the quilt backing (see Photo 3K, *left*). For large dowels or decorative curtain rods, allow extra ease in the side of the sleeve away from the quilt back.
Note: *Before stitching down the long folded edge, fold it up about ½", then stitch in place. This will prevent the rod from creating a ridge on the front side of the quilt when it is hanging.*

Stitch the short hemmed edges of the hanging sleeve to the backing where they touch.

7. Slide a wooden dowel or slender piece of wood that is 1" longer than the finished sleeve into the sleeve and hang the quilt.

Adding a Hanging Sleeve After Binding

1. Measure the quilt's top edge. Cut a 6- to 10"-wide strip that is 2" longer than the quilt's top edge.

2. Fold under 1½" on both short edges. Sew 1¼" from each folded edge.

3. Fold the hemmed strip in half lengthwise with the wrong side inside; pin. Join the long edges using a ¼" seam allowance to make a hanging sleeve. Press the seam allowance open and center the seam in the middle of the sleeve.

4. Center the hanging sleeve on the quilt backing about 1" below the top edge of the quilt with the seam facing the backing. Sewing through the backing and batting, hand-stitch the sleeve to the backing along both long edges and the short edges that touch the backing (see Photo 3L, *below*).
Note: For large dowels or decorative curtain rods, allow extra ease in the side of the sleeve away from the quilt back.

Before stitching down the second long edge, fold it up about ½", then stitch it in place. This will prevent the rod from creating a ridge on the front side of the quilt when it is hanging.

5. Slide a wooden dowel or slender piece of wood that is 1" longer than the finished sleeve into the sleeve and hang the quilt (see Photo 3M, *below left*).

Adding Hanging Loops
For quilts 35" square or less, you may wish to use hanging loops instead of a full hanging sleeve.

1. Cut several 3½x5½" rectangles. Turn each rectangle's long edges under ¼"; press. Stitch ⅛" from the folded edges. Repeat with the short edges of the rectangles.

2. Evenly space the hemmed rectangles across the quilt backing 1" from the inner edge of the binding. Hand-stitch the top and bottom edges of each rectangle in place (see Photo 3N, *below*).

TIP: For quilts more than 60" wide, make two or three sleeves. This allows for more nails or brackets to hold the hanging rod and more evenly distribute the quilt's weight.

To make multiple sleeves, divide the quilt's top edge measurement by 3. Add 2" to the new measurement and cut three fabric pieces this length. Make the sleeves as previously instructed.

Photo 3L

Photo 3M

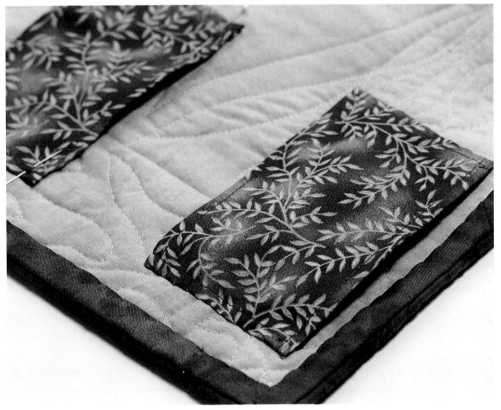

Photo 3N

Adding Hook-and-Loop Tape

This hanging method eliminates the need for a dowel but requires that a lattice strip be mounted to the wall.

Photo 3O

1. Measure the quilt's top edge. Cut a 1½"-wide strip of hook-and-loop tape 2" shorter than that measurement.

2. Cut a 2"-wide wooden lattice strip the same length as the hook-and-loop tape strip.

3. Separate the tape halves so there is one strip with hooks (stiffer strip) and one with loops (softer strip). Center the hook strip across the quilt backing ½" below the top edge of the quilt. Hand-stitch the entire strip to the backing, making sure the stitches don't show on the front of the quilt (see Photo 3O, *left*).

4. Aligning the edges, attach the loop strip to the lattice strip using a staple gun. ***Note:*** *A hot-glue gun may be used for this step to hang a small, lightweight quilt.*

5. Measure, mark, and anchor the lattice strip securely to the wall with the loop strip facing out. Place nails 1" or so in from each lattice end and in the center. Add nails, or the appropriate fastener for the wall type, between those already placed, dividing and subdividing spaces. Use as many nails as needed to make sure the lattice can support the weight of the quilt (see Photo 3P, *left*).

6. Mount the quilt by aligning the hook-and-loop tape halves; press together firmly.

LABELING YOUR QUILT

Since the quilts you make may outlive you, it makes sense to preserve their heritage for future generations by marking them with your name, your city, and the date at a minimum. Adding other information, such as a poem, a good-will wish for the recipient, a special-occasion note, or even the fabric content and care instructions, further personalizes the quilt.

There are several ways to permanently mark a quilt. You can sign directly on the quilt using a fine-tip permanent fabric marking pen, cross-stitch, or embroidery.
Note: *Be sure to test any marking pen on a scrap of fabric identical to the quilt fabric to check for bleeding before writing on the actual quilt. (See Putting Pen to Fabric, opposite, for more information.)*

Photo 3P

As a guide for embroidering or cross-stitching a signature, write on tissue paper first, then stitch directly through the paper onto the fabric. After completing the stitching, gently pull away the paper. You can also sew a separate label to the quilt backing. Purchase a premade label, or design one yourself. The fabric content of the attached label should be compatible with the quilt fabric and should be colorfast. For example, a satin or wool label on a cotton quilt might complicate the cleaning process.

To affix the label, turn under the raw edges. Using a traditional appliqué stitch (see Chapter 6—Appliqué Techniques for more information) or other decorative stitch (see Chapter 10—Specialty Techniques for more information), sew through the folded label edge, catching the quilt backing and batting in your stitches.

However you choose to label your projects, it's important to do so. It's a thoughtful act for present and future generations who may want to know: Who made this quilt?

Putting Pen to Fabric

Whether you're making one label or a whole quilt of signature blocks, use these tips to write successfully on fabric.

1. Choose a smooth, high-quality, 100%-cotton fabric. Select a fabric color that will allow the ink to show. Avoid white-on-white prints because the pattern is painted on, rather than dyed into, the fabric, which makes writing difficult and inhibits the ink penetration.

2. Prewash the fabric; cotton fabrics usually contain sizing that acts as a barrier to ink penetration.

3. Use a permanent-ink pen designed for use on fabric. A fine point (.01 mm diameter) writes delicately and is less likely to bleed. Lines can be made thicker by going over them more than once. For larger letters or numbers, a pen with .05 mm diameter works well.

4. Test the pen and fabric together. Write on a fabric sample, then follow the manufacturer's directions for setting the ink. Wait 24 hours for the ink to set, then wash the sample as you would any fine quilt. The extra time it takes to run such a test will pay off in years of durability.

5. Stabilize the fabric and create guidelines with freezer paper. Cut a piece of freezer paper large enough to cover the fabric's writing area. Use a ruler and thick black marker to draw evenly spaced lines on the freezer paper's dull side (see Photo 3Q, *above right*).
Note: This works only with light-color fabrics, which allow the lines on the freezer paper to show through.

6. Iron the freezer paper to the fabric's wrong side with a hot, dry iron (see Photo 3R, *right*).

7. Write slowly and with a light touch. This allows time for the ink to flow into the fabric and lets you control the letters (see Photo 3S, *below right*).

Photo 3Q

Photo 3R

Photo 3S

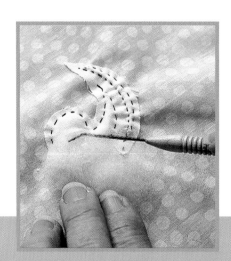

Chapter 10

SPECIALTY
TECHNIQUES

Explore new ideas and design options that
will help you keep your quilts and quilting
fresh and alive with your personal touch.

PERIWINKLE

The same pattern can be known by many different names at different times and in different parts of the country. This design is known as Periwinkle, Hummingbird, Slave Chain, Texas Tears, Snowball, and other names. Snowball refers to the white octagons between the colorful blocks; the other names identify the blocks themselves. There is no evidence that this pattern was known in the first half of the 19th century, however, so why it's called Slave Chain isn't clear. Examples are usually from the 1920s and later. Usually this pattern is made of two pieces in a solid color and two pieces in a coordinating print. Black is a color not often seen in quilts, so its use in some of the blocks in this 1930s quilt adds visual interest.

Specialty *Techniques*

As the art of quilting has expanded over the years, so have the design options and techniques that are available. Whether you're looking for instructions on assembling a classic Log Cabin block, want to attempt trapunto for the first time, or are just ready to try something new, you'll find a host of ideas and explanations in this chapter.

TRAPUNTO

Preparing the Quilt Top

Quilting adds texture to a quilt's surface. For even more relief, trapunto, or dimensional quilting, is a technique to try. By stuffing or filling an area, then quilting it, a raised surface, or relief, is formed that gives shape to stems, leaves, or other motifs.

1. Select a quilting design with trapunto in mind. Choose a design that has definite shapes stitched around all sides, as the trapunto will bring those areas into relief. If you wish, choose one of the patterns specifically created for trapunto quilting. *Note: If you choose to do machine trapunto, steps 2 through 6 are not necessary. See page 277 for machine trapunto instructions.*

2. Transfer the design onto the quilt top using a nonpermanent marking tool. (See Chapter 8—Quilting Ideas for information on transferring a design onto fabric.) Cut out a muslin underlining to cover the trapunto design area. This muslin will form the backing for the area that will be stuffed. *Note: After the trapunto is completed, the quilt top will be layered with batting and backing and finished as any other quilt.*

3. Baste the muslin underlining to the wrong side of the marked design. To prevent shifting while basting, tape the corners of the muslin down, then tape the marked quilt top to a work surface.

4. Using a smaller than normal basting stitch and contrasting thread, sew just inside the marked lines of the design or motifs (see Photo 1A, *below, far left*).

5. Turn the fabric layers with the muslin side faceup. If the finished project will be hand-quilted, use small sharp embroidery scissors to carefully trim away the muslin underlining, except what's behind the design motifs, retaining a ¼" seam allowance (see Photo 1B, *below left*). Leave small areas where it is not possible to leave a ¼" seam untrimmed. *Note: Trimming the muslin is done to reduce the bulk for hand quilting and does not have to be exact. It is not necessary to trim the muslin for machine quilting.*

6. There are several ways to create the raised surface—channel, stuffed, and machine trapunto. Descriptions of each method follow. Choose one or more than one to stuff the basted shapes.

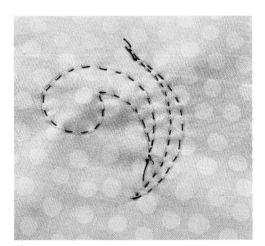

Photo 1A

Photo 1B

Photo 1C

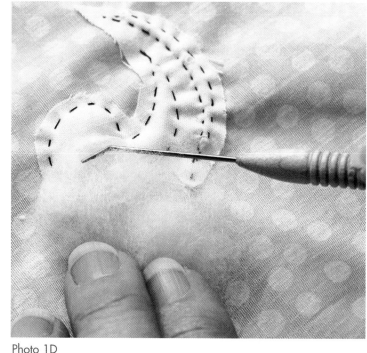

Photo 1D

Channel Trapunto

To fill thin areas, such as leaf stems or veining, use channel trapunto.

1. Prepare the quilt top for trapunto. (See Preparing the Quilt Top on *page 275*.)

2. Thread a darning needle with 12 to 16" of cotton yarn. Working from the wrong side of the quilt top, slip the needle under the muslin underlining but not through the quilt top. Pull it through a basted channel, leaving a 1 to 2" tail of yarn at the beginning (see Photo 1C, *above*).

3. Move in and out of the muslin underlining until the channel is filled with the yarn. For wider channels, pass through the area a second time. It is best to pass through the channel twice with a single strand rather than using a doubled strand of yarn once.

4. Repeat to fill all the desired motifs, then complete the quilt as desired. (See Chapter 7—Assembling the Quilt Top and Backing for more information.)

5. Remove the basting threads.

Stuffed Trapunto

To fill larger design motifs, use stuffed trapunto.

1. Prepare the quilt top for trapunto. (See Preparing the Quilt Top on *page 275*.)

2. Working from the wrong side of the quilt top, use small embroidery scissors to cut a small slit in the muslin underlining in the center of a motif, such as a leaf, or a section of a motif. Be careful not to cut into the quilt top fabric.

3. Working on a flat surface, insert small bits of fiberfill into the cavity with the aid of a blunt stuffing tool (see Photo 1D, *above*). Stuff only small bits at a time until the design is lightly but evenly stuffed. Avoid overfilling, which may cause the fabric surrounding the design to pucker.

4. Turn the project over from time to time to check for distortion. If necessary, adjust the amount of fiberfill.

5. Once a motif is stuffed, use a needle and thread to whipstitch the opening in the muslin underlining closed.

6. Repeat to fill all the desired motifs, then complete the quilt as desired. (See Chapter 7—Assembling the Quilt Top and Backing for more information.)

7. Remove the basting threads.

Photo 1E

Photo 1F

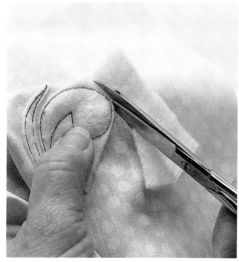

Photo 1G

Photo 1H

Trapunto By Machine

To do trapunto completely by machine, use water-soluble thread.

1. Transfer the design onto the quilt top using a nonpermanent marking tool. (See Chapter 8—Quilting Ideas for information on transferring a design onto fabric.)

2. Cut a piece of batting the size needed to cover the design area. Place the batting over the design area on the wrong side of the quilt top. Baste the batting in place.

3. Using water-soluble thread in the needle and cotton thread in a color to match the quilt top in the bobbin, stitch around a motif that will be stuffed (see photos 1E and 1F, *above* and *above right*). *Note: For illustration purposes only, contrasting thread was used in the photographs.*

4. When stitching is complete, trim the batting away around the shape next to the stitching line, leaving the batting inside the stitching lines secured (see Photo 1G, *above right*).

5. Repeat to fill all the desired motifs, then complete the quilt as desired. (See Chapter 7—Assembling the Quilt Top and Backing for more information.)

If you're machine-quilting, be sure to stitch over the water-soluble thread around each shape to secure the trapunto batting piece.

To make the raised areas even more prominent, quilt more heavily around each motif with closely spaced stitches, such as small stippling (see Photo 1H, *right*).

6. After the quilting and binding are complete, wash the quilt or spritz the trapunto areas with water to remove the water-soluble thread.

CRAZY QUILTING

In the late 1800s and early 1900s, quilters went a little crazy, using an array of fabrics and embellishments in their projects which came to be known as crazy quilts. Each block showcased the needlework skills of its maker. Although this quilt style was popular, the finished projects were more for decoration than for function.

One advantage of crazy quilting is that it uses foundation blocks, enabling quilters to more easily work with angled, bias-edge fabric pieces. Another attraction of this technique is that it offers the opportunity to use a variety of fabrics, such as silk, taffeta, and velvet, which aren't typically found in pieced quilts (see Photo 1I, *below*). The following steps describe crazy quilting.

Photo 1I

1. For each block, cut a muslin square the desired size of the finished block plus ½" for seam allowances. These are the block foundations.

2. Cut a variety of fabric pieces in assorted shapes and sizes. The pieces must be cut with straight, not curved, edges.

3. Place a fabric right side up in the center of a muslin foundation square. Place a second piece right side down over the first piece, aligning straight edges along one side. Sew along the aligned edges with a ¼" seam (see Photo 1J, *below left*).

4. Press the top piece open. Trim the ends of the larger piece so that they're even with the smaller piece.

5. In the same manner, position a third fabric piece right side down on the pieced unit, aligning a pair of edges. Sew along the aligned edges with a ¼" seam. Press open and trim as before.

6. Repeat the process to fill the entire muslin foundation, trimming any fabric pieces that extend past the foundation edges (see Photo 1K, *below*).

7. Hand- or machine-embellish the finished block as desired with decorative stitches along the seam lines. (See Decorative

Stitches by hand, which begins *below*, or Decorative Stitches by Machine on *page 282* for stitch ideas.)

8. Repeat to create the desired number of blocks. When the crazy quilt blocks are finished, lay them out as desired and sew together into a quilt top. Complete the quilt as desired. (See Chapter 7—Assembling the Quilt Top and Backing for more information.) If desired, stitch across the block seams or add ribbons, beading, buttons, or charms as embellishments (see *page 284* for information on surface embellishments).

DECORATIVE STITCHES BY HAND

Hand-stitching embellishment options are as limitless as the available thread types, making decorative stitches an extremely personal form of expression. Although decorative stitching has long been associated with crazy quilting, it can be found in quilts ranging from traditional to contemporary, whether embellishing seam allowances or in place of the usual straight quilting stitches.

Instructions for some more common decorative stitches follow.

Backstitch
To backstitch, pull the needle up at A. Insert it back into the fabric at B, and bring it up at C. Push the needle down again at D, and bring it up at E. Continue in the same manner (see Illustration 1 and Photo 1L, *opposite*).

Photo 1J

Photo 1K

Blanket Stitch (Buttonhole Stitch)

To blanket-stitch, pull the needle up at A, form a reverse L shape with the thread, and hold the angle of the L shape in place with your thumb. Push the needle down at B and come up at C to secure the stitch. Continue in the same manner (see Illustration 2, *right*, and Photo 1M, *far right*).

You may wish to make all of the stitches the same length, as shown in the illustration, or to vary the lengths, as shown in Photo 1M.

Chain Stitch

To chain-stitch, pull the needle up at A, form a U shape with the thread, and hold the shape in place with your thumb (see Illustration 3, *right*, and Photo 1N, *far right*). Push the needle down at B, about ⅛" from A, and come up at C. Continue in the same manner.

Chevron

To chevron-stitch, pull the needle up at A, then push it down at B (see Illustration 4, *right*, and Photo 1O, *far right*). Holding the thread out of the way with your thumb, make a small stitch by bringing the needle up at C, pulling the thread taut. Then push the needle down at D and bring it up at E (same hole as B). Next push the needle down at F, pull it up at G, push it down at H, and bring it up at I (same hole as F). Pull the thread taut. Continue in the same manner.

Cross-Stitch

To cross-stitch, pull the needle up at A, then push it down at B (see Illustration 5, Step 1, *right*, and Photo 1P, *far right*). Bring the needle up at C, then push it down at D. Continue in the same manner.

At the end of a row of stitching, push the needle down at H, pull it up at I, push it down at J (same hole as F) to make an X, and pull it up at K (same hole as G) (see Illustration 5, Step 2, *right*). Continue in the same manner.

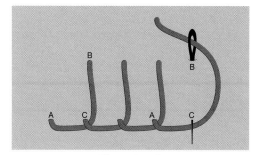

Illustration 1

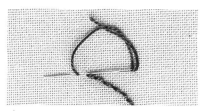

Photo 1L

Illustration 2

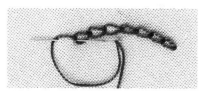

Photo 1M

Illustration 3

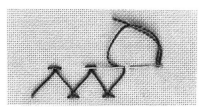

Photo 1N

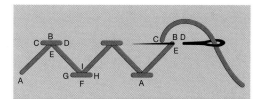

Illustration 4

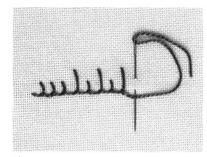

Photo 1O

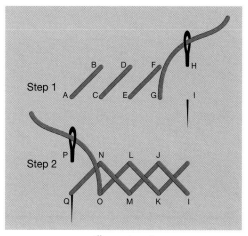

Illustration 5

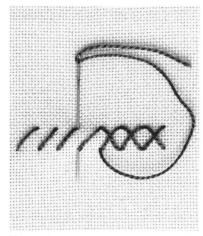

Photo 1P

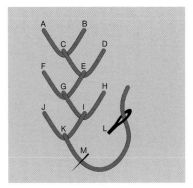

Illustration 6

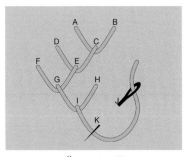

Photo 1Q

Illustration 7

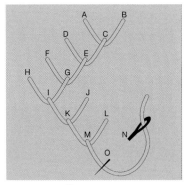

Illustration 8

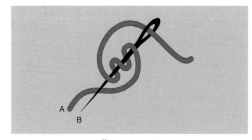

Illustration 9

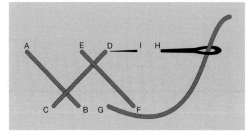

Photo 1R

Illustration 10

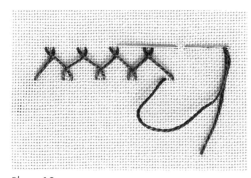

Photo 1S

Featherstitch

To featherstitch, pull the needle up at A, form a V shape with the thread (pointing in either direction), and hold the angle in place with your thumb (see Illustration 6, *far left*, and Photo 1Q, *below, far left*). Push the needle down at B, about ³⁄₈" from A, and come up at C. For the next stitch, form a V shape with the thread, insert the needle at D, and bring it out at E. Continue in the same manner.

There are many variations of the featherstitch. If all the V shapes fall on the same side of a seam, it looks similar to a blanket stitch. For a double or triple feather-stitch, work two or three stitches on the right side of a seam, followed by two or three on the left side (see Illustrations 7 and 8, *below, far left*).

French Knot

To make a French knot, pull the thread through at the point where the knot is desired (A) (see Illustration 9, *above left*, and Photo 1R, *left*). Wrap the thread around the needle two or three times. Insert the tip of the needle into the fabric at B, ¹⁄₁₆" away from A. Gently push the wraps down the needle to meet the fabric. Pull the needle and trailing thread through the fabric slowly and smoothly. Repeat for as many French knots as desired.

Herringbone Stitch

To herringbone-stitch, pull the needle up at A, then push it down at B (see Illustration 10, *above left*, and Photo 1S, *left*). Bring the needle up at C, cross the thread over the first stitch, and push the needle down at D. Pull the needle up at E, cross the thread over the second stitch, and push the needle down at F. Pull the needle up at G and continue in the same manner.

Lazy Daisy Stitch

To make a lazy daisy stitch, pull the needle up at A and form a loop of thread on the fabric surface (see Illustration 11, *right*, and Photo 1T, *right*). Holding the loop in place, insert the needle back into the fabric at B, about $\frac{1}{16}$" away from A. Bring the needle tip out at C and cross it over the trailing thread, keeping the thread as flat as possible. Gently pull the needle and trailing thread until the loop lies flat against the fabric. Push the needle through to the back at D to secure the loop in place. Repeat for as many lazy daisy stitches as desired.

Running Stitch

To make a running stitch, pull the needle up at A and insert it back into the fabric at B, $\frac{1}{8}$" away from A (see Illustration 12, *below right*, and Photo 1U, *below right*). Pull the needle up at C, $\frac{1}{8}$" away from B, and continue in the same manner.

Star Stitch

To star-stitch, or double cross-stitch, pull the needle up at A, then push it down at B (see Illustration 13, *above, far right,* and Photo 1V, *far right*). Bring the needle up at C, cross it over the first stitch, and push the needle down at D to make a cross. Pull the needle up at E, push it down at F, bring the needle up at G, cross it over the last stitch, and push the needle down at H to make an X. Continue in the same manner.

Stem Stitch

To stem-stitch, pull the needle up at A, then insert it back into the fabric at B, about $\frac{3}{8}$" away from A (see Illustration 14, *above, far right,* and Photo 1W, *far right*). Holding the thread out of the way, bring the needle back up at C and pull the thread through so it lies flat against the fabric. The distances between points A, B, and C should be equal. Pull gently with equal tautness after each stitch. Continue in the same manner, holding the thread out of the way on the same side of the stitching every time.

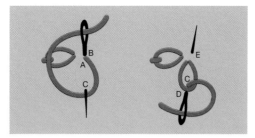

Illustration 11

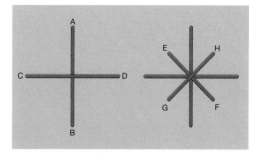

Illustration 13

Photo 1T

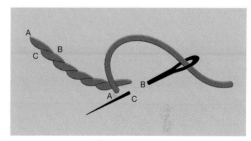

Photo 1V

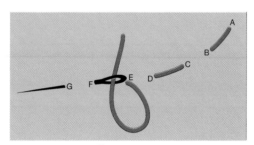

Illustration 12

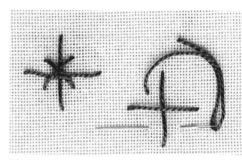

Illustration 14

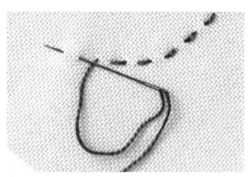

Photo 1U

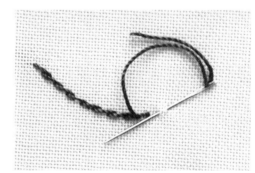

Photo 1W

DECORATIVE STITCHES BY MACHINE

Decorative stitches are built into many sewing machines and can be used for embellishing or quilting. Practice your machine stitches on scraps of quilted fabric so you have a sample of the stitches available (see Photo 1X, *below*). When finalizing a design, the stitched sample will provide you with a variety of choices.

Experiment by adjusting the width and length of the decorative stitches when possible. Some stitches that look less desirable at their normal width and length take on a whole new look once you alter one or both factors. Be sure to mark on the stitch sample the settings used.

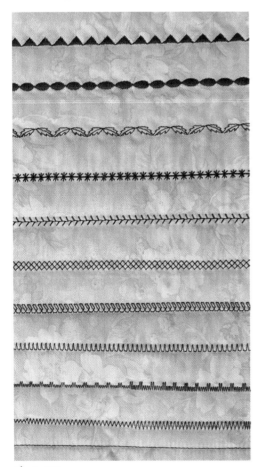

Photo 1X

YO-YOS

A perennial favorite, the yo-yo is a circle of fabric that has been gathered to form a smaller, three-dimensional circle. Yo-yos can be sewn together to make a quilt (see Photo 1Y, *below*) or used as an embellishment.

Yo-yos are traditionally made by hand, and many quilters find them a good project for travel or television time. They can be made from any size fabric circle. The finished size of a yo-yo will be slightly less than half the size of the fabric circle. For example, a 3"-diameter circle will make a yo-yo that is approximately 1½" in diameter.

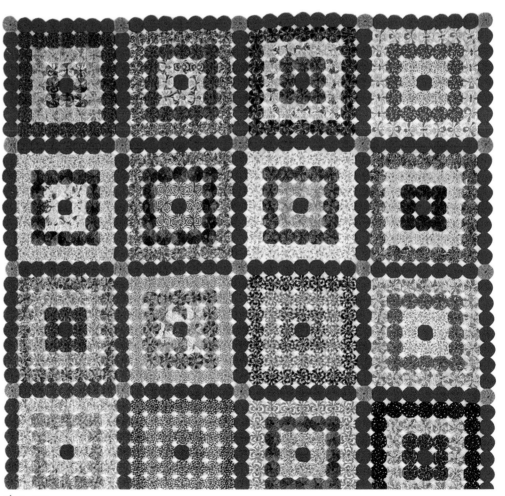

Photo 1Y

1. Cut the desired-size fabric circle using a template.

2. Begin with a sewing needle and sturdy, 100% cotton thread. Knot the end of the thread tail. While folding the raw edge of the fabric circle ¼" to the wrong side, take small, evenly spaced running stitches near the folded edge to secure it, as shown in Photo 1Z, *opposite*. (See the description of the running stitch on *page 281*.)

3. End the stitching just next to the starting point. Do not cut the thread. Gently pull the thread end to gather the folded edge until it forms a gathered circle (see Photo 2A, *opposite*). The right side of the fabric will develop soft pleats as you gather the edge. The folded-under seam allowance should roll to the inside of the yo-yo. Take a small tack stitch to hold gathers in place, then knot the thread and cut off thread tail.

4. To stitch yo-yos together, place the yo-yos with the gathered fronts together. Using matching thread, whipstitch them together for about ½" (see Photo 2B, *below right*).
Note: *For photographic purposes only, contrasting thread was used.*

Make rows of yo-yos the desired width of the finished quilt, then sew the rows together in the same manner.

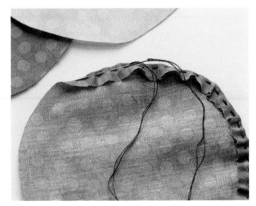

Photo 1Z

Photo 2A

Photo 2B

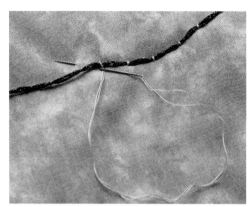

Photo 2C

Photo 2D

SURFACE EMBELLISHMENTS

Surface embellishments are finishing touches that can add texture and an element of surprise to a quilt. From buttons to beads, the options are many. Use your imagination as you search for items to stitch onto a quilt.

Couching

Fastening a thread, ribbon, or trim to a quilt's surface with small, evenly spaced stitches—couching—adds texture and dimension to a project. Couching can be done by hand or by machine and with clear monofilament or contrasting thread, depending on whether you want the anchoring stitches to show or not.

Couching by Hand
Position the decorative thread on the quilt top. Use fine thread to work small stitches ¼" to ⅜" apart over the decorative thread (see Photo 2C, *left*).

Couching by Machine
Position the decorative thread on the quilt top. Set the machine for a zigzag stitch that is slightly wider than the thread being couched. Adjust the upper tension, if necessary, or run the bobbin thread through the finger on the bobbin to increase its tension. This will pull the needle thread to the quilt back, preventing the bobbin thread from showing on the quilt top. Zigzag-stitch over the decorative thread, making sure the swing of the needle pivots to either side of the couched thread as you stitch (see Photo 2D, *left*).

Many sewing machines have special couching feet available, which places the decorative thread or trim in a groove that stabilizes it beneath the presser foot.

Practice on scraps of quilted fabric to get the appropriate stitch width, length, and tension setting when machine-couching. Some decorative threads may flatten during couching, so it is important to stitch test samples. If the thread is being flattened too much, try a blind hem stitch rather than a zigzag stitch.

Beads, Buttons, and Charms
Beads, buttons, and charms add sparkle, dimension, and texture to a quilt. Generally, it is best to add these embellishments to quilts that will not receive much handling, such as wall hangings.

Sew on the beads, buttons, or charms after quilting is complete to avoid damaging items. The method you choose for attaching them usually is driven by the desired finished effect.

Note: With the following methods, stitches will show on the quilt's back. If you wish to hide the stitches, modify the techniques to run the needle through the quilt top and batting only.

Adding Round or Seed Beads Individually
Attaching single beads to a quilt surface can be tedious, but if precise placement is important, this may be the best option.

1. Thread a beading needle with matching-color cotton or monofilament thread and knot one end. Push the needle through the quilt top to the back at the point where the first bead is desired. *Note: The knot will be covered by the first bead.*

2. Take a few tiny stitches on the quilt back.

3. Push the needle from the quilt back through to the quilt top right next to the knot, and slip the first bead on the thread (see Illustration 15, *below*).

4. Place the needle into the quilt top close to the bead and pull the needle through to the back. Pull the thread taut, but do not pull too tightly or you may distort or pucker the quilt top.

5. Repeat to add additional beads. Take a

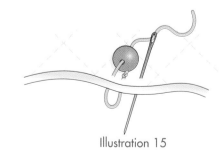

Illustration 15

backstitch after three or four beads to secure them. To backstitch, bring the needle up from the back of the quilt and thread it back through the last bead (see Illustration 16, *below*).

To travel short distances between beads, slide the needle between the quilt top and batting to the point of the next bead. Do not carry the thread for long distances between beads. Instead, knot the thread and begin again.

Adding Long or Bugle Beads Individually
Long, thin beads or bugle beads require a sewing technique different from round beads so they'll lie flat on the quilt.

1. Thread a beading needle with matching-color or monofilament thread and knot one end. Push the needle through the quilt top to the back at the point where the first bead is desired.
Note: The knot will be covered by the first bead.

2. Take a few tiny stitches on the quilt back.

3. Push the needle from the quilt back through to the quilt top right next to the knot, and slip the first bead on the thread.

4. Place the needle into the quilt top close to the bead and pull the needle through to the back.

5. Push the needle to the quilt top one

bead width away, as you would for a backstitch (see Illustration 17, *below*). Pull the thread taut, but do not pull too tightly or you may distort or pucker the quilt top. Make sure the bead lies flat against the quilt top.

6. Repeat to add additional beads. Take a backstitch after three or four beads to secure them. To backstitch, bring the needle up from the back of the quilt and thread it back through the last bead.

Couching a String of Beads
Attaching a string of beads by couching them to a quilt surface can be faster than adding them one at a time.

1. Thread a single strand of matching-color or monofilament thread onto a beading needle and knot one end. Bring the needle from the quilt back to the quilt top. String the desired number of beads onto the thread, leaving a few inches of thread near the needle without beads.

2. Secure the bead strand by parking the needle in the quilt. Do not remove the needle.

3. Thread a single strand of matching-color or monofilament thread onto a second beading needle and knot one end. Starting near the knotted end of the bead strand, bring the needle up from the quilt back to the quilt front.

4. Make a couching stitch (see Couching, *opposite*) over the bead-strand thread right next to the first bead. Push the needle through to the quilt back. Pull the thread taut so that no thread shows on the quilt top near the first bead (see Illustration 18, *below*).

5. Slide the second bead next to the first and couch over the bead-strand thread right next to the second bead. Repeat to couch the remaining beads in place.

6. Once the bead strand has been couched, bring the couching thread to the quilt back and knot it off. In the same manner, bring the parked needle and bead-strand thread to the quilt back and knot the thread.

Adding Buttons and Charms
Folk art quilts often feature buttons as embellishments. In some cases, buttons are part of a quilt's ties, rather than thread alone. For added dimension, buttons can be layered one on top of another.

Charms often appear on crazy quilts. (See *page 278* for information on crazy quilts.) Add charms to a theme quilt to enhance the design and provide another element of interest. Quilt and crafts stores often carry packages of metal charms that work well on quilts or needlework.

Depending on the finished look desired, use matching- or contrasting-color thread to attach the buttons or charms to a quilt.

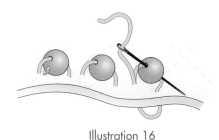

Illustration 16

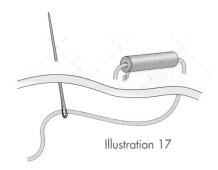

Illustration 17

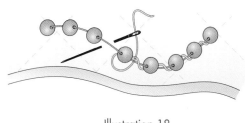

Illustration 18

Photo 2E

Machine Embroidery

Computerized sewing machines and the expanded availability of specialty threads to noncommercial sewing enthusiasts has opened up many machine embroidery options to quilters (see Photo 2E, *left*). You may wish to use the preprogrammed designs available from sewing machine and independent software design companies. For example, sewing machines with computer programs and embroidery images make it possible to stitch designs. You also can create your own designs using free-motion or freehand embroidery.

Most often machine embroidery is added to a quilt top before the quilt layers are assembled. Pay special attention to the stabilizer and the density of the designs. If the stabilizer is not removed or the designs are too dense, there may be undesirable stiffness in the embroidered areas of the finished quilt.

If the machine does not have computerized embroidery capabilities, try freehand embroidery—with a darning foot and the feed dogs dropped—which enables you to create embroidered designs.

SPECIALTY QUILT STYLES

There are numerous specialty quilt styles. Though this book does not provide step-by-step instructions for the techniques, the information that follows can help you identify particular specialties. Many books and patterns are available that give how-to instructions for each of these types of quilting.

Creative Tip

If it is difficult for you to get a row of French knots

to be uniform, use a small bead instead. It adds a

nice embellishment to a simple piece.

—*SHARON, SALES ASSOCIATE*

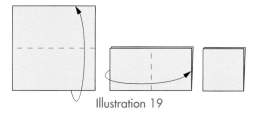

Illustration 19

Photo 2F

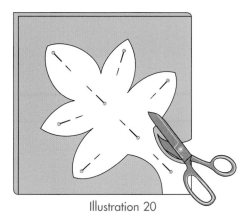

Illustration 20

Illustration 21

Bargello

Bargello quilts—those with a zigzag or flame pattern—look complicated but are actually quite simple. First, strips of fabric are sewn together. Then the pieced strips are cut into different widths and sewn together in a prescribed order. The peaks and valleys in the design are created by staggering the strips and varying the strip widths. Bargello variations abound.

Broderie Perse

Fabrics with attractive motifs take on a second life when the motifs are cut out and appliquéd to another fabric in a technique called broderie perse (see Photo 2F, *above*). This technique was popular in the mid-1800s when the motifs generally were cut from a small piece of an expensive fabric or one that was in short supply. The motifs were then buttonhole-stitched to a less expensive fabric. Floral motifs are commonly used in broderie perse.

Celtic (Bias Tube Method)

Celtic quilts have geometric designs and an architectural flair. Much like stained-glass quilts in technique, this type of Celtic quilt has a linear design theme. These designs often are applied to quilt tops with thin tubes of bias-cut fabric. (See Chapter 6—Appliqué Techniques for information on making bias strips and using bias bars.)

Hawaiian Appliqué

Intricate, symmetrical designs are the hallmark of a Hawaiian appliqué quilt. The designs result from a process similar to cutting snowflakes from paper.

To create a Hawaiian appliqué design, first make a pattern by folding a large, square piece of paper in half two times (see Illustration 19, *above top*).

Draw an appliqué design on the paper with the design's base positioned where all the folded edges meet (see Illustration 20, *above left*). Cut out the design and unfold it to see the complete motif. If you're pleased with the shape, cut the paper apart on the folds to make quarter-size patterns.

Fold the appliqué fabric in half two times. Align the cut edges of a quarter-size paper pattern with the folded edges of the folded fabric and pin in place. Cut out the appliqué shape, adding a seam allowance around the outer edges. Unfold the fabric to reveal the appliqué shape (see Illustration 21, *above*).

Baste the appliqué shape to a foundation fabric and stitch it in place using needle-turn appliqué. (See Chapter 6—Appliqué Techniques for information on needle-turn appliqué.)

Photo Transfer

Photographic images can be transferred to fabric, resulting in a highly personalized quilt. With access to a photocopier or computer and printer, you can make your own photo transfers.

Select photo-transfer paper that is specific to or compatible with the equipment you are using. The computer or copier needs to be able to produce a mirror image of the photo or design. Otherwise, the finished photo transfer will be a reverse image of the photograph, a concern if there is lettering on a garment or a sign in the photo (see Photo 2G, *below right*).

Making a photo transfer is a two-step process. First, copy the image onto the transfer paper, then press the transfer paper onto a foundation fabric using dry heat and sufficient pressure (see Photo 2H, *below, far right*). Follow the directions that accompany the product for transferring the image and caring for the final product.

Raw Edges

For a casual look, try leaving raw edges of a quilt exposed. Sew the blocks with their wrong sides together so that the seams show on the quilt top. Press the seams open. Clip the seams to fringe them, or let the washer and dryer do the unraveling work.

Redwork

Traditionally, white squares of fabric with images embroidered in red thread or floss became the basis for redwork quilts. The quilter added stitches to preprinted squares and sewed them together in a red and white quilt.

Today, quilters use a variety of white to off-white fabrics as the foundation for redwork stitches—most often stem stitches. The embroidered designs can be combined with pieced blocks into a quilt top or joined with sashing strips. When blue thread or floss is used, the technique is aptly called bluework. (See Decorative Stitches by Hand, which begins on *page 278,* for embroidery ideas.)

Sashiko

What began as a method to mend and reinforce indigo-color work clothes in Japan—sashiko—has evolved into a quilting technique.

Sashiko is done today over one or two layers of fabric with or without a batting. It also can function as a quilting stitch. Sashiko uses thick white thread and solid-color fabrics; it involves fewer stitches per inch—five to seven stitches—than traditional quilting. The decorative patterns tend to be geometric or reflect items found in nature. Designs need to be transferred and the stitching sequence determined prior to beginning stitching.

Signature Quilt

When the settlers headed west across America, many carried a quilt signed by members of the community that they were leaving. Scores of these signature quilts can be found in antique shops, and more are being produced by quilters today. Names and notes are inscribed on the blocks in these

Photo 2G

Photo 2H

quilts with embroidery, permanent ink, or machine stitching. (See Chapter 9—Finishing Techniques for information on putting permanent signatures with pen on fabric.)

Stained-Glass Quilt

The makers of stained glass and stained-glass quilts have a history of sharing patterns and designs, even though making a quilt look like a stained-glass window is a relatively new concept.

To make a stained-glass quilt, strips of ¼"-wide black bias tape are positioned over areas where different colors of fabric meet (see Photo 2I, *right*). The strips are machine-stitched down with a double needle and black thread or are stitched along each edge by hand or machine. The bias tape bends smoothly around curves and other shapes, imitating the look of leading in a stained-glass window (see Photo 2J, *right*).

Bias tape specifically designed for stained-glass quilts is available at quilt shops. (See Chapter 6—Appliqué Techniques for information on making your own bias strips or tubes.)

String Piecing

Similar to piecing a crazy quilt, string piecing involves sewing fabric strips to a foundation fabric. The strips, or "strings," can be any color combination, from scrappy to graduated color families.

The strips do not need to be a uniform width, as the foundation will prevent bias edges from distorting. This is an excellent technique for using scraps from previous quilt projects.

To begin, place two strips with right sides together atop a muslin foundation piece cut to the desired finished shape, including seam allowances. Sew along a pair of long edges, then press open the top strip. Place a third strip on the second strip with right sides together. Sew together a pair of long edges, and press open the top strip (see Photo 2K, *below*). Continue to add strips in the same manner.

Trim the strip-pieced unit even with the foundation edges, then join the trimmed units to make blocks (see Photo 2L, *below right*).

Watercolor or Color-Wash Quilt

When an assortment of busy print fabrics is cut into small pieces and carefully positioned in a quilt top, the look of a watercolor painting emerges. Prints with multiple colors and varying values, such as florals, work well for watercolor, or color-wash, quilts.

Generally, the quilts are made from 2" squares of fabric. The key to a successful watercolor quilt is a large value range in fabric choices. (See Chapter 2—Fabric and Color for more information about color values.) To accumulate enough prints, consider a fabric exchange with other quilters. Use a design wall to plan the design and avoid fabrics that appear solid when viewed from a distance.

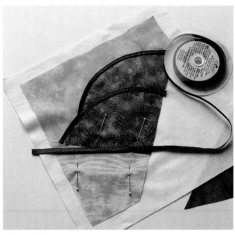

Photo 2I

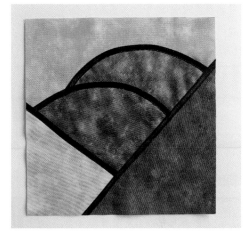

Photo 2J

Photo 2K

Photo 2L

Glossary

A

Acrylic ruler: A ruler of thick, clear plastic used to make straight cuts with a rotary cutter. Available in a variety of sizes and shapes.

Acrylic template: Thick, durable plastic pattern used to trace and/or cut around. Available commercially in a variety of shapes and patterns. Can be used with a rotary cutter.

Allover quilting: Stitching that covers the entire quilt without regard for block shapes or fabric design. Can be quilted from either the top or the back side.

Alternate blocks: Plain, pieced, or appliquéd blocks between a quilt's primary blocks. Also called alternate squares or setting squares.

Analogous color: The colors located on either side of a color on the color wheel.

Appliqué: Fabric motifs sewn by hand or machine to a foundation fabric.

Appliqué template: A pattern used to trace shapes onto fabric.

Asymmetry: When one-half of an image or block does not mirror the opposite half, the image is asymmetric.

B

Background quilting: Stitching in open interior spaces, such as in setting squares. Squares, diamonds, clamshells, or other small regular shapes are commonly used as background quilting. The closely spaced lines tend to flatten the area being quilted, creating a low-relief, textured appearance.

Backing: The layer of fabric on the back of a quilt. It can be a single fabric, pieced from multiple fabrics, or created using extra blocks.

Basting spray: Adhesive available in a spray can that may be used to hold the layers of a quilt together instead of basting.

Basting stitch: A large, loose stitch used to hold together layers of fabric or fabric and batting. Basting stitches are usually removed after the layers are permanently joined.

Batting: The material used between the quilt top and quilt back. Commercial battings are available in a variety of fiber contents. Flannel fabric is sometimes substituted for traditional batting.

Bearding: The appearance of batting on the quilt surface, showing through the holes where the needle pierced the quilt top or back during the quilting process. Also called fiber migration.

Betweens: Short, fine needles used for hand piecing, hand quilting, appliqué, and sewing on binding.

Bias: Any diagonal line between the crosswise or lengthwise grain line in woven fabric. The bias grain has more stretch and is less stable than the crosswise or lengthwise grain. See also "True bias."

Bias binding: Binding strips cut on the true bias grain, resulting in a binding that can be easily positioned around curved edges. When striped fabrics are cut on the bias, the result is a "barber pole" effect.

Bias strips: Long, thin pieces of fabric cut on the bias grain.

Big stitch: Large, evenly spaced hand quilting used in folk art.

Binding: The finishing band of fabric that covers the raw outer edges of a quilt.

Blanket stitch: A decorative machine or hand stitch used to outline appliqué pieces. Also called buttonhole stitch.

Block: The basic unit, usually square and often repeated, from which many quilts are composed. May be pieced, appliquéd, or solid.

Bobbin case: The portion of the sewing machine that holds the bobbin. Bobbin cases may be fixed or removable, depending on machine style and manufacturer.

Bobbin case finger: The part of the bobbin case that projects upward in some machines. It contains a hole for threading the bobbin thread through to increase the lower thread tension.

Bobbin-fill thread: A lightweight thread used in the bobbin for machine embroidery, machine appliqué, or decorative stitching. Also called lingerie thread.

Border: The framing on a quilt that serves to visually hold in the design and give the eye a stopping point.

Broderie perse: A technique in which individual motifs are cut from one fabric and applied to another fabric foundation.

Butted corners: Border pieces that meet at a 90° angle or binding pieces that overlap in the corner at a 90° angle, rather than being mitered.

Buttonhole stitch: See "Blanket stitch."

C

Chain piecing: Sewing patchwork pieces in a continuous chain from edge to edge without backstitching. Short lengths of thread link the pieces.

Channel stitching: Parallel rows of straight-line quilting that go in one direction across a quilt top.

Chenille needle: A long, oval-eye needle used for heavyweight thread, embroidery, and tying quilts.

Chevron stitch: A zigzag-type embroidery stitch used for decorative embellishment.

Color retention: A fabric's ability to retain its color in the wash.

Color wheel: Device used to demonstrate the relationships of primary, secondary, and tertiary colors and the tints and shades of each.

Complementary colors: Pairs of colors that are opposite one another on the color wheel.

Continuous bias binding technique: A method of marking, sewing, and cutting a square of fabric into one long bias strip.

Continuous sashing: Strips of fabric that separate entire rows either vertically or horizontally.

Contrast: The differences between color values, described as light, medium, or dark. Contrast clarifies design and makes depth apparent.

Corner matching points: Marks made on templates and pattern pieces to indicate where corners come together. Especially important when hand-piecing, as stitching stops at the marks.

Cornerstones: Squares of fabric pieced within sashing that align at the block corners.

Couching: Stitching thick threads, ribbons, beads, and other items to a quilt surface.

Covered cording: A trim or binding made by covering cording with fabric. Also called piping.

Crazy quilting: Popularized in Victorian times. Odd-shaped pieces of fabric sewn onto a foundation and embellished with embroidery, ribbons, and beading. Silk, velvet, cotton, and other fine fabrics are typically used in crazy quilting.

Crocking: The rubbing off of color from one fabric to another, caused when fabrics rub against one another during handling or washing.

Crosswise grain (cross grain): Threads that run perpendicular to the selvage across the width of a woven fabric.

Curve, concave: A curve that bows inward.

Curve, convex: A curve that bows outward.

Curved rulers and templates: Made of acrylic plastic, to ease rotary-cutting of intricate, curved pieces.

Cutting mat: Surface used for rotary cutting that protects the tabletop and keeps the fabric from shifting while cutting. Often labeled as self-healing, meaning the blade does not leave slash marks or grooves in the surface even after repeated usage.

D

Darning foot: An open-toe sewing machine foot for free-motion quilting.

Design wall/surface: A vertical surface used to position and view fabric choices to see how they might appear in a quilt.

Diagonal set: Quilt top with blocks set "on-point" in diagonal rows.

Directional borders: Borders that have designs running in a particular sequence or order.

Directional clipping: Snipping seams on the bias to prevent raveling of fabric edges, such as in appliqué.

Directional pressing: Ironing seams in a designated direction to limit bulk in certain areas of a block. Commonly used in diamonds and other center-intersecting blocks.

Directional stitching: Sewing seams in a designated direction when piecing to prevent puckering. Commonly used in sewing diamonds and other center-intersecting blocks.

Dog-ears: Long points that extend beyond the seam allowance, block edge, or quilt top edge after the pieces are stitched together. Usually trimmed off to make aligning subsequent pieces easier.

Double-appliqué method: Finished-edge appliqué pieces faced with a lightweight interfacing, then stitched to a foundation fabric.

Double-fold binding: A fabric strip that is folded in half then used to bind the quilt. Also called French-fold binding.

E

Easing: Working in extra fabric where two pieces do not align precisely, especially when sewing curves.

Echo quilting: Multiple lines that follow the outline of an appliqué or other design element, echoing its shape.

Embellishment: Adding decorative items or stitches to a quilt top. May include buttons, beads, heavyweight threads, or charms.

Embroidery: A type of embellishment or stitchery that can be created by hand or machine using a variety of threads.

English paper piecing: Technique of stabilizing fabric over a paper template. Frequently used for designs with set-in corners such as the hexagon shape.

Ergonomics: The study of workspace design to prevent injury.

Extra-fine pins: Pins with a thinner shaft than standard pins, thus leaving smaller holes in fabric.

F

Fat eighth: A 1/8-yard fabric cut crosswise from a 1/4-yard piece of fabric for a finished size of approximately 9×22".

Fat quarter: A 1/4-yard fabric cut crosswise from a 1/2-yard piece of fabric for a finished size of approximately 18×22".

Featherstitch: A decorative embroidery stitch.

Feed dogs: The sawtooth-edge machine component that rests under the throat plate and aids in moving fabric beneath the presser foot.

Felted wool: Wool fabric that has been machine-washed and dried to create a napped, no-fray material.

Finger-pressing: The process of pressing a small seam using a finger to apply pressure. Also called finger-crease.

Flannel: A 100%-cotton fabric that has a brushed, napped surface.

Foundation piecing: A method of sewing together fabric pieces on the reverse side of a paper pattern or foundation fabric. Sometimes preferred for joining very small or irregularly shaped fabric pieces.

Four-Patch unit: A block or unit of four equal-size squares sewn in two horizontal rows, often with alternating color placement.

Glossary

Free-motion embroidery: Machine embroidery done with the feed dogs disengaged and using a darning presser foot so the quilt can be moved freely on the machine bed in any direction.

Free-motion quilting: Machine quilting done with the feed dogs disengaged and using a darning presser foot so the quilt can be moved freely on the machine bed in any direction.

Freezer paper: Paper commonly available at grocery stores that can be used to make appliqué patterns. The shiny coating on one side temporarily adheres to fabric when pressed with a warm iron.

French-fold binding: See "Double-fold binding."

Fusible web: A paper-backed adhesive that can be ironed to the back of fabric that is then cut into shapes. These fused shapes can be adhered to a background fabric by pressing them with a warm iron. Frequently used in appliqué projects.

Fussy cutting: Isolating and cutting out a specific print or motif from a piece of fabric.

G

Glass-head pins: Pins with a glass head that won't melt when pressed.

Grain (grain line, on grain, or grain perfect): Reference to the lengthwise or crosswise threads in a woven fabric.

Greige goods: Fabric in a raw, unfinished state. Pronounced "gray-zh" goods.

Grid quilting: Quilting in vertical and horizontal lines across the quilt top. Also called cross-hatch.

H

Half-square triangle: The 90° triangle formed when a square is cut in half diagonally once.

Hand-appliqué: Sew fabric pieces by hand onto a fabric foundation.

Hand-piece: Sew seams by hand to make a quilt top.

Hand-piecing templates: Patterns used to trace and cut patches for hand-piecing projects. The shapes do not include seam allowances.

Hand quilting: Series of running stitches made through all layers of a quilt with needle and thread.

Hanging sleeve: A piece of fabric sewn to the back of a quilt. The fabric holds a rod so a quilt can be hung for display.

Hawaiian appliqué: Intricate, symmetrical appliqué designs. The pattern-making process is similar to that used to create paper snowflakes.

I

Inset seam: See "Set-in seam."

Intensity: The amount of pure color (saturated or brilliant) or muted color (grayed or subdued) in a fabric.

In-the-ditch quilting: Stitching just next to the seams on the quilt surface often used to define blocks or shapes. Also called stitch-in-the-ditch quilting.

Ironing: Moving the iron while it has contact with the fabric, which can stretch and distort fabrics and seams. Ironing is distinctly different from pressing.

Isosceles triangle: A triangle with two equal sides whose sum is longer than the base.

K

Kaleidoscope: A quilt block pattern in which fabric is pieced so that it resembles the variegated image seen through a kaleidoscope.

Knee-lift presser foot: A device attached to a sewing machine that allows the quilter to raise the machine presser foot with the knee, leaving the hands free to manipulate or hold the fabric.

Knife-edge self-binding: Quilt top fabric and backing fabric are turned under to meet evenly at the edges of the quilt, leaving the quilt edges without an additional strip of binding fabric.

L

Lap quilting: Hand quilting done while holding the quilt loosely in the lap without a hoop.

Lengthwise grain: Threads that run parallel to the selvage in a woven fabric.

Light box: A translucent surface that is lit from below and is used for tracing patterns onto paper or fabric.

Loft: The thickness of the batting.

Long-arm quilting machine: A quilting machine used by professional quilters in which the quilt is held taut on a frame, allowing the quilter to work on a large portion of the quilt at a time. The machine head moves freely, allowing free-motion quilting in all directions.

M

Machine-appliqué: Sew fabric motifs onto a fabric foundation using a sewing machine.

Machine-piece: Sew patchwork pieces together with ¼" seam allowances, using a sewing machine, to make a quilt top.

Machine quilting: Series of stitches made through all layers of a quilt sandwich with a sewing machine.

Machine tension: The balancing forces on the needle and bobbin threads that affect the quality of its stitch. Tension may be affected by the machine parts, how the machine and bobbin are threaded, thread type, needle type, and fabric choice.

Marking tools: A variety of pens, pencils, and chalks that can be used to mark fabric pieces or a quilt top.

Matching point: Where the seam line joining two pieces begins or ends. Also known as a joining point.

Meandering stitch: An allover quilting pattern characterized by a series of large, loosely curved lines that usually do not cross over one another. Commonly used to cover an entire quilt surface without regard for block or border seams or edges.

Metallic needle: A needle with a large eye for use with metallic thread.

Metallic thread: A synthetic thread with a shiny, metallic appearance.

Milliners needle: A long needle with a small round eye used for basting, gathering, and needle-turn appliqué. Also called a straw needle.

Mirror image: The reverse of an image or how it might appear if held up to a mirror.

Mitered borders: Border strips that meet in the corner at a 45° angle.

Mock-hand appliqué: Using clear, monofilament thread in the needle, cotton thread in the bobbin, and a blind-hem stitch to make virtually invisible appliqué stitches by machine.

Monochromatic: Use of a single color, which may include tints and shades of that color.

Monofilament thread: A clear or smoke-colored thread made of polyester or nylon used for machine quilting. Finished stitches are virtually invisible.

N

Napping: Brushing the fabric surface to create a soft texture. Process used to create flannel.

Needle-punching: A process used in batting manufacturing to entangle the fibers and stabilize the batting.

Needle threader: A device that helps in getting thread through the eye of the needle. Available for both hand and machine sewing.

Needle-turn appliqué: An appliqué method in which the seams are turned under with the needle tip just ahead of the section being stitched.

Nine-Patch: A block or unit comprised of nine squares of fabric sewn together in three horizontal rows, often with alternating color placement. A common block configuration in quilting.

Novelty print: Fabric designed with a theme that may include holiday symbols, hobbies, or pet motifs. Also called a conversation print.

O

Off grain: When the lengthwise and crosswise grains of fabric don't intersect at a perfect right angle.

On point: Quilt blocks that are positioned on the diagonal are on point.

Outline quilting: Quilting done ¼" from a seam line or an edge of an appliqué shape.

P

Paper foundation: A thin piece of paper with a pattern that becomes the base for a quilt block when fabric is sewn directly onto it.

Partial seams: A two-step process of seaming to avoid set-in seams.

Perle cotton thread: A soft, yarnlike cotton thread used for quilting, decorative stitching, or embellishment. Available in a variety of thicknesses.

Photo transfer: Technique for transferring photo images onto fabric for use in a quilt top.

Pin-baste: Basting together quilt layers with pins (often safety pins).

Pinking blade or shears: Rotary-cutter blade or scissors with edges that cut a zigzag pattern in fabric.

Piping: See "Covered cording."

Ply: A single strand of fiber. Several are twisted together to create a thread.

Polychromatic combination: A multicolor mix.

Pounce: A chalk bag that can be patted over a stencil to transfer a pattern to fabric. Also called stamping powder.

Prairie points: Folded fabric triangles used as a border or embellishment.

Preshrinking: Washing and drying of fabric to remove finishes and shrink fabric before it is cut and sewn.

Presser foot: The removable machine accessory that holds fabric in place against the machine bed and accommodates the needle. (A variety of presser-foot styles are available for most machines.)

Pressing: Picking up the iron off the fabric surface and putting it back down in another location, rather than sliding it across the fabric. See "Ironing."

Primary colors: The three main colors from which all others come—red, blue, and yellow.

Q

Quarter-square triangle: The 90° triangle formed when a square is cut diagonally twice in an X.

Quilt center: The quilt top before borders are added.

Quilt sandwich: The three parts of a quilt layered together—the quilt top, batting, and backing.

Quilt top: The front of a quilt prior to layering and quilting. It can be pieced, appliquéd, or made of a single piece of fabric.

Quilter's knot: A knot used frequently in quilting in which thread is wrapped around the needle, then the needle is pulled through the wraps to create a knot. Also known as knot on the needle.

Quilting distance: The space between quilting stitches. Different distances are recommended for specific batting.

Quilting frame/hoop: Two pieces of wood or plastic that are placed on the top and bottom of a quilt to hold the fabric taut for quilting or surface embellishment.

Quilting stencils: Quilting patterns with open areas through which a design is transferred onto a quilt top. May be purchased or made from sturdy, reusable template material.

Quilting templates: Shapes that are traced around to mark a quilt top for quilting. May be purchased or made from sturdy, reusable template material.

Glossary

R

Reducing lens: A device that allows quilters to view fabric and projects as if they were several feet away. Distance may be valuable in determining design qualities.

Repeat: Repetitions of a pattern or design in a fabric or repetition of a quilting design or motif.

Reproduction fabrics: Re-creations of fabrics from different time periods, such as the Civil War era or the 1930s.

Resiliency: The ability of a batting to resist creasing and regain its loft.

Reverse appliqué: An appliqué method in which the foundation fabric is on top of the appliqué fabric. The foundation is cut away to reveal the appliqué fabric underneath.

Right triangle: A triangle with one 90° angle.

Rotary cutter: Tool with a sharp, round blade attached to a handle that is used to cut fabric. The blade is available in different diameters.

Rotary-cutting mat: See "Cutting mat."

S

Sandpaper: Typically used in woodworking and crafts. The fine-grit type can be used in quilting to hold fabric while marking to prevent distortion.

Sashiko: A type of Japanese embroidery traditionally using a thick white thread on layered indigo-color fabric to create geometric patterns.

Sashing: Strips of fabric used to separate or set off block designs.

Satin stitch: A compact zigzag stitch often used around appliqué pieces to enclose raw edges and attach the appliqués to a foundation fabric.

Scale: The size of a print in relationship to other fabrics.

Scalloped border: A border with multiple curves around the quilt's outer edges.

Seam allowance: Distance between the fabric's raw edge and the seam line. Typically ¼" in machine piecing.

Seam line: The straight or curved line on which the stitches should be formed.

Seam ripper: A sharp, curved-tip tool used to lift and break thread when removing a seam.

Secondary colors: Colors created by combining the primary colors—orange, violet, and green.

Self-binding: Using backing fabric as binding, rather than attaching a separate binding strip.

Selvage: The lengthwise edge of woven fabric.

Set: How blocks are arranged in a quilt top.

Set-in seam: The type of seam used when a continuous straight seam is not an option. Separate steps are necessary to sew a piece into an angled opening between other pieces that have already been joined.

Setting a seam: The first pressing of the seam as it comes from the sewing machine to lock threads together, smooth out puckers, and even out minor thread tension differences before pressing the seam open or to one side.

Setting squares: Solid, pieced, or appliquéd squares placed between the focal-point quilt blocks to set off a design.

Setting triangles: Triangles used to fill out a design when blocks are set on point. Also called filler triangles.

Shade: Black added to a color or hue creates a darker shade of that color.

Sharp: A thin hand or machine needle with an extremely sharp point that is used to piece woven fabrics.

Silk pins: Thin-shaft pins with sharp points for easy insertion. Creates tiny holes in delicate fabrics.

Single-fold binding: A single-thickness fabric strip used to enclose quilt edges. Most commonly used for quilts that will not be handled frequently.

Sizing: Product used to add body or stability to fabric, making it easier to handle.

Slipstitches: Small stitches used to stitch down binding.

Spacer border: Plain border sewn between a quilt center and an outer pieced border.

Split complement: A color grouping utilizing a primary, secondary, or tertiary color and the colors on either side of its complement.

Spray starch or spray sizing: Liquid starch or sizing that can be sprayed over fabric to stabilize it before cutting.

Stabilizer: A product used beneath an appliqué foundation to eliminate puckers and pulling on the fabric while machine-stitching. Stabilizers are often tear-away or water-soluble for easy removal after stitching is complete.

Stippling: An allover quilting pattern characterized by a series of randomly curved lines that do not cross. Stippling is used to fill in background areas, which allows motifs to be more prominent. Also called allover meandering or puzzle quilting.

Stitching sequence: A designated order in which appliqué pieces should be stitched to the foundation fabric. Normally notated on appliqué patterns or pieces by a number.

Stitch-in-the-ditch: See "In-the-ditch quilting."

Stitch length: The number of stitches per inch. On a sewing machine, stitch length is often in millimeters.

Stitch width: A term generally applied to machine satin or zigzag stitching where the stitch width can be adjusted.

Straightedge: A ruler or other rigid surface that can be placed on template material or fabric to position a cutting tool or draw a line.

Straight grain: See "Lengthwise grain."

Straight set: A quilt top setting with blocks aligned side by side in straight, even rows without sashing.

Straight-set borders: A border that has been added first to the top and bottom of the quilt, then to the side edges, or vice versa.

Straight-stitch throat plate: A sewing machine throat plate with a small round hole for the needle to pass through. This allows less area for the sewing machine to take in or "swallow" the fabric as it is being stitched.

Straw needle: See "Milliners needle."

String piecing: Sewing multiple strips of fabric to a foundation piece for use in a block.

Strip piecing: A process for accurately and quickly cutting multiple strips and joining them together prior to cutting them into units or subunits for blocks. Also known as the strip method.

T

Tapestry needle: A needle with an oval eye that accommodates thick thread and creates a hole in the fabric big enough for thick or coarse fibers to pass through.

Template: A pattern made from paper, plastic, cardboard, or other sturdy material, used to cut pieces for patchwork or appliqué.

Template plastic: Easy to cut, translucent material available at quilt shops and crafts supply stores. Designs can be traced onto its surface with a marking tool to make templates, pattern pieces, or quilting stencils.

Tension: See "Machine tension."

Tension dial: A sewing machine part that allows for adjustment of the upper thread tension. Important to achieving a balanced stitch.

Tension discs: Sewing machine parts that hold the thread and keep the tension appropriate for the stitch being sewn.

Tertiary colors: Colors that are combinations of primary colors (red, blue, yellow) and secondary colors (green, orange, violet)—red-orange, red-violet, blue-violet, blue-green, yellow-green, and yellow-orange.

Tetrad: A combination of four colors that are equidistant on the color wheel.

Thimble: A device to protect finger pads from needle pricks. Can be made of metal, leather, plastic, or rubber.

Thread-basting: Basting quilt layers together using a needle and thread and extra-long stitches that will be removed after the quilting is complete.

Thread count: The number of threads woven into a fabric. A higher number designates a more tightly woven fabric.

Throat plate: The removable plate on the machine bed that covers the bobbin and has an opening for the feed dogs and needle. Throat plates can be changed depending on the type of project.

Tint: White added to a color or hue creates a lighter tint of that color.

Topstitch: A machine straight stitch typically done on the right side of a project close to a seam.

Tracing paper: A thin, translucent paper used for copying patterns.

Trapunto: A method of adding raised texture to quilts by stuffing design areas. Trapunto is used frequently in stems, leaves, and other motifs.

Triad: Three primary, secondary, or tertiary colors that are equidistant on the color wheel.

Triangle-square: The square unit created when two 90° triangles are sewn together on the diagonal.

True bias: Intersects the lengthwise grain and crosswise grain at a 45° angle.

Tying: Taking a stitch through all three layers of the quilt and knotting it on the quilt surface. Tying creates a loftier quilt. Also called tufting.

U

Unit: A combination of at least two pieces of fabric sewn together that form part of a block.

Utility stitch: See "Big stitch."

V

Variegated thread: Thread in which the color changes throughout the strand.

W

Walking foot: A sewing machine foot that has grippers on the bottom that act in tandem with the machine's feed dogs to evenly feed multiple layers of fabric and batting beneath the foot. Effective for machine quilting. Also called an even-feed foot.

Water-soluble: Threads, stabilizers, or marks that dissolve when wet.

Y

Yo-yos: Three-dimensional gathered fabric circles that may be sewn into quilt tops or used for decorative embellishments.

Z

Zigzag stitch: A side-to-side stitch that can be used for machine appliqué. It can be shortened and very closely spaced to create a satin stitch.

Index

Index

The Fabric of Success

The Story of JO-ANN® Stores, Inc.

A young boy busies himself straightening the shelves of notions in his family's shop. It is Saturday, and the store is humming with its familiar sounds: customers chatting while they thumb through patterns; scissors cutting fabric from broad, colorful bolts; children tugging on their mothers' sleeves, asking for a drink of water.

Feeling a familiar tap on his shoulder, the boy turns. A dollar bill and a handwritten note are pressed into his hand. The note bears a cryptic message that he quickly decodes: "Butterick, 5562, size 12." He understands his mission instantly, and darts out of the store. A customer has requested a pattern, and his grandmother has learned she does not have it in stock. She has quietly dispatched him to buy the pattern her customer seeks from the five-and-dime across the way.

He returns quickly, transferring the package to his grandmother's hand; there is a brief, unspoken exchange of covert victory between the two of them. She will make no money on that sale today, but she has kept a customer happy. Instinctively, she knows this decision is sound business, as surely as she knows cotton from silk.

The boy, watching the customer smile as she thanks his grandmother and pays for the pattern, listens and learns. He has witnessed, again, what lies at the core of his family's business ethic, and it will stay with him always.

The boy in this 1950s story is Alan Rosskamm, current chairman, president, and chief executive officer of Jo-Ann Stores, Inc. The story is a company legend of sorts. It captures the essence of Jo-Ann's renowned mission of superior customer service during sixty years of business, an anniversary the company celebrates this year. Founded in 1943, the company that would become the nation's largest fabric and crafts retailer was begun by two families, the Reichs and the Rohrbachs, out of a single shop in Cleveland, Ohio.

But who is the grandmother tapping young Alan on the shoulder? She is the late Hilda Reich, matriarch of the Reich family and a founding member of the company. "My grandmother was all about doing whatever it took to meet the needs of her customers," Alan Rosskamm recalls, nodding toward the

Founded in 1943, the company has become the nation's largest fabric and crafts retailer.

bronze bust of Hilda Reich that hangs on the wall to the right of his desk. She is a constant reminder of the legacy he aims to see reflected in every decision made at the company he runs, from the boardroom to the buyers' offices to the button department.

A MATTER OF "HERSTORY"

All of the surviving members of the Rohrbach and Reich families give great credit to the business savvy and expertise of their men, but the stories they share reveal that the roots of Jo-Ann Stores, Inc. lie in a story about women. It was strong, creative women, undaunted by challenges and with a bent for hard work, who ran the business for many years. They built a large base of loyal customers who were and are, for the most part, also women. The business itself was eventually named for two daughters of the founding families, Joan Zimmerman and Jackie Ann Rosskamm. And women in large numbers continue, both inside and outside the company, to steer the company in its mission to serve and inspire creativity.

So, Jo-Ann's story is a matter of "herstory" as much as it is "history."

MOTHERS AND DAUGHTERS, HUSBANDS AND SONS

Hilda and Berthold Reich were running a small cheese and fancy-food business in

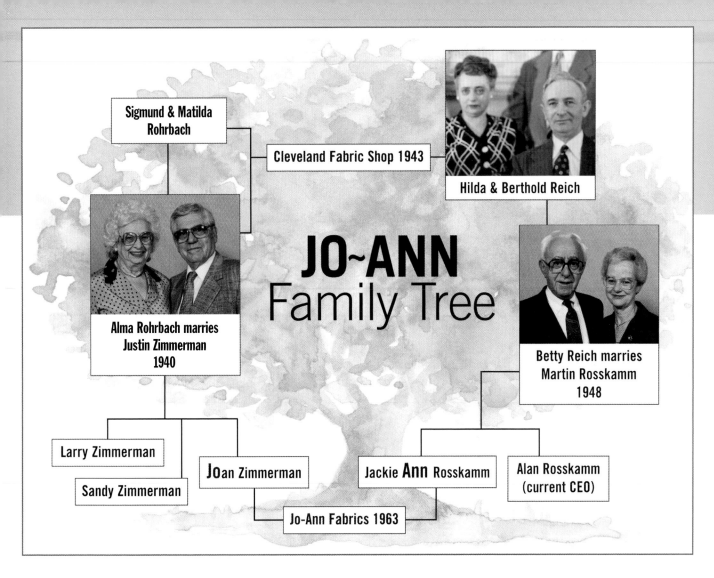

Sigmund & Matilda Rohrbach

Cleveland Fabric Shop 1943

Hilda & Berthold Reich

JO~ANN
Family Tree

Alma Rohrbach marries Justin Zimmerman 1940

Betty Reich marries Martin Rosskamm 1948

Larry Zimmerman

Sandy Zimmerman

JOan Zimmerman

Jackie Ann Rosskamm

Alan Rosskamm (current CEO)

Jo-Ann Fabrics 1963

Cleveland when they were approached by Sigmund and Matilda Rohrbach, who inquired about selling fabrics in the shop. The families decided to move fabrics to the front of the store, and eventually the food business moved to a different location. In 1943 the two couples celebrated the opening of what was then called the Cleveland Fabric Shop.

It was a year when the presence of women in the work force was unquestioned. With men at war, all hands were needed on the home front. Later, of course, women were urged to return fully to their domestic duties. But Hilda, Betty and Alma were not

among them. They were busy keeping up with customer demand in the business in which they and their husbands were partners.

SOMETIMES A GREAT NOTION

Sigmund and Matilda Rohrbach's daughter, Alma, would grow to be a significant contributor to the success of the business, as would her husband, the late Justin Zimmerman, who would eventually serve in the role of executive vice-president.

Alma Zimmerman recalls thinking, during the store's early years, "As long

as the customer is in here buying fabric, why not sell them patterns and buttons and so forth?" She persisted in her idea to add notions to the store's offerings. "Nobody else wanted to do it, so I got stuck with it," she smiles.

She is being rather modest.

"Alma was renowned in the industry," says Alan Rosskamm. "She built our entire notions department from nothing to a huge part of our business."

Alma Zimmerman's life, too, has been shaped by her family's powerful work ethic. She recalls her youth in Germany, which she left at age 22 to come to America: "I took a lot of training, because it was hard to get work, so whatever you knew was helpful. My father had approached the owner of a very fine fashion, fabric and lingerie store, and asked if I could work there, not for pay, just to learn. At the end of six weeks, the owner said to my father, "You asked me not to pay your daughter, but I must. You see, she does better than some of my employees." Alma worked there for four years while going to school.

Alma, an emeritus board member who served as a director for more than thirty-five years, still keeps regular office hours at Jo-Ann Stores' corporate headquarters. She recently celebrated her 90th birthday. She remembers without hesitation the circumstances, as well as the address, of her family's first place of business in Cleveland: "We first set up at 12708 Superior Avenue. I was pregnant, helping a customer on Sunday, the day before the store even opened. On Monday morning, my daughter Joan was born."

During their journey toward prosperity, the Rohrbachs and Reichs thought less about greatness than the important matters at hand: "We simply came to work each day and did what needed to be done. Hours didn't mean anything. We learned what we had to learn and did it," Alma says.

MOVING HEAVEN AND EARTH

Hilda and Berthold Reich's daughter, Betty, worked in the store from its early days. She later met and married Martin Rosskamm, who encouraged his father-in-law to expand the business, and would join it full-time in 1966. Martin Rosskamm served as president, chairman and CEO for many years. He retired in 1985, and died in August of the same year. "I was 16 when my family got involved in the business," Betty recalls. "I started by typing invoices after school. I've always enjoyed working."

Betty recalls, "I started by typing invoices after school. I've always enjoyed working."

Her values, too, were shaped in great measure by her mother, Hilda. "My mother ran the messiest store we ever had," recalls Betty in her forthright manner. "But she would move heaven and earth to take care of a customer. She did more volume per square foot than any store we've ever had. She lived till she was 87, and she was still running the store five days before she died."

EMBRACING CHANGE AND TECHNOLOGY

Poised and polished in a bright red jacket, today Betty Rosskamm sits in a dark paneled conference room and speaks vividly of the early days. But she is clearly more riveted by the present than the past. At 75, she continues to put in full days as senior vice-president and director of special orders at the company's headquarters in Hudson, Ohio. Like Alma Zimmerman, she recently completed more than thirty-five years of service on the board of directors and retains an emeritus board position.

Undaunted by change, she regularly puts technology's power to work for her. "The potential of technology is incredible; we can't even imagine yet how our world can change from it," Betty Rosskamm asserts. "I can look at numbers on computer-generated reports and pick up problems. Last week I earned my keep by finding something no one else found; I told Alan I earned my year's salary that day." She smiles, then adds modestly: "But I have the time that others might not."

WORKING MOTHERS IN THE '40s AND '50s

Both Alma's and Betty's memories of motherhood are intertwined with their work lives. "When the third store opened, I was pregnant with Alan, and I ran that store," Betty recalls. "Then we opened our fourth store, our first shopping center location. A week before Alan was born, I was trimming the window of that store."

How did they manage? Like the working mothers of today, they cobbled together a way of life that was part juggling act, part serendipity, part hired help, and a large measure of personal commitment and family support.

"When I wasn't working, I was home with my children," remembers Betty. "I cooked big meals around every weekend. We celebrated every holiday together. We had good family time. I don't think my children suffered because I worked." Alma Zimmerman echoes similar memories. "If I wasn't working, I was home," she says. "I went to all the PTA meetings. I had my mother at home—she lived with us for thirty-six years. She was like a parent to my children while I took care of the business. That was a huge blessing. Then, when we moved out of the apartment and into a house of our own, I had help, so there was always someone for the children to play with."

It wasn't always easy.

"I knew I was different from the other mothers, the mothers of my children's friends," says Alma. "I wasn't playing bridge. I never ran around at night. No, I don't think my children suffered from my working, either. They think they did"—she laughs at this candid admission—"but at least they'll talk about it honestly."

Betty's husband, the late Martin Rosskamm, was particularly supportive of his wife's business skills, especially for a man living in 1940s America. "Right before Alan was born, my husband said to me, 'Just in case you want to return to work, I want you to have full-time help,'" she recalls with a smile.

MARRIED TO THE BUSINESS AND EACH OTHER

Betty and Martin thrived together as business partners, each balancing out the other's strengths and weaknesses ("I was up; he was down. I was the optimist; he was the pessimist," she says.) After Betty convinced her husband to give up his lucrative career as a vice-president of a sweater mill, Martin came on board full-time and the business became their shared passion.

"Our whole life was built around the business. On vacation, how did I entertain him? I'd drive him around to see all the fabric shops. He would start waiting on people." She smiles at the memory. "But we had a good time."

Alma and Justin Zimmerman, too, married business with pleasure. For years, Mr. Z, as he was known to many, bought candy to hand out to his customers' children. Vendors and customers alike were proud to call him a friend.

"We had our fun while we worked," says Alma. "We didn't know any better. We didn't have as many other hobbies as other people we knew." She adds an expression of gratitude about her husband: "We've had a wonderful sixty-three years together." Her recollections now seem particularly poignant. Just one day after she retold these stories in an interview, Justin Zimmerman died, at the age of 90.

THE VISION CONTINUES TO EXPAND

Jo-Ann Stores, Inc. continues to grow and refine its abilities to provide women with the resources they want and need to pursue their creative endeavors. And Betty Rosskamm and Alma Zimmerman remain as passionate as ever about the future of the company they forged with their families.

They urge team members at every level to base their actions on the values that allowed a tiny shop in Cleveland to grow into a thriving network of more than 900 stores serving the creative consumer.

Betty Rosskamm sums it up this way: "Everything you do in business must take care of the customer, and the customer is not just the lady in the store. It's anyone in the company who needs something from you. We are all serving the customer. The end result filters down to the lady in the store, but there are a million steps in between to get that customer's need filled."

That, in essence, is the heritage of Jo-Ann family members who carry the company into the future: doing whatever they can to serve and inspire creative dreams.

When visiting a Jo-Ann Store to choose a luxurious fabric, craft a gift in someone's honor, or assemble supplies for a project with the help of a Jo-Ann employee, the customer continues a venerable tradition—joining the long line of women being celebrated for sixty years of passion, hard work, and creativity. ✀

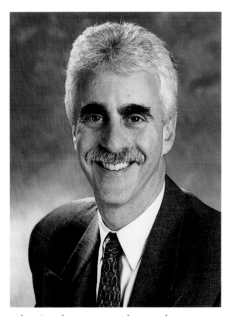

Alan Rosskamm, president and CEO, Jo-Ann Stores, Inc.

JOANN®

It is our sincere hope that after reading this book
you will feel challenged to try new techniques, learn by doing,
create from the heart, be more determined when you fail,
and rejoice in your creativity—

❧

Your journey has just begun…

 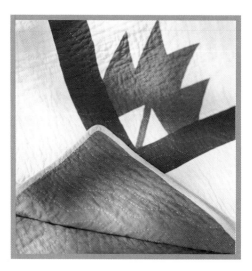 

Cutting · Piecing · Appliquéing · Quilting